BEADING WITH ALGORITHMS

Cellular Automata in Peyote Stitch

BEADING WITH ALGORITHMS

Cellular Automata in Peyote Stitch

Gwen Fisher

Roger Antonsen

World Scientific

NEW JERSEY · LONDON · SINGAPORE · BEIJING · SHANGHAI · HONG KONG · TAIPEI · CHENNAI · TOKYO

Published by

World Scientific Publishing Co. Pte. Ltd.

5 Toh Tuck Link, Singapore 596224

USA office: 27 Warren Street, Suite 401-402, Hackensack, NJ 07601

UK office: 57 Shelton Street, Covent Garden, London WC2H 9HE

British Library Cataloguing-in-Publication Data
A catalogue record for this book is available from the British Library.

BEADING WITH ALGORITHMS
Cellular Automata in Peyote Stitch

ISBN 978-981-98-1487-9 (hardcover)
ISBN 978-981-98-1575-3 (paperback)
ISBN 978-981-98-1488-6 (ebook for institutions)
ISBN 978-981-98-1489-3 (ebook for individuals)

For any available supplementary material, please visit
https://www.worldscientific.com/worldscibooks/10.1142/14357#t=suppl

This book is dedicated to my friend and coauthor, Roger Antonsen, who passed in the Spring of 2024 before we could complete it. May the legacy of his work herein continue to inspire us.

Preface

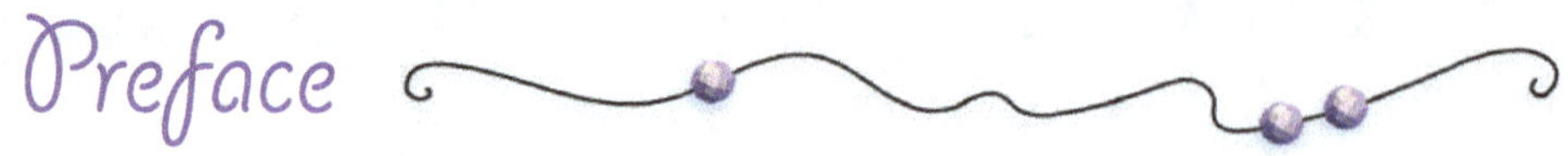

What this book is

This book is the first to explain how to weave beads using the algorithms of cellular automata (CA). This is a how-to-craft book that describes this specific connection between math and art, emphasizing the art more than the mathematics. We include enough mathematics so that readers can understand how to use and manipulate the algorithms to make their own art, patterns, and jewelry. Contained on the pages are a wide range of CA rules and the beautiful designs we made with them. The reader will learn techniques to make their own beaded artwork using these methods. Moreover, the ideas described in this book can be applied to a variety of art media. In particular, the rules described in this book can be used to color on the included coloring pages (see the appendix), paint pictures, lay tile, crochet, and piece quilts.

Who this book is for

This is an introductory book on one-dimensional CA in which no prior knowledge is assumed. This book is for bead weavers, crafters, designers, and other makers, especially those with an interest in visual patterns, mathematics, or computer science. There are very few resources for mathematically inclined girls that give them an opportunity to develop their mathematical reasoning while making crafts and having fun. So, in addition to math lovers and crafters purchasing this book for themselves, we hope mothers and aunts will buy this book for their daughters and nieces.

This book could be used in a university course on math and art, computer science and art, or computer-assisted design. It could also be used as a supplementary text for a course in liberal arts, especially aimed at art or textile majors or graphic designers.

What this book contains

Chapters 1 through 6 are the main body of the text. These six chapters are ordered from simple to complex. This book took over a decade to create because the algorithms tell a story with lots of forks in the road. To understand this story, we recommend reading the text from the beginning straight through, at least for the first two or three chapters. At the same time, we include more complex CA recipes in all the chapters that are ready to be followed by an eager maker with beads or a handful of colored pencils, tiles, fabric, or whatever art medium you choose.

The last chapter, Chapter 7, is on the tools, materials, and techniques for weaving beads into fabrics, jewelry, and other art objects. This chapter can be read at any time the reader wants to learn more about the craft of weaving beads. Included is a detailed discussion on choosing colors.

The coloring pages that you can color directly with colored pencils, crayons, or markers appear in the appendix. We recommend that you make copies of these pages before coloring them for repeated use.

This book is full of original illustrations, paintings, and photographs by Gwen Fisher. That is only half of the art.

The Software

The other half of the art in this book is computer-generated, with software written by Roger Antonsen using Gwen's ideas. The software is available at *BeadingWithAlgorithms.org*. Many of the images in this book that were created from the software have a two-letter short code next to them. Go to the website, click on the airplane button, and in the text box, type in that short code and then click enter. That image will load in the software, and you can edit it there. The menus on the left include Basics and Styling, which are both self-explanatory if you click on the tools to see what they do. The rest of the sections are more complicated, and some of the software features have caution tape around them because they might contain bugs or cause the software to seize up if you ask it to do too much too quickly. If that happens, simply reload the page. This book is not intended to be an explicit how-to manual for the software, and the software does not do everything described in this book.

Acknowledgments

Special thanks to Zelda Lin, who did the graphic design and layout of this book using Adobe's Creative Suite and also helped with the user experience of the software. Zelda also helped to make several of the images in this book. This book is profoundly more beautiful because of Zelda's design wizardry and skill. More of Zelda's work can be found at *zeldalin.com*.

Thank to the geniuses who inspired this book, including Susan Goldstine, Ellie Baker, and Stephen Wolfram. This book never would have existed if Susan had not asked Gwen if she could bead in such a way that each stitch was determined by what beadwork had come before it. Susan probably would not have asked Gwen if it were not for her conversations with Ellie about beading and CA. As for Stephen Wolfram, he wrote and distributes freely the primary resource book on the larger subject of CA, called *A New Kind of Science*. That book laid a foundation for this whole conversation.

Thanks to Tom Davis, who wrote the first round of custom software that allowed Gwen to test and explore her algorithms with the help of a computer.

Thanks to our proofreaders, Rebecca K. Brent, Gregory Lee, Cindy Holsclaw, Ellie Baker, and Laura Taalman, for your sharp eyes, great minds, thoughtful comments, and attention to detail.

Thanks to Scott Vorthmann for shepherding the software into a usable form after Roger's passing.

Thanks to our partners, Paul Brown and Kelly Nelson, for giving us the time and space to work on this years-long labor of love.

$\mathcal{C}$ontents

BEADING WITH ALGORITHMS

A New Kind of Peyote Stitch

An algorithm is a process or a set of instructions for solving a problem or making an object. The focus of this book is on algorithms called *cellular automata*, which create complex visual designs. You can make any of the designs in this book with colored markers and one of the coloring pages in the appendix. However, the real inspiration for this book is what happens when we use cellular automata with beads and thread. The starting beads—also called *cells*—and the rule uniquely determine the pattern. This book explains the connection between beaded peyote stitch and cellular automata, presents many beautiful designs, and gives techniques for how to make beaded artwork and jewelry.

Cellular automata, or just CA for short, are algorithms that provide a new way for bead weavers to select colors *while* weaving beads. The beads are sewn to each other, one at a time, with a needle and thread. To choose colors for a new bead, you first look at the colors you have already beaded. Then, you use that information and a rule (which can have several parts) to determine which color to pick up in the next stitch. This rule specifies the algorithm. This is different from the way we bead with a beading chart, where you see the complete arrangement of colors before you ever start stitching. With a chart, you know how the design will look before picking up a bead. In contrast, with CA, the mosaic of colors emerges, bead by bead, or cell by cell, as you weave. When using CA, the colors of the cells happen *automatically*, according to your rules, hence the name "cellular automata."

CA beadweaving can look intricate and complicated, but the actual bead weaving is remarkably intuitive. We hope you will find that beading with CA is beautiful, meditative, and magical. You might even find that beading with CA can be a little addictive because every row ends with a cliff-

"I am open to the guidance of synchronicity, and do not let expectations hinder my path."
- Dalai Lama

Introduction
The Structure of Peyote Stitch

Everything in this book was inspired by one of the simplest forms of beading, called *beaded peyote stitch*. If you are new to peyote stitch, or could just use a refresher, here is a brief overview to get you started. For more details, we refer you to the chapter dedicated to beading with peyote stitch. Chapter 7 gives information on materials, tools, techniques, and projects, including jewelry, keychains, and pouches.

Peyote stitch is a two-dimensional weave of beads and thread. It creates a colored mosaic of beaded fabric that can be flat or tubular. The tools needed are simple: a needle, scissors, and a bead mat.

hanger. What will the design look like next? You won't know until you bead it.

We start by stringing the first two rows of beads on a thread. Beads are stitched to each other in staggered rows, added from the top down. We use a black arrow to show which side to start each pattern and which direction to go. The beads in any column sit between adjacent beads in the row added before and the row added after, ignoring the beads on the left- and right-most edges. At the end of each row, the thread switches direction which is simply called a *turn*.

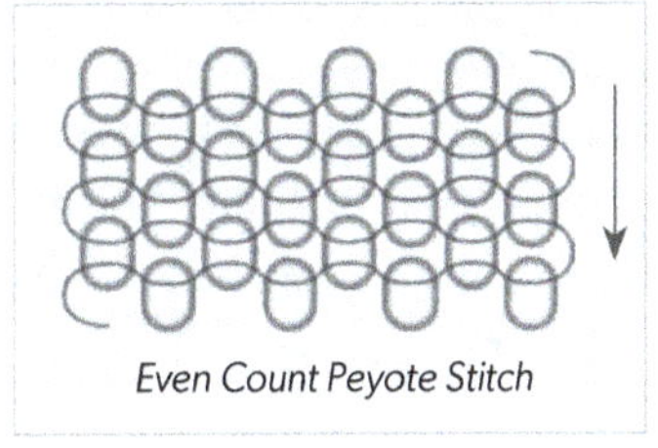
Even Count Peyote Stitch

Each new bead attaches to the beads directly to its left and right with thread. The new bead touches both of these beads as well as the bead directly above it. We call these three beads the **left bead,** the **above bead**, and the **right bead**. As we stitch, we will use the rules of CA to determine the color of each new bead based on the colors of its left, above, and right beads.

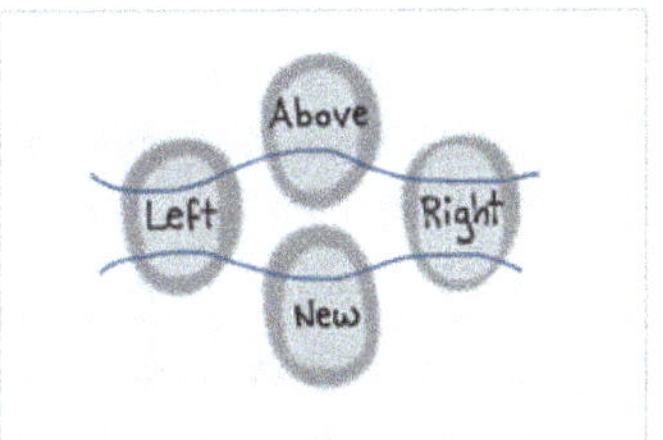

Counting along a diagonal gives both the number of columns and the number of rows in a patch of peyote stitch. The rows are staggered, meaning each row contains beads in every other column, and each column contains beads in every other row.

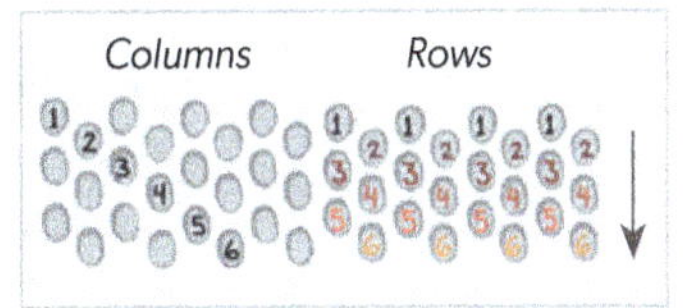

We characterize peyote stitch as either "even" or "odd" by the number of columns. Most of the beadwork in this book uses even-count peyote stitch because the turns are neat and easy. See the chapter on peyote stitch for odd-count turns.

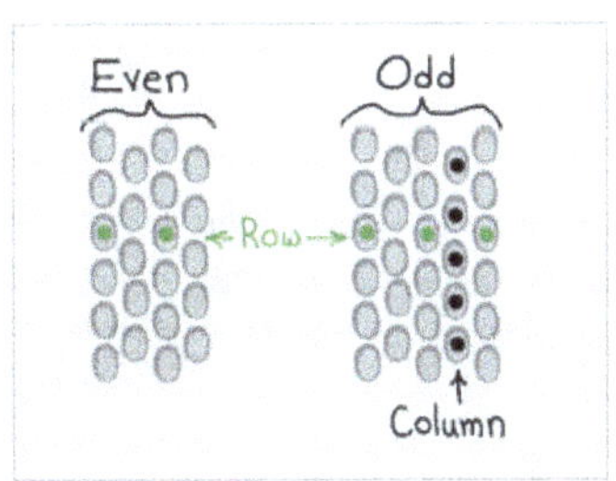

The Beauty of Cellular Automata

The technique of cellular automata allows us to pick bead (cell) colors automatically. In other words, we choose a rule, or a set of instructions, to decide how to determine the color of each bead as we stitch. The rule gives us a method for how to color the beadwork. For example, below you can see a patch of peyote stitch woven from the top down. Here, and throughout the book, we use an arrow to show the direction a piece is made so that you know which way to follow the rule.

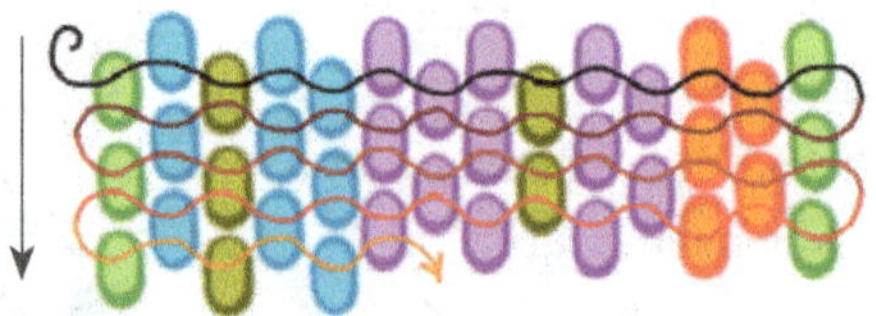

Think about this rule for choosing colors: **On each stitch, choose the color of the new bead to be the same color as the bead above.** If you follow this rule, you get a patch of beadwork with a pattern of vertical stripes, as shown on the left.

Of course, you can use the same rule with different starting rows. If you start with a different set of colors in the first rows, or with more or fewer beads, then the rule will make a different patch of beadwork—but it will still be stripes. In other words, we can use the same rule to make a lot of different patches of striped beadwork. As long as we apply the same rule, the design of stripes only depends upon what colors and how many beads are in the first two rows, so those rows are super important. We call the first rows the *initial state* or *initial condition*. You can choose your initial state carefully, to make the stripes just as you like, or you can make the initial state random and just go from there. The choice is yours. The rule can be applied in any case, and it will always make a striped patch of beadwork, even if it makes just one fat stripe because you started with an initial state that was all one color.

Now, stripes are fine, but it turns out that there are easy algorithms that will create designs that are much more interesting than stripes. For the first several chapters of this book, we will focus on the simplest rules and the designs that they make. These rules are our favorites because they are easy to follow, and they make designs that we think are pretty.

Traditionally, beaded peyote stitch patterns are recorded with a bead chart, like the one here. The chart shows precisely how to arrange two colors of beads to make a flat patch of beaded peyote stitch. Of course, you don't need to use pink and gray; you can use this chart with any two colors you want. The point of this book is that we can also make this pattern exactly, specifying just an initial state and a rule, instead of using a chart.

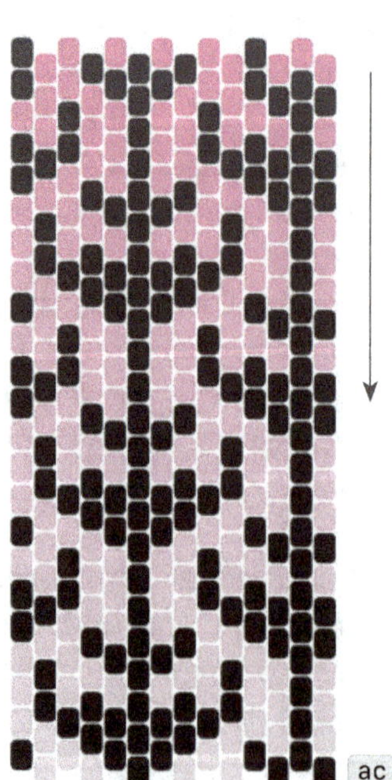

The algorithm we used here is one we call *Roots*, which we will explain in great detail next. The rule for *Roots* is so simple that you can easily memorize it.

NOTE: *The images in this book that were created from the software at beadingwithalgorithms.org each have a two-letter short code. Click on the airplane icon on the website, and type the short code in the text box. That image will load in the software, and you can edit it there.*

An Amazing Rule: Roots

Imagine you are weaving peyote stitch with two colors: pink and gray. On each stitch, your thread exits one bead, you pick up a new bead, and you pass through a bead. The bead you exit from and the bead you pass through are the *left* and *right* beads, in some order.

Now, either the left and right beads are the same color, or they are different colors.

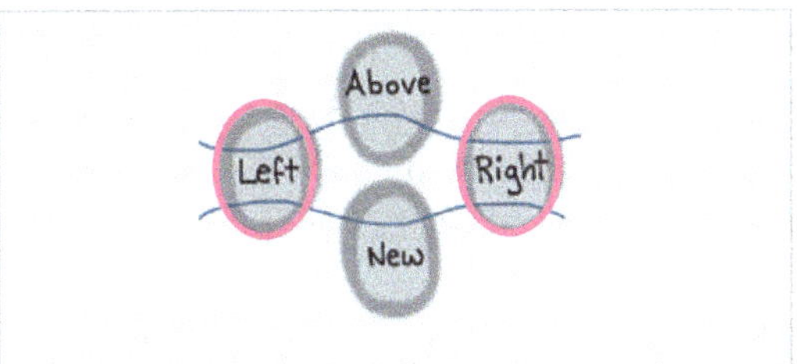

Roots rule: If the left and right beads are the same color, then pick up gray (1). If they are different, pick up pink (0).

We think of this as a *"same/different* rule." When we apply this rule to the left and right beads, we call it *Roots* for short, because it makes patterns that look like tree roots. It is one of the simplest rules that does some really amazing things. Below is the rule for *Roots* written in two different ways that convey the same information: beads (or blobs of color) on the left, and numbers on the right.

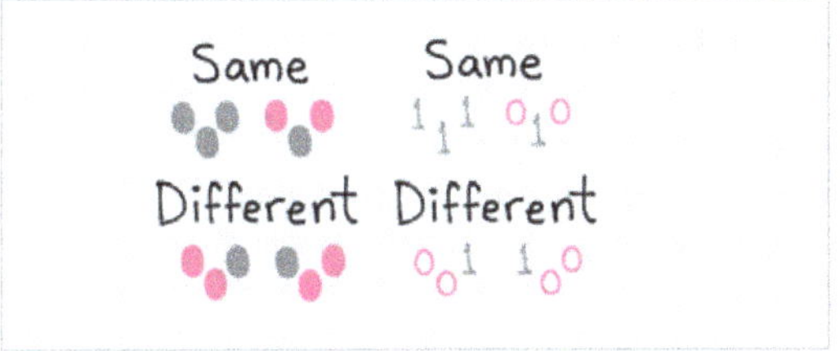

We use both notations for different reasons. The bead notation (on the left) is easy to follow while beading, but it is hard to write on paper without colored pencils. The number notation (on the right) is easy to write, and it is easier to translate the numbers into other color schemes rather than translating colors into other colors. To prepare for beading, we draw a color chart with blobs of colors that match the colors of our beads. Colored pencils work well for this.

Here is the correspondence between the two notations, part for part.

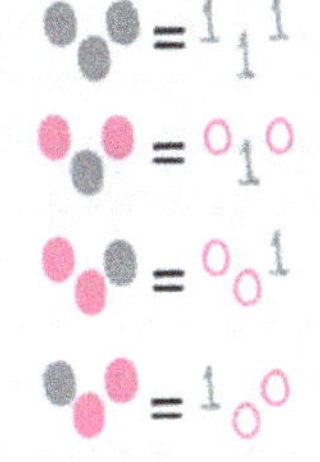

To understand how these parts work, consider the fourth line above, which gives this part.

The top two beads show the input for the part. In other words, the beads you exit and enter look like this.

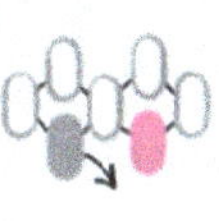

Then, the bead you pick up looks like the one on the bottom.

This is how the stitching looks, whether you stitch from the left or right.

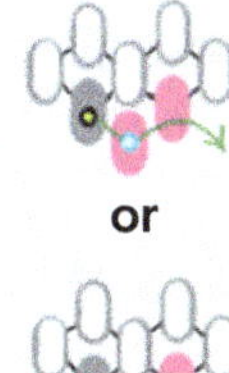

Next, you will learn to bead this patch of Roots:

How to Peyote Stitch with Roots

This section explains how to do even-count peyote stitch, and we leave other techniques of peyote stitch to the chapter dedicated to that purpose. For now, just remember that **you can weave all the CA rules in this book by starting with the three rows described next.**

Rows 1 and 2:
Starting even-count peyote stitch

In general, an even-count peyote stitch starts with an odd number of beads (because even-count peyote stitch starts with two rows that are the same size, plus the first bead of row three). The length of your starting strand of beads dictates the width of the strip, and it can be as long or as short as you want. If this is your first beading project, we suggest you start by threading your needle with about a yard (meter) of thread, and then string 15 beads in one color. A long strand will make a wide panel of beadwork, and a short strand will make a narrow panel. Wide panels are especially good for complex rules with lots of interesting substructures, but short strands are easier to manipulate and best for learning the technique.

Pass back through the third-to-last bead and pull the thread tight, leaving a tail that is long enough for you to thread onto a needle and weave into the beadwork (6 to 8 inches, or 15 to 20 cm). You will do that later. Hold the tail so the beads don't slide off. You can wrap the tail around your finger or add a stop bead.

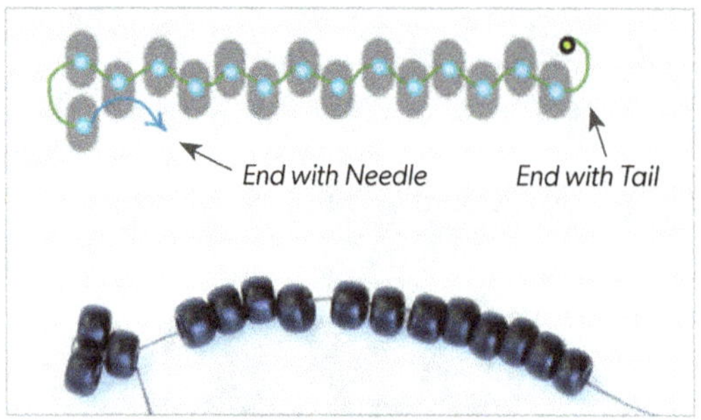

It is worth mentioning that the first 14 of these beads are not part of the pattern, but the last bead you strung is in row 3, making it part of the initial state. We'll talk about this next.

Row 3: Initial state

We add the initial state to the third row of peyote stitch. The initial state is any sequence of beads we choose, using our colors: 0 (pink) and 1 (gray). For example, say we want our initial state (row 3) to be 1000010 or ●●●●●●●. We already have the 1 on the left added. This was the last of your first 15 beads.

The next bead we string is color 0. Now, skip a bead on the strand and pass through the next bead. *That is a peyote stitch with color 0.*

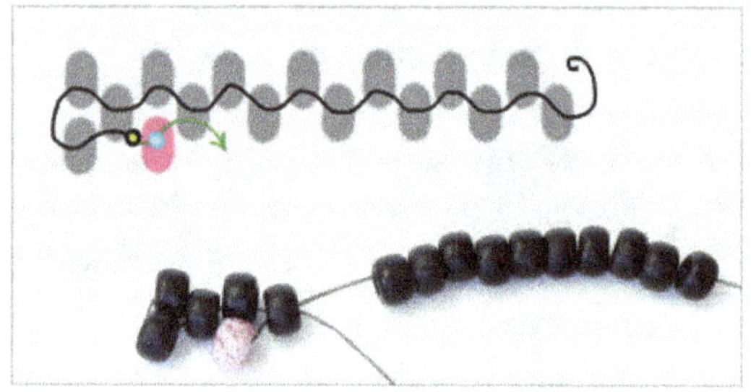

Add another peyote stitch with color 0. Repeat two more times, then peyote stitch with color 1. Finally, peyote stitch with color 0. You have completed the initial state when you get to the end of the row.

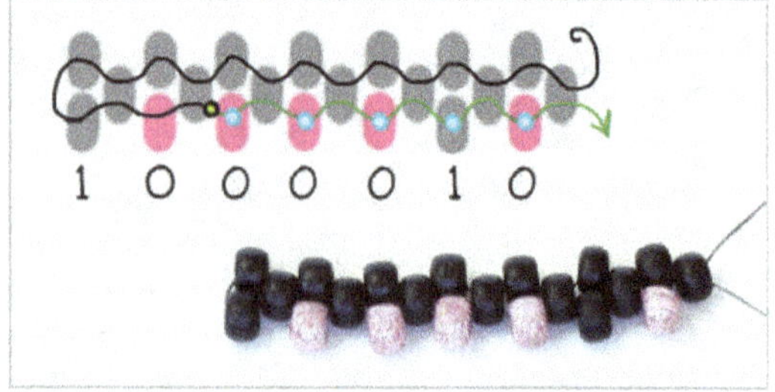

You might be wondering why we waited until row three to introduce the initial state beads rather than starting them at the very beginning. You can certainly choose your first two rows freely and consider them to be your initial state. However, it can be challenging to keep the beads in rows 1 and 3 from twisting, and if they are different colors, you will have to be sure to keep them in position.

To make things easier, we recommend starting with at least two plain rows before adding the initial state that starts the color pattern. If you want the pattern to start right at the top edge of the finished beadwork, you can always rip out the first rows of beads later, before you weave in the tail of thread. Just be sure that your needle doesn't pierce the thread, and the beads should pull out easily.

Rows 4 and beyond for Roots

Remember the two ways to write the rules for *Roots:* with beads (left) and with numbers (right). Label your x piles. Gray is "same," and pink is "different."

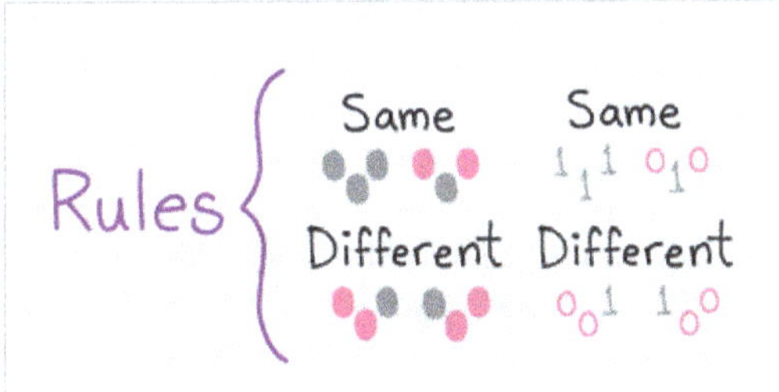

A. **Follow the rule: If the left and right beads are the same color, string a bead from the pile labeled "same." If they are different, string a bead from the pile labeled "different."** When you start a new row, you'll need a simple idea to figure out which color to start with: imagine that the beadwork is a tube where the left and right sides connect. Then, compare the colors of the first and last beads of the previous row (the outlined beads).

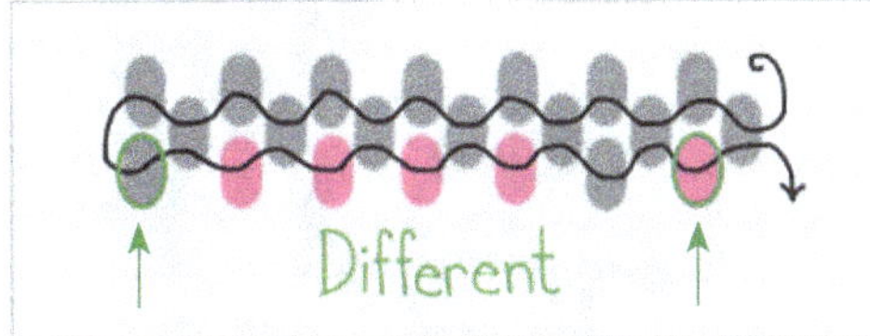

In the pictures, they are different, so we string a pink. Reverse direction, and pass through the last bead on the previous row. That's a turn. Pull the thread tight.

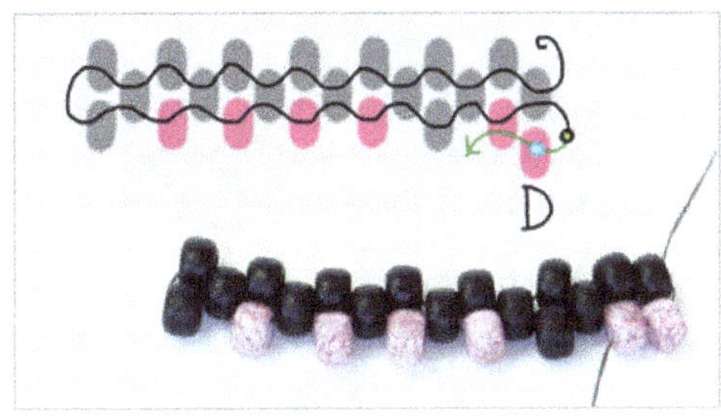

B. Look at the bead your thread currently exits and the next bead you will pass through (the outlined beads). Follow the rule from step A. In the pictures, they are different...

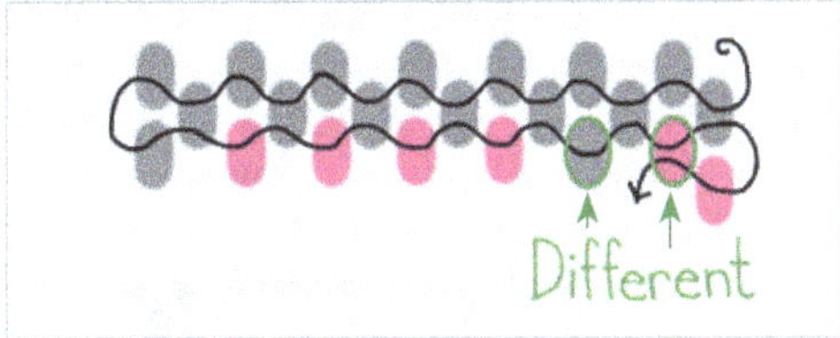

...so the new bead is pink.

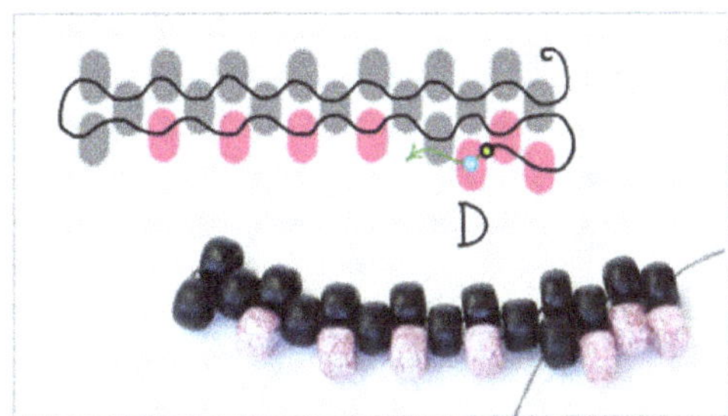

C. Repeat step B until you finish the row.

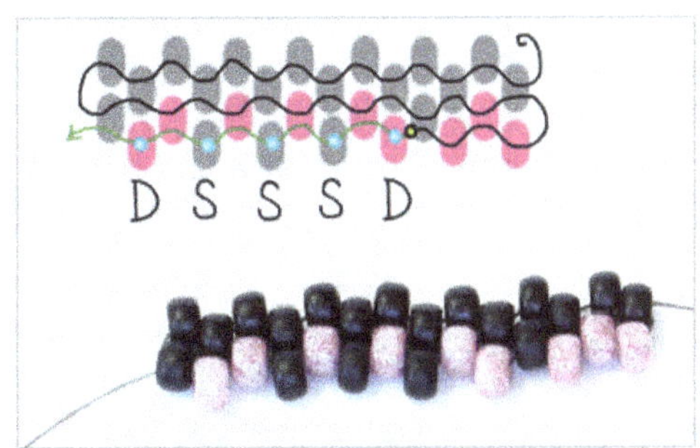

D. Repeat step A.

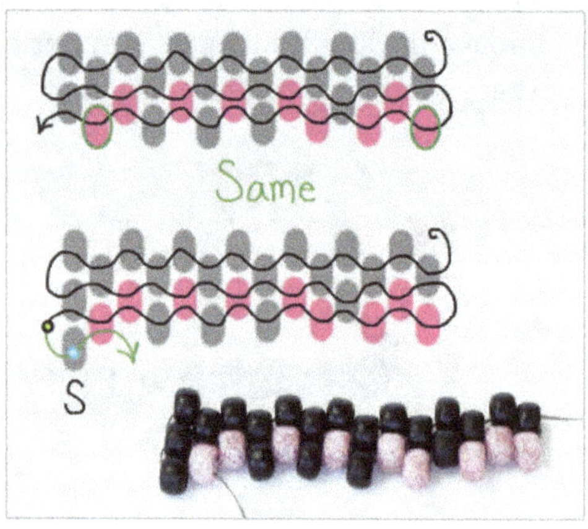

E. Repeat step B until you finish the row.

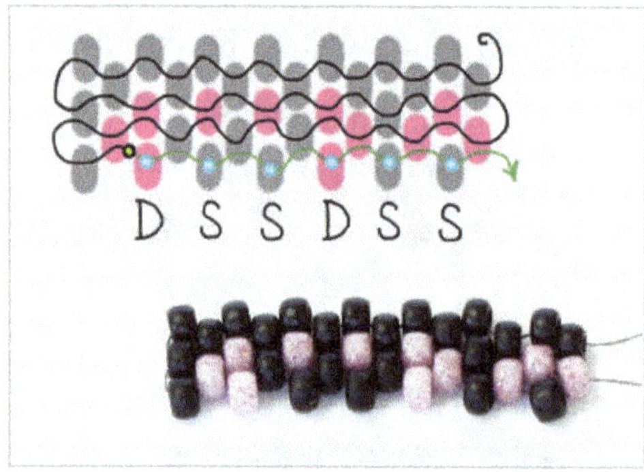

F. Repeat steps A and B.

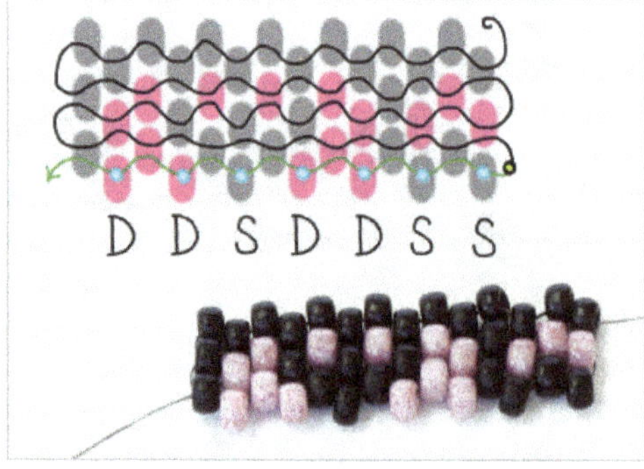

Continue to repeat steps A and B to make the strip as long as you want. This is what the beadwork looks like with seven rows. It is easiest to count the rows diagonally.

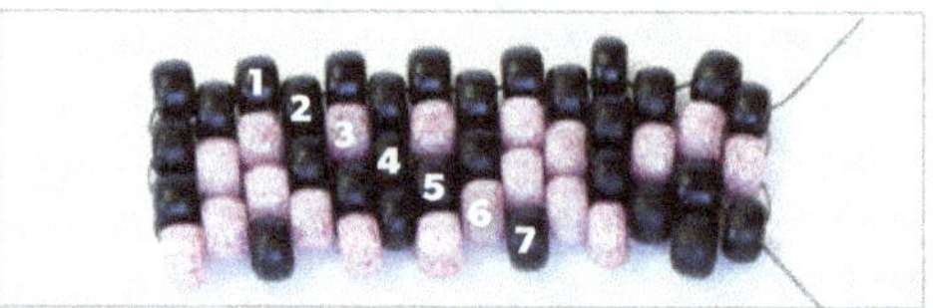

G. One yard (or one meter) of thread and size 8° (size 8/0) seed beads made the patch below with enough thread to weave in and secure both ends of the thread. This is 19 rows. If you don't like that the first two rows are all the same color, you can rip them out before securing the tail.

Below is a drawing of the same patch done on a computer. The drawing omits the first two rows and continues for many more rows. See how the pattern repeats? We will talk about repeats later.

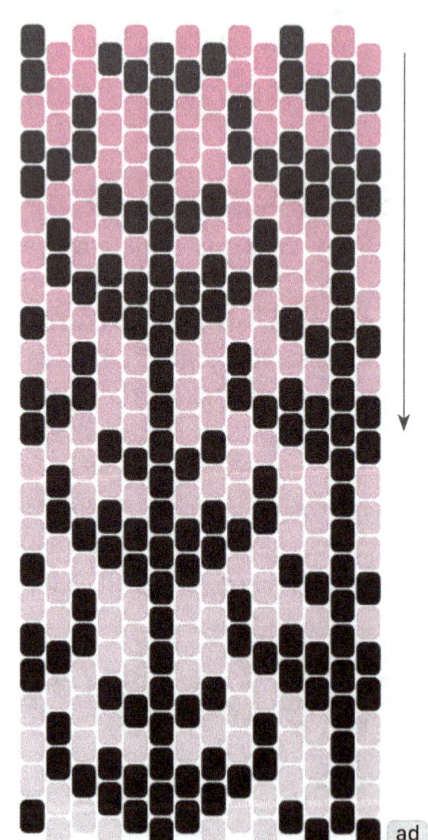

In step A on the previous page, we chose the first bead of the new row so the design would wrap around the left and right sides, as if we were beading a tube that had been sliced open to lie flat. Here we show an easy alternative, an example of *Roots* with borders on the left and right edges. To make this border, the first bead added on each row is color **1**, the color labeled "same." Both patches shown here have the same initial state except for one bead on the border. The different border treatments eventually have a huge effect on the color pattern of the individual beads. Even though the two versions are very different from bead to bead, the overall feel of the two versions is still very similar: The algorithm makes the same design motifs in both versions.

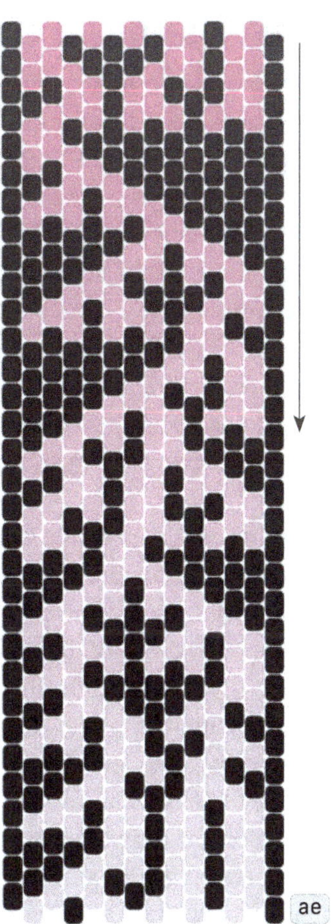

Examples of Roots

There are countless examples of *Roots*. We call it *Roots* because when you bead it from the top down, the patterns look like roots or dangling vines.

Beaded from the bottom up (because direction matters), *Roots* makes designs that look like a sea of jellyfish or a fleet of space invaders flying toward Earth.

Panel Width and Repeats

There is much to be explored in the interplay among initial states, patch width, and repeating designs in peyote stitch beaded with CA.

If you bead a rectangle, then the number of beads in the initial state determines exactly which designs are possible. Moreover, you will eventually start repeating rows. In other words, as long as your patch is a rectangle, a repeating design will always emerge if you make the rectangle long enough.

For example, the panel of *Roots* below begins without a repeat, but after a few rows, the repeat starts, as indicated by the top of the red line. The length of the repeat is the length between hash marks on the red line at the left. The pattern shows two staggered repeats horizontally and five repeats vertically. If you continue to follow *Roots*, the pattern will repeat forever. If you don't want your design to repeat, simply break a rule somewhere. If you don't want it to be obvious where you are breaking a rule, break it when adding the first bead in a row because it's almost impossible to notice errors on a boundary.

ai

Narrow patches reveal the basic repeating motifs of CA rules. For example, imagine using *Roots* on a patch that is just one stitch per row (two columns of beads). No matter how you start, you will end with all one color.

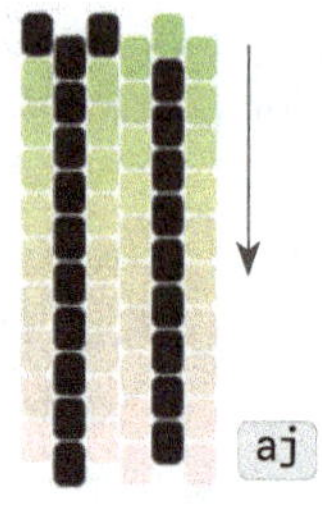

3 stitches/row

Start with two stitches per row (four columns), and again, you get all one color, no matter how you start. With three stitches per row (six columns), some initial states still lead to all one color, but we also find vertical stripe designs, shown here. The first two rows show how *Roots* makes stripes in more than one way.

Use *Roots* on any patch with four stitches per row (8 columns), and eventually you will get all one color. With five stitches per row (like the figure to the right), *Roots* finally creates

5 stitches/row

something novel that looks like *Roots*. We think this looks like two vertical stems that are five columns apart and staggered vertically.

With six stitches per row, we get another staggered stem design. Here, the vertical stems are six columns apart. With six stitches per row, we can also get the same stripe design that we got with three stitches per row. Upon closer inspection, this shouldn't surprise us since six is a multiple of three. Similarly, if you start with any multiple of five stitches per row, you can use *Roots* to create a panel of the repeating stem design made with five stitches per row.

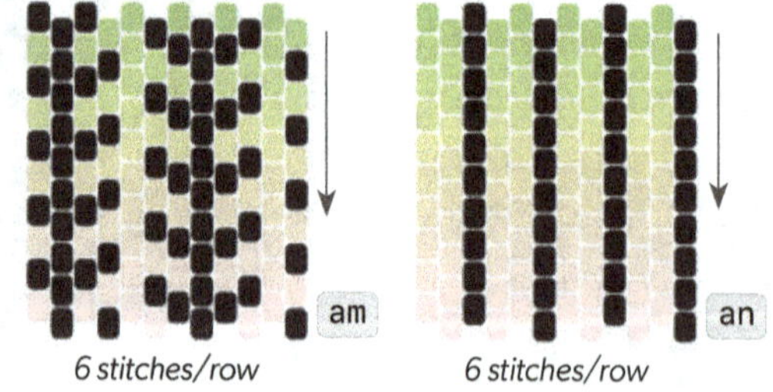

6 stitches/row   *6 stitches/row*

With seven stitches per row, we find the pretty design shown below. Now we have diagonal stems that repeat vertically and diagonally. With seven stitches per row, *Roots* also makes another staggered stem design, shown below on the right. It is more complex than the others. The vertical stems are seven columns apart.

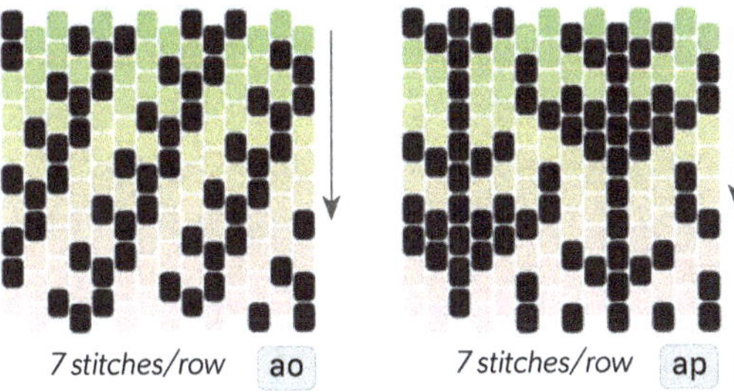

7 stitches/row ao   *7 stitches/row* ap

To see better how this design repeats, we can use a panel with 14 stitches across (since 14 is a multiple of seven). Any multiple of seven will work.

aq

14 stitches/row

Don't bother to make a patch with *Roots* that is 16 or 32 stitches across, since no matter how you start, the pattern eventually becomes all one color. In fact, this is true for any power of two. On the other hand, most patches of *Roots* with 18 or more columns will create a variety of beautiful designs. Wider patches have more possible row states than narrow patches. Consequently, it will usually take longer to randomly land on a repeating cycle if we are weaving a wide patch. Also, wider patches tend to have longer repeats; that is, it takes more rows (patch length) before the pattern will repeat. If we weave a wider patch, there is a better chance we can finish our project before we hit a repeat. We can find exceptions to some of these generalizations, but they are still good guidelines to consider when we design our beadwork.

Most of the time, when we use *Roots*, regardless of the initial state, we get something that looks like a tree's roots. When we flip it upside down, we will see space-invading jellyfish monsters. The point here is that you don't have to plan your initial state and patch width if you don't want to. Feel free to start beading a random initial state of a random width, and just see what happens. Letting the design emerge without expectation is part of the joy of beading with CA.

"Do not dwell in the past, do not dream of the future, concentrate the mind on the present moment."
- Buddha

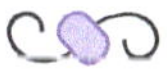

Initial State

Before we can apply a CA rule, we need to start with an initial state. For *Roots*, the initial state is the first row, but in many of our later rules, the initial state will be the first two rows. Here are a few classes of initial states to consider.

Seed

If the initial state is all one color, except for one bead, which is a *seed* state. If you apply *Roots* to a seed, the result looks like a Sierpiński triangle with its nested triangles that repeat forever in scaled copies of itself.

If we add more rows and zoom out, it looks like this.

If you use a seed as your initial state, the designs often emerge at an angle. Fortunately, we can make these angles, without the solid background, in beaded peyote stitch by using so-called *increases* to make beaded shapes such as triangles and trapezoids. *Roots* with a seed start makes an obtuse angle of about 115°, depending upon the particular beads you use. Here, you can see a beaded version.

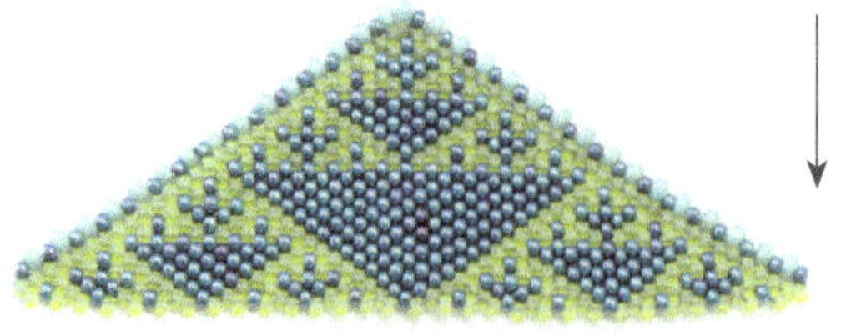

Below are drawings that show how to peyote stitch the beaded triangle with *Roots*. To create this obtuse angle, we stitch an increase at the beginning of each row. Make the first stitch with three beads: Pick up green, blue, green, and pass back through (in the opposite direction) the first bead you just picked up. Each new row begins by picking up those same three beads (green, blue, green) on the first stitch to make an increase. Peyote stitch to the end of the row using the *Roots* algorithm. The chapter on peyote stitch gives more details.

Roots with an obtuse angle start

Random

A random sequence of colors for the initial state will often create a seemingly random version of the design. That said, no matter how wide your strip is, if you bead long enough without any errors, the pattern will eventually start repeating. The reason is the *Pigeonhole Principle*, which states that if *n* pigeons are put into m holes, and n is greater than m, then at least one hole will have more than one pigeon. In terms of beads, if we add enough rows, eventually we will run out of combinations of colors, and we will have to repeat a row. When that happens, we will build that row in the same way we did the first time, so the pattern starts to repeat.

Symmetric

To make a beaded patch with a perfect line of mirror symmetry down the middle column, we must use odd-count peyote stitch and a symmetric initial state. It is possible to create lines of mirror symmetry with even-count peyote stitch, but the pattern's centerline won't fall on the beadwork's centerline, which lies between beaded columns. Instead, you have to imagine the beadwork wrapped into a tube, joining the left and right edges; there, any tube will have an even number of lines of symmetry. (Recall that zero is even.) For example, the top patch to the right has two lines of mirror symmetry, indicated by the pink lines.

The black lines indicate lines of glide reflection symmetry. A *glide reflection* is a combination of a reflection over a line and a translation parallel to the same line. Lines of glide reflection are common in peyote stitch with CA because of the staggering of the rows.

The middle patch is the same as the top patch, but the design is shifted horizontally; the middle patch also has two lines of mirror symmetry. The bottom patch has four lines of mirror symmetry. Lines of mirror symmetry always lie on a column of beads, while lines of glide reflection can lie on or between columns of beads.

Other initial states

There are certainly other ways to choose an initial state. One that we think is worth exploring is a symmetric initial state, such as **110011** or **1010000101**.

The Pigeonhole Principle

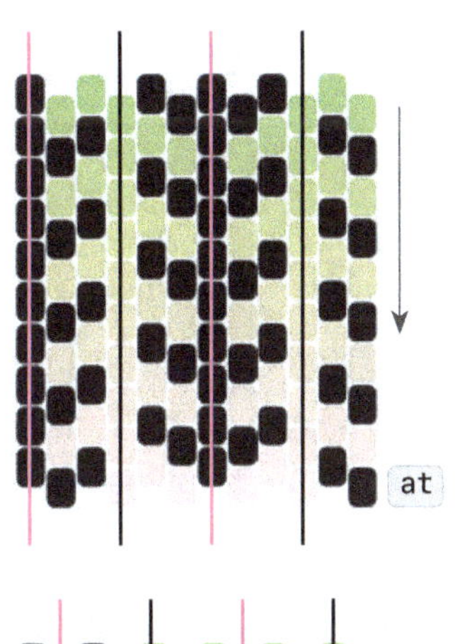

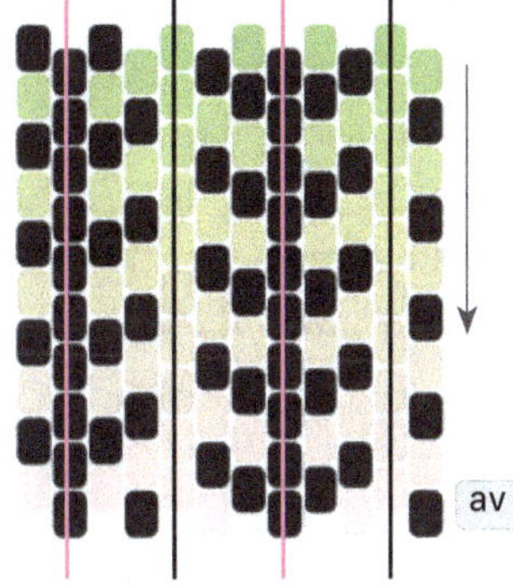

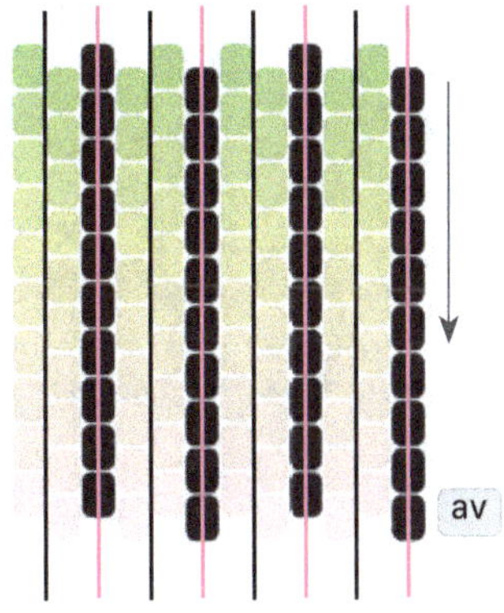

Color Cycling and Shading

Even though the same-different rule uses just two colors, you can actually use it with as many colors as you want. An easy way to do this is by picking beads that are almost the same color, like the different blue/green beads in the piece below. In each row, we used just one kind of blue bead but we switched *which* blue bead after every two or three rows, cycling through the various blues, in the same order, going down the rows. The color change doesn't have to happen on a repeat.

In the following two patches of beadwork, we have swapped the roles of light and dark. To make the patches look like mirror images, we also reflected the initial state. So, for example, if the left had started with **110001**, the right patch would start with **011100**.

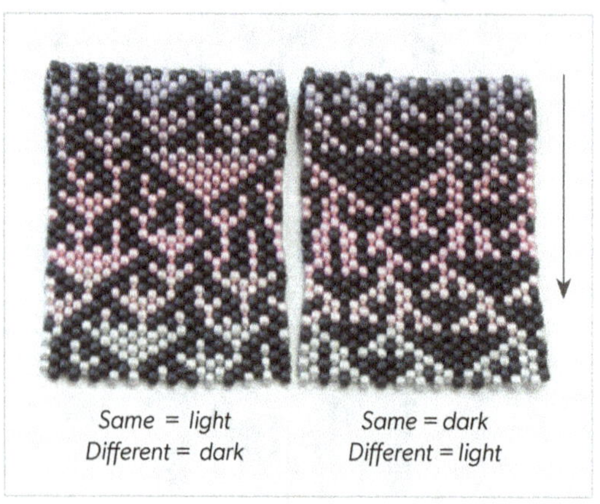

Below is an example of *Roots* that is beaded with 14 different colors of beads. To make this, start by choosing beads in two values: lights and darks. For color **1** (same), use light colors like white, cream, gold, silver, pale blue, pale green, and yellow. For color **0** (different), use dark colors like black, navy, forest green, and gray. For rows 1, 2, and 3, start with black (not shown in photo). For the initial state in row 4, use black for color 0 and opaque white for color **1**. Stitch another row with those two colors. Then, use navy blue for color **0** and silver-lined opal for color **1**, and stitch a couple of rows. Change to gold for color **1**, and stitch a couple more rows. After every two or three rows, switch to a new color for **0** or **1** or both.

Below are two views of the same pouch, front and back. This pouch shows a color shading of seed beads. Shading is like color cycling without a repeat.

Color Splitting

Next, we explain another way to use a two-color rule with more than two colors. The bottom section of the bracelet below uses *Roots* with three colors.

In the same/different sense of the rule, the black beads are the output for *different*. The green and gold beads are both the output for *same*. By splitting one color into two, we turn a rule for two colors into a rule for three colors. Below is the three-color rule, substituting colors for the beadwork above. The next few pages explain how this works.

Consider *Roots* as a visual design in two colors: blue and gold.

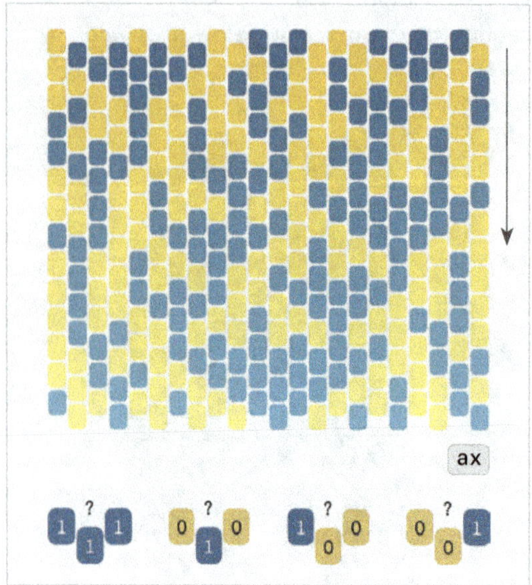

The blue region has a lot of different parts that are visually distinct. We see baskets, vines, and vine tips. We can emphasize these different features with another color. For example, let's split the color blue into two colors: blue and pink. You can choose either blue or pink for the outputs that were originally all blue.

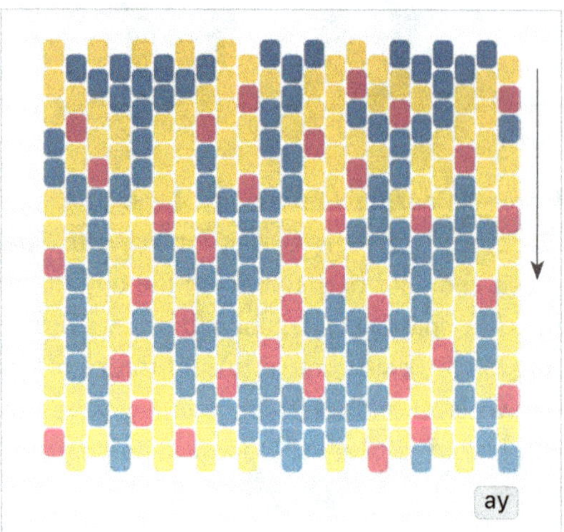

See how we colored all of the vine tips pink to make them look like flowers? This makes pink the output of this part of the rule.

Where this part of the rule had two inputs (left and right), we now consider three inputs (left, above, right) for this part of the rule. In particular, we replace [figure] with [figure].

When a color has been split into two colors, both colors behave in the same way when used as inputs. So, when pink beads are the inputs to the rule, they behave just as blue beads do. We can also look at the patch directly in order to see what comes after pink, and identify the other parts of the new rule in this way.

For example: because **1** and **2** behave similarly, from [figure], it follows that [figure].

Similarly, [figure] implies [figure].

The complete rule for the pink-tipped vine has 11 parts.

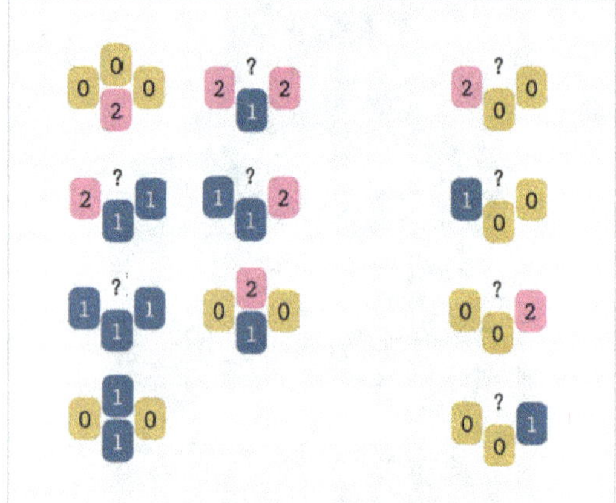

Taking advantage of the color split for blue and pink, we can shorten the rule to just five parts, small enough to fit on a sticky note.

Notice that if you make all of the pink beads blue again, you would be back to the rule for *Roots*.

Many of the beading illustrations in this book, like the one on the right, are coded with oval dots of color. The green dots show where the thread starts in each step. The pale pink dots show the new beads added in each step.

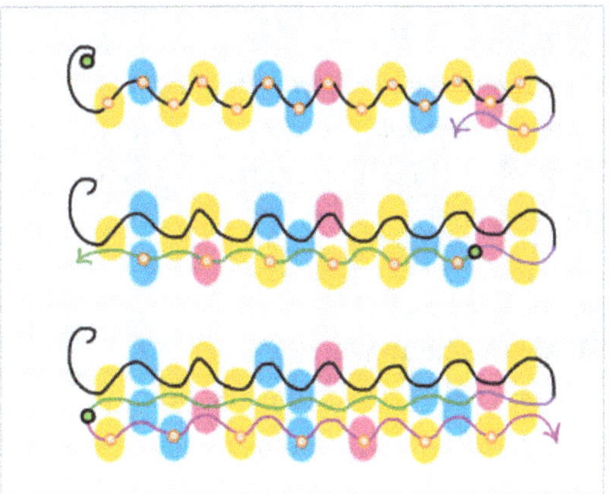

Four Pendants

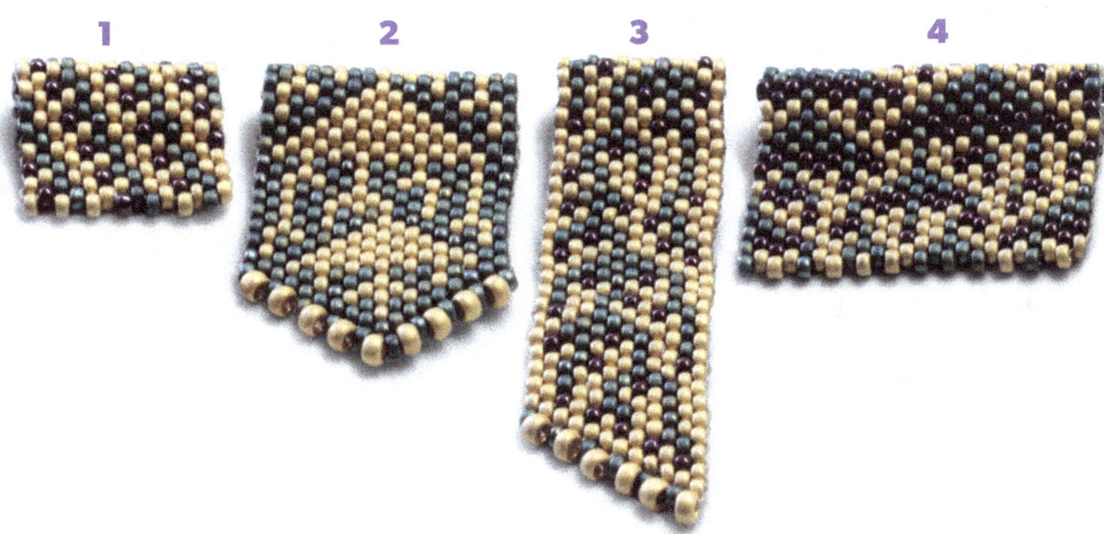

1. The **small rectangle** is seven stitches across (14 columns). At the top of this page, you can see how to stitch the first four rows. The rule is *Roots* plus the one level of color splitting we just described, repeated here.

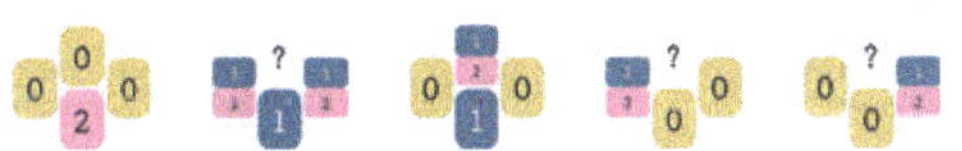

2. The **pentagon** has an obtuse angle start as described earlier. It is nine stitches across (18 columns). The rule we used is *Roots,* in which gold is *same,* and blue is *different.*

3. The **trapezoid** has an acute angle start as described on the next page. It has six stitches across (12 columns). The rule is given on the previous page.

4. The **large rectangle** is 12 stitches across (24 columns). The rule is *Roots* plus the two levels of color splitting described after the acute angle start.

Acute Angle Start

These instructions give the start for the trapezoid pendant, beaded upside-down from the photo. Colors are **(Y)ellow**, **(B)lue**, *and* **(P)ink**.

Rows 1, 2, and 3

Make an increase: Pick up **YBY**, and pass back through the first bead (in the opposite direction) that you just picked up.

Row 4

Make a turn: Pick up **Y** and pass back through the last bead you picked up in the previous stitch.

Row 5

Make an increase.

Then pick up **P**, and peyote stitch by skipping a bead and passing through the next bead.

Row 6

Make a turn, then pick up **Y** and peyote stitch. Make sure your increase isn't twisted.

Row 7

Make an increase.

Pick up **P**, and peyote stitch. Pick up **B**, and peyote stitch.

Even rows (green thread)

Make a turn, and peyote stitch to the end of the row, using the rule to determine which color to pick up on each stitch.

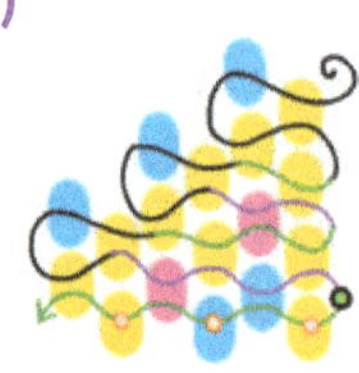

Odd rows (black and blue threads)

Make an increase. Peyote stitch to the end of the row.

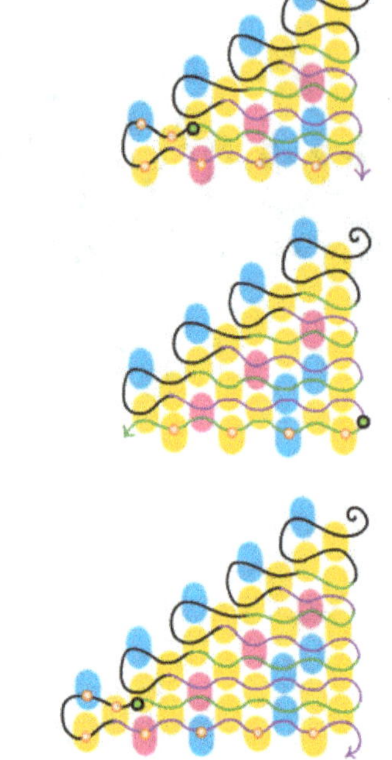

Use peyote stitch to finish the edge by adding larger (green) beads between the blue beads from the increases.

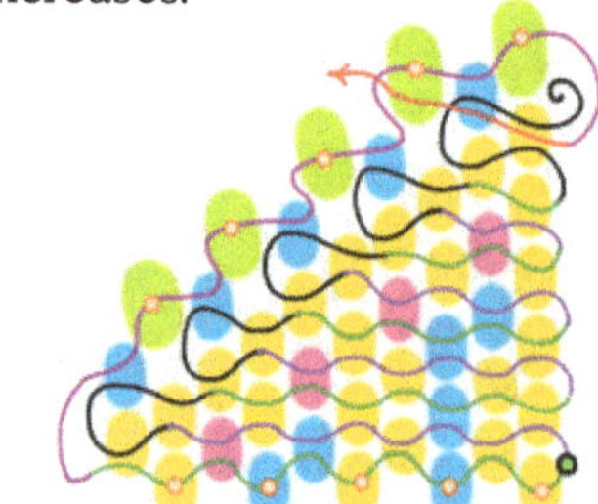

Pendant Four

Here, we explain the rule for the large rectangular pendant. To make the tops of the baskets pink, replace 2?112?2 with 2?211?22.

az

Below is the complete rule for this patch.

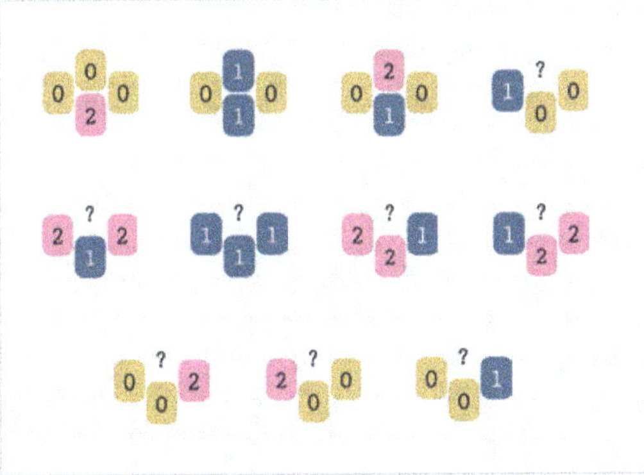

If we take advantage of the color splitting, we can represent the same rule with just eight parts.

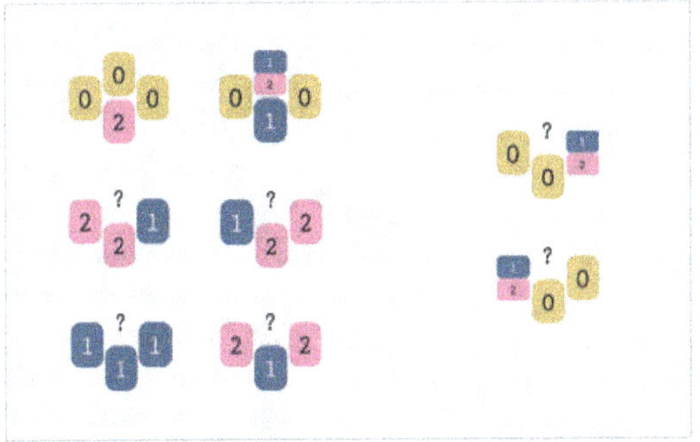

Another Pendant

This pendant shows *Roots* with both color splitting and shading. The pink (or lilac) and green beads are the color split, while the black and blue beads are shaded.

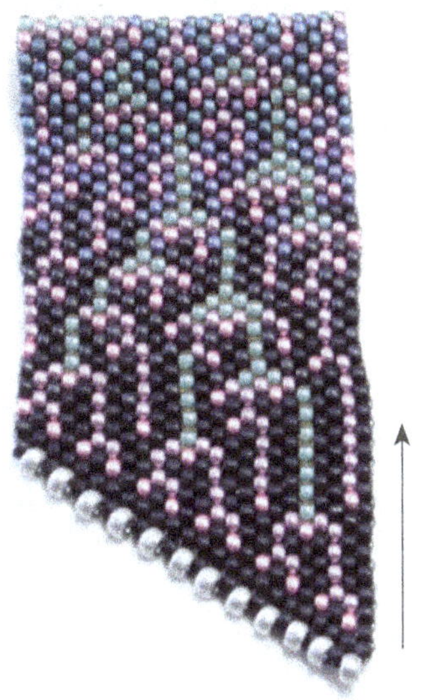

Here is the complete rule for this patch.

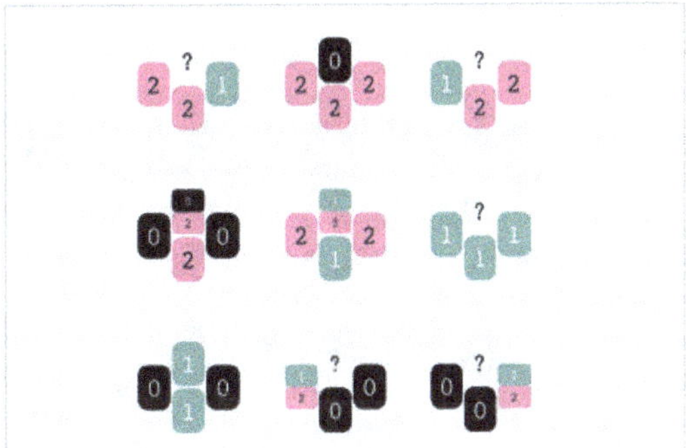

Here is a computer-generated patch that starts just like the beaded pendant above, but without any errors.

bd

The Roots algorithm generates all these patterns, and many more.

Chapter Two
TRIANGLE PARTY

Another Same-Different Rule

In beaded peyote stitch, each *new* bead in the interior touches exactly three beads already stitched in place. As long as we keep the front side in front, we can uniquely describe these three beads as *left*, *above*, and *right*. For *Roots*, we compared the beads on the left and right to see whether they were the same or different to decide the color of the *new* bead.

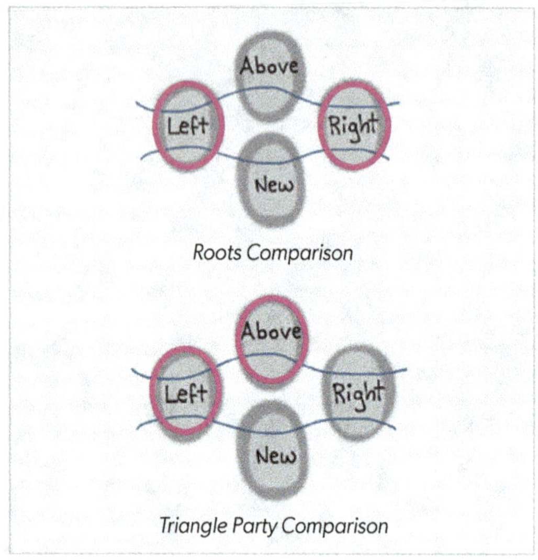

Roots Comparison

Triangle Party Comparison

In contrast, for *Triangle Party*, we compare the color of the left bead with the above bead. **If the left and above beads are the same, pick up 1 (light). If they are different, pick up 0 (dark).** To the right is this rule, written in two more ways: with blobs of color and with numbers. The Xs are placeholders that indicate that the right bead can be any color (Sometimes we use ?s instead of Xs).

The *Triangle Party* algorithm makes a sea full of triangular islands surrounded by rivers. The tightly packed triangles are color **1**, and the narrow rivers are color **0**. The beads that are the same color amass in patches of land. The rivers, just one bead wide, are on the boundary between triangles. Thus, the rivers are in the different color.

Triangle Party Variation with 12 Colors and Diamond Cells

How to Bead Triangle Party

Now we will make a patch of beadwork using the rule for *Triangle Party*, shown below on the left with beads and below right with numbers.

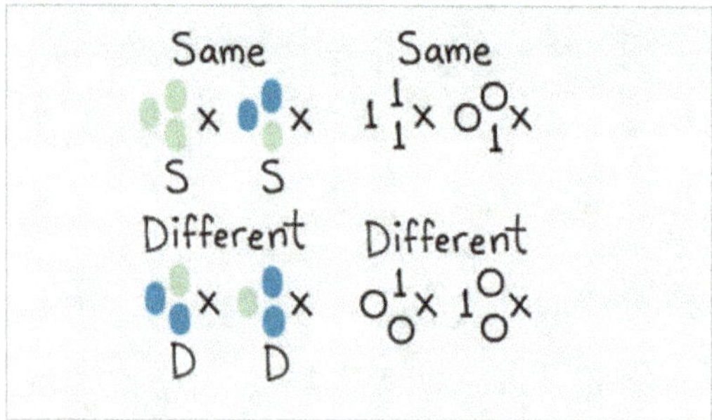

Rows 1 and 2: Waste beads

Label your bead piles "same 1" and "different 0." Thread your needle, and pick up 15 beads (or any odd number, to make an even number of columns) in color **0** for rows **1** and **2**. Here, the first two rows are waste beads that you can rip out later if you want. Start row 3 by passing back through the third-to-last bead.

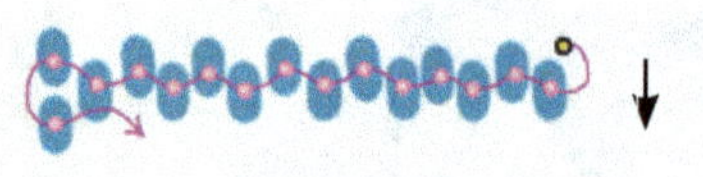

Continue row 3: The initial state

Pick up a bead (color **1**), skip a bead, and pass through a bead.

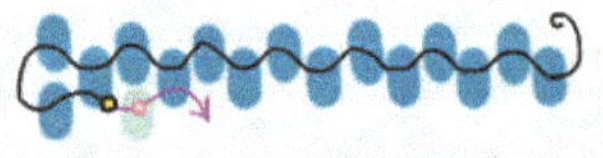

Complete row 3 with peyote stitch using any (possibly random) sequence of colors **0** and **1** you choose. The choice of colors in this row will determine the pattern of triangles that emerges in the following rows.

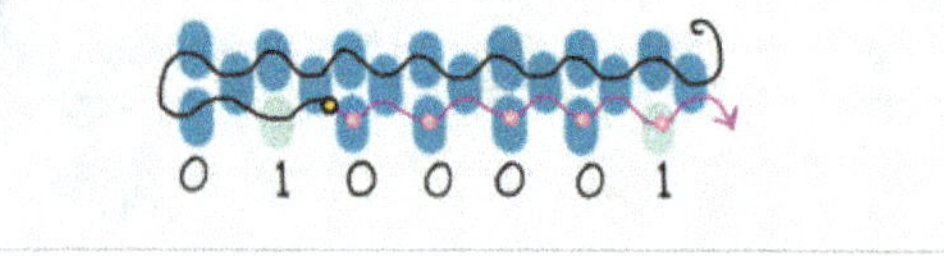

Rules that use the left and above beads require two rows for the initial state, so reverse direction and stitch row 4 using any sequence you choose. We have not yet been following the rule. We will begin following it on the next row.

A. To be sure the front side is facing you, make sure the thread tail is on the top right. To start the next row on the left edge, we want to compare the left and above beads, but there is no left bead on that edge. So use the bead on the bottom right as your left bead as if wrapping the beadwork into a tube. Compare this bead with the above bead (the last bead you passed through).

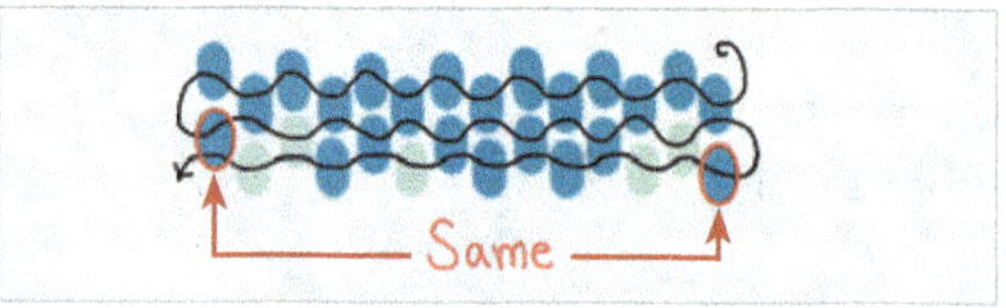

In our case, they are the same color, so we pick up color **1**. If they were different, we would pick up color **0**.

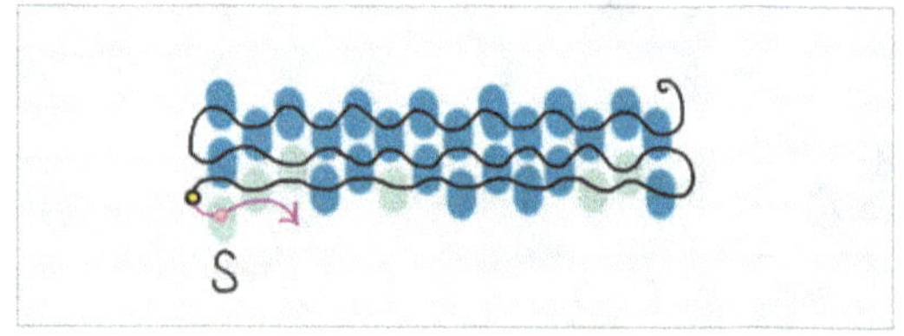

B. Compare the colors of the next left bead (the one you just exited) and the above bead. Here, they are the same color, so we pick up color **1**. If they were different, we would pick up color **0**.

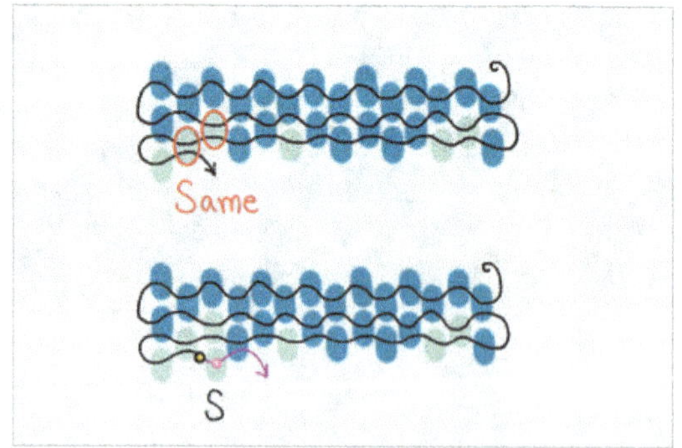

C. Repeat step B until you finish the row. **Do not flip the beadwork over. The tail should always be on the top right.**

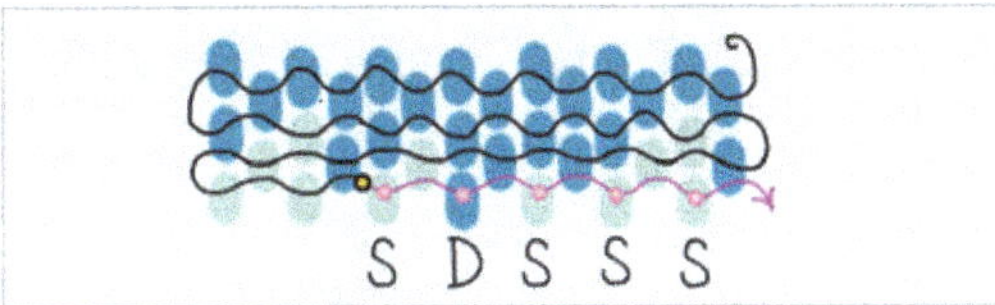

D. To start the next row on the right edge, compare the left bead (the last bead you picked up) with the above bead (the last bead you passed through). Unlike on the other edge, here the left bead is where we expect it to be.

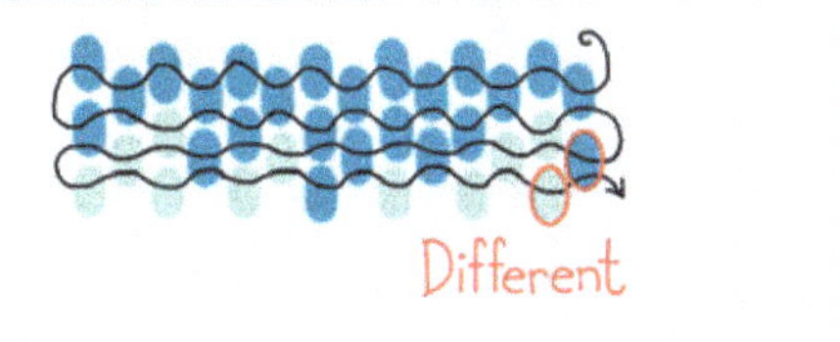

Since the left and above beads are different colors here, we pick up color **0**. If they were the same, we would pick up color **1**.

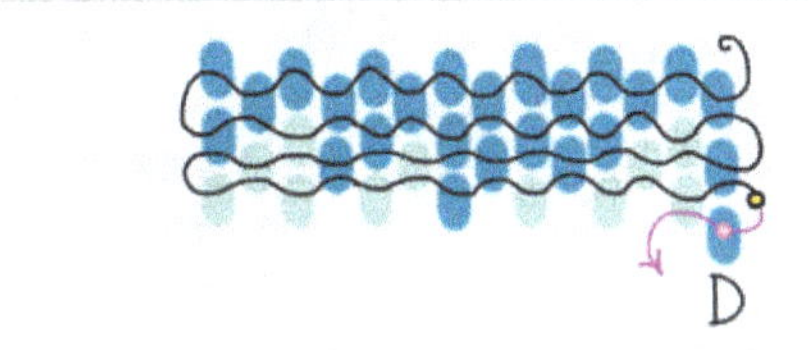

E. Compare the colors of the left bead (the one you will pass through) and the above bead. If they are the same color, pick up **1**. If they are different colors, pick up **0**.

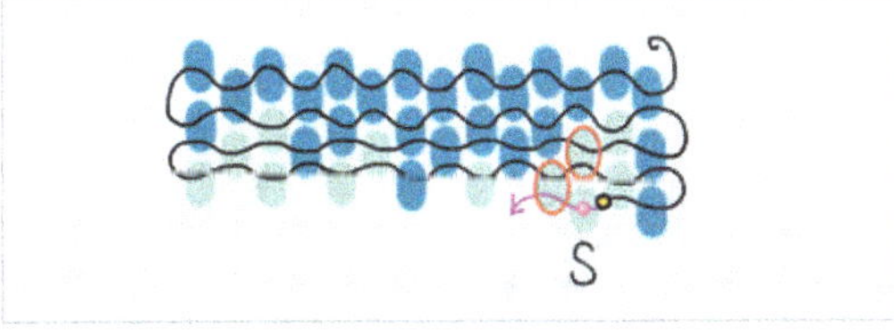

F. Repeat step E until you finish the row. Do not flip the beadwork over.

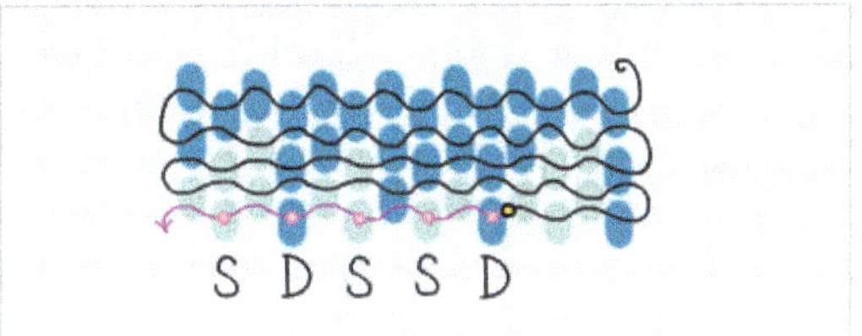

G. Repeat steps A through F to make the strip as long as you want.

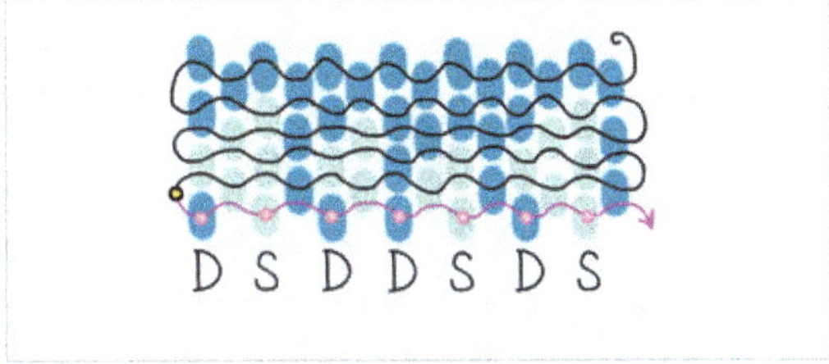

This is what the pattern looks like, using our initial state and colors.

Repeating Patterns

If you use a specific repeating sequence of colors for the initial state, *Triangle Party* produces beautiful repeating patterns. Here are a few of our favorites, each marked with the number of columns in its period, or repeating unit.

We used the following repeating version of *Triangle Party* to make the beaded bead below with three colors. The beaded tube has 24 columns of beads. The pattern repeats seamlessly around the tube because 24 is a multiple of 6, the period.

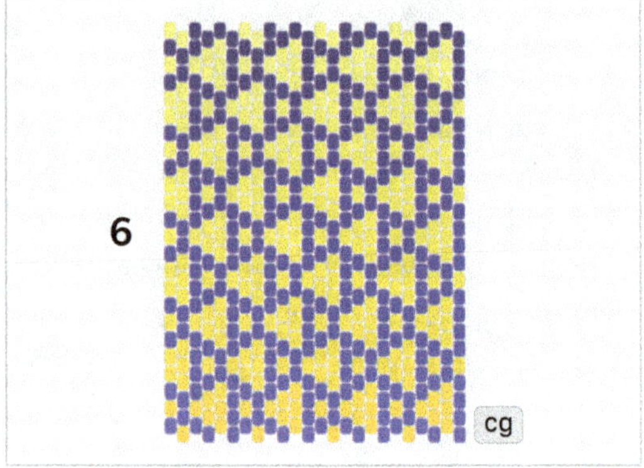

To help it hold its shape, this beaded bead contains a bit of plastic straw layered with electrical tubing.

The ends of the beaded bead are hexagonal. Below left is the hexagonal start, and below right is the hexagonal finish. The dots show the increases and step-ups (left) and decreases and step-downs (right). See the chapter on peyote stitch for more information.

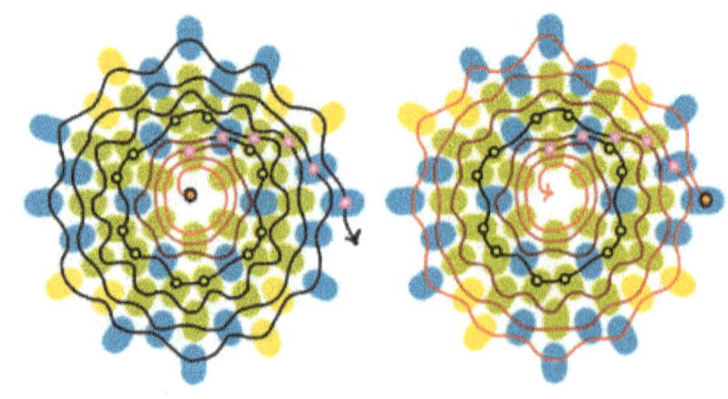

Color Blocking

In *Triangle Party* patterns, the triangles in the patch below are all disjointed, meaning they don't touch each other. Because they don't touch, we can make each triangle a different color, and it's even easy to do this while beading. In particular, we add two parts to the rule for *Triangle Party*: **If the left, above, and right beads are all red, then pick up a non-red color. Continue using that color until you finish that triangle.**

A *bail* is a loop at the top of a pendant. The patch below is a pendant with a fold-over bail at the top. This piece was beaded from the center out (see arrows) with a single piece of thread, by leaving the thread tail attached to its spool. Use the first end of the thread to bead the triangles and the fold-over bail. Finish off the first end. Then, pull the tail end off the spool, and rip out the first rows, those before the initial state. Stitch enough rows to complete all of the triangles plus one row of all red, and finish with the blue flower trim.

Color Shading

The patch of beadwork below is an application of the *Triangle Party* rule with lots of different colors—and several mistakes. Can you find them? We counted six.

Use darks (for different) and lights (for same), with a large range of hues for each. The darks shade with black, blue, and lilac. The lights shade with white, cream, gold, orange, red, and burgundy. The first three rows are all black. Then, for the initial state, bead two random rows with black and orange. After every two or three rows, switch to a new, related color for one of the colors in use. Continue switching after every few rows. We like to use a color for about two to five rows before switching.

Human eyes see change in a value more than a change in color. If we keep the light beads lighter than the dark beads, especially where they touch, then it helps us see the underlying design better. The patch below has some regions that do that and other regions that don't, so the triangles are sometimes hard to distinguish.

Mirror Symmetry

We applied a *same-different* rule in two ways, for *Roots* (using left and right beads) and for *Triangle Party* (using left and above beads). One important difference is that the rules for *Roots* have mirror symmetry, and the rules for *Triangle Party* do not. To see this, swap the left and right beads in the rule for *Roots*. We get the same four parts. Because the order of the inputs doesn't matter, we don't have to pay attention to which side is the front when beading *Roots*. In contrast, the order of the inputs matters in *Triangle Party*, so the algorithm does not have mirror symmetry. This is why the beadwork must not be flipped (i.e., the tail kept at the top right) while beading unless the rules are flipped as well.

If we swap the left and right beads, a left-above rule turns into a right-above rule, so we have to be careful. If we flip the beadwork, we must also flip our rule, or the rule won't work as intended. This makes rules with mirror symmetry easier to bead with than those without. For this reason, most of the rules in this book have mirror symmetry.

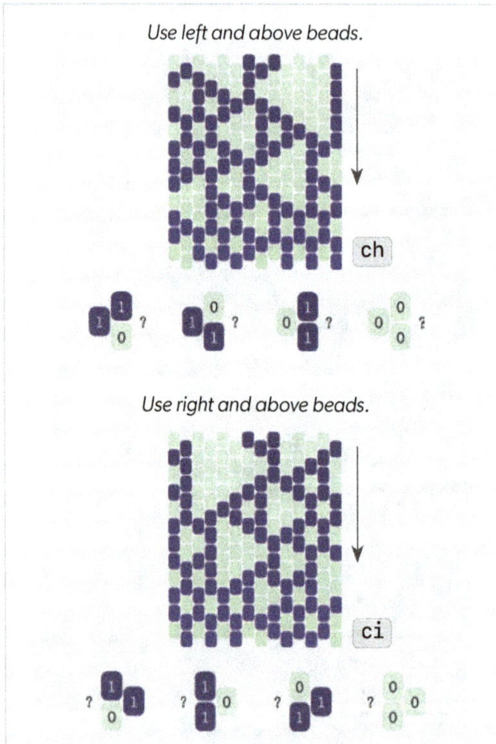

Use left and above beads.

Use right and above beads.

Reversibility

If you make a patch of beadwork with *Triangle Party* and flip the beadwork over, top to bottom, the triangles point in the same direction as before. You will also find that the rule for *Triangle Party* still applies. We say that the rule for *Triangle Party* is *reversible*. Reversability is a useful property. When a rule is reversible, you can generate the pattern from the center out, which means you can add new beads along both the top and bottom.

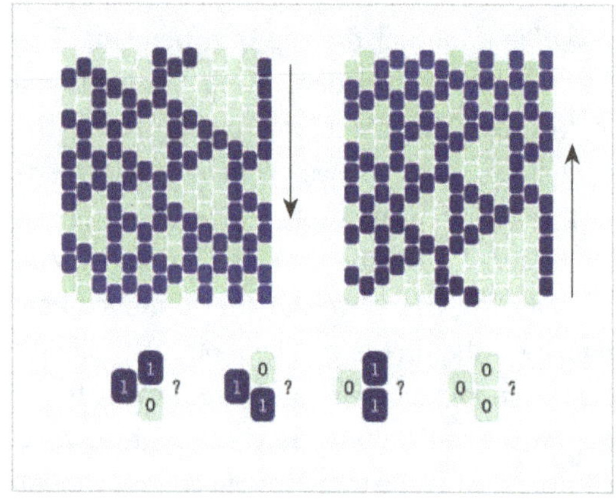

Reminders...
Do not flip the beadwork from side to side when beading *Triangle Party*.

For the left-above rule...
When you weave peyote stitches to the left, the left bead is the bead *you stitch into*.

When you weave peyote stitches to the right, the left bead is the bead *the thread is coming out of*.

For the right-above rule...
When you weave peyote stitch to the left, the right bead is the bead *the thread is coming out of*.

When you weave peyote stitches to the right, the right bead is the bead *you stitch into*.

The patch of beadwork below shows silver dots and blue triangles in a sea of black. To do this, we started with the rule for *Triangle Party* in two colors, and then split it. Here is the right-above version of *Triangle Party* in two representations.

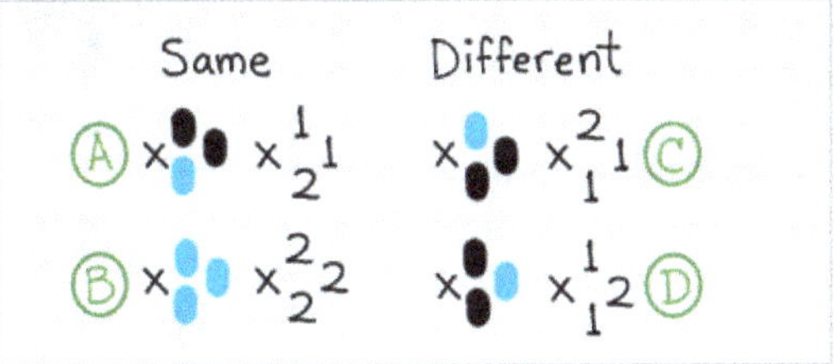

Using the rule above, each triangle after the initial state starts with a blue (**2**) bead. In contrast, in the beadwork below, each triangle starts with a silver (**0**) bead. Here, we split blue into two colors, silver (**0**) and blue (**2**). In particular, if the left, above, and right beads are all black (**1**) (which happens only when we are starting a new triangle), then pick up a silver (**0**) bead.

Below is this rule for *Triangle Party* with three colors. The silver beads act just like the blue beads when used as inputs for the two-color rule for *Triangle Party*. The letters A–D show the correspondence between the original rule and its color split, but they are not otherwise used in the algorithm.

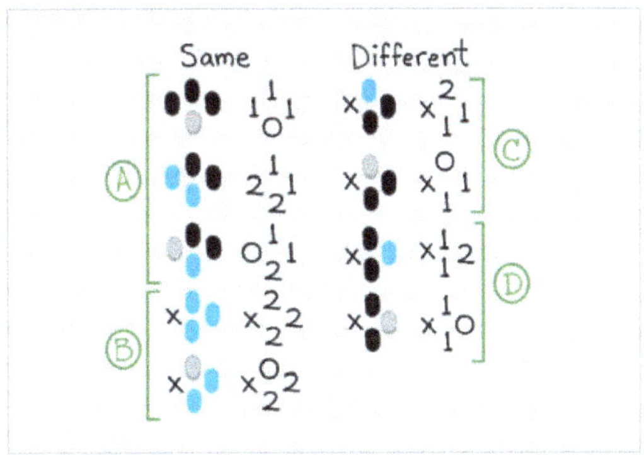

In theory, we need two more parts to complete splitting section B in the rule above, but in practice, the two parts below aren't used, unless you force their use with your initial state.

Below is another three-color version of *Triangle Party* with striped triangles. The two left-most parts on the bottom row are not needed unless they are required by the initial state.

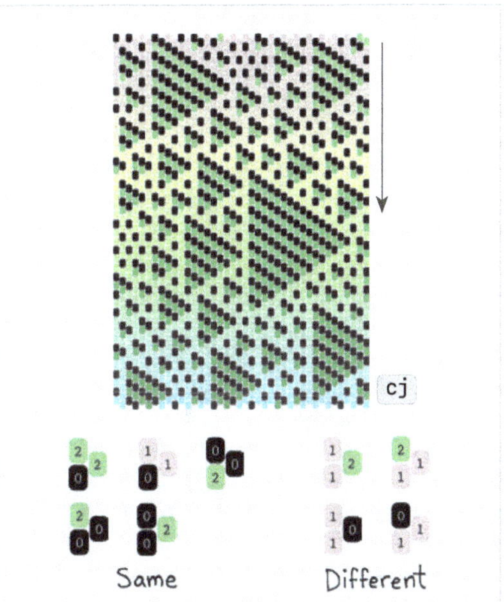

Seed State

If the initial state is all one color, except one bead, that is a *seed* state. When we apply *Triangle Party* to an initial state that is a seed, a beautiful version of the Sierpiński triangle emerges. The nested triangles that make up the Sierpiński triangle are angled with sides on the vertical, like pennants in the wind.

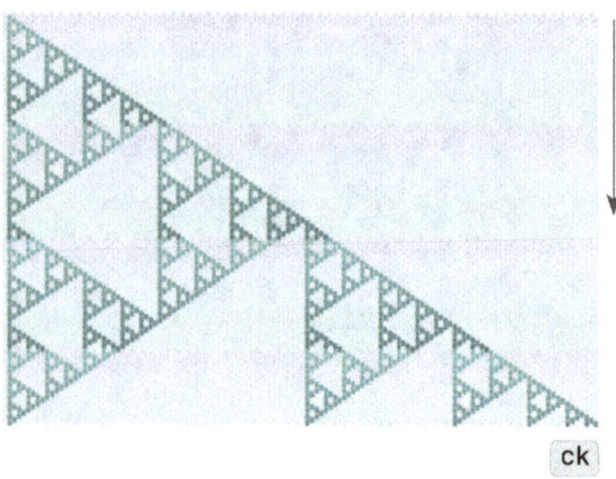

Here is a set of three pendants using *Triangle Party* and seed starts. The center pendant uses an obtuse angle start; the side pendants use acute angle starts.

Acute Angle Start

Rows 1, 2, and 3

Make an increase: Pick up three dark beads, and pass back through the third to last bead.

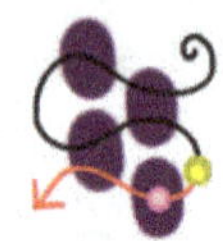

Row 4

Make a turn: Pick up one dark bead and pass back through the last bead you picked up in the previous stitch.

Row 5

Make an increase. Pick up one gold bead and continue the peyote stitch. This is where we start to follow the *Right-Above* rule for *Triangle Party*.

Even Rows

Make a turn, and follow the rule to peyote stitch to the end of the row (blue).

Odd Rows

Make an increase (red). Follow the rule to peyote stitch to the end of row (orange).

Triangle Party with an Acute Angle Start

Use these instructions to construct the pendants on the left: Reverse the shaping and use the *Left-Above* rule for *Triangle Party* to make the pendant on the right. To make the middle pendant, use an obtuse angle start as shown in Chapter 1, increasing at the beginning of every row. Also, use the dark beads to make a line of symmetry down the center. Use the *Left-Above* rule for *Triangle Party* on one side of the line, and use the *Right-Above* rule for the other side, switching rules on each row, immediately after passing the line of symmetry.

RULES WITH TWO COLORS

The Beauty of Multisets

Consider a rule that uses the colors from three beads, taken in any order, as the inputs to determine the color of the new bead, the output. For example, if a part of a rule looks like this:

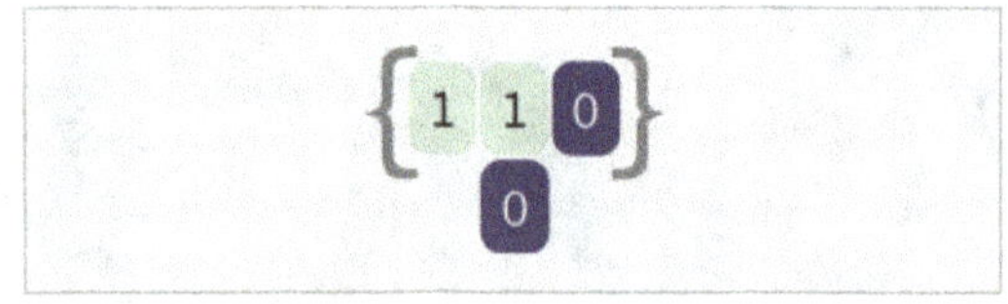

then the beadwork can look like any of these:

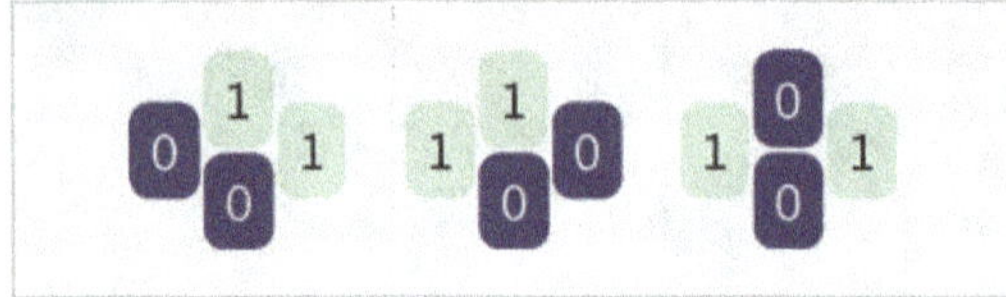

In words, if two of the input beads are light, and one is dark, then the new bead is dark. The brackets indicate that the input is a *multiset*, meaning the colors of the inputs can be applied in any order. A useful property of a multiset rule on three beads is that the rule is symmetric, meaning we can flip the beadwork over after every row, and the same rule still applies.

The example above is one part of a multiset rule that we call *Minority Wins,* with code **0011**. This rule behaves just as the name implies: "Go with the color that appears the **least** number of times." Here are all four parts of the rule for *Minority Wins*, given as a bead diagram, with numbers and colors. Notice that the inputs are written in decreasing order, and the outputs, read in order, give the code **0011**. Remember, the brackets indicate that the input for each part can be taken in any order.

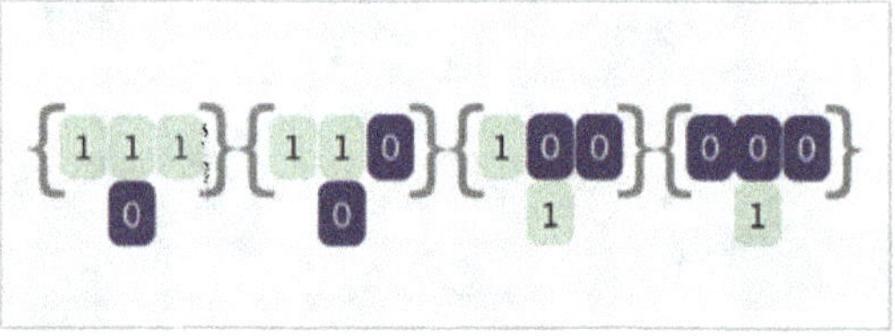

We like to use this rule, in particular, with errors added on purpose. It turns out that some rules make more exotic and compelling designs when used with errors, and *Minority Wins* is one of them. Figure 1 shows a typical patch of the kind of patterns *Minority Wins* makes: simple stripes with diagonal jogs. However, Figure 2 shows what happens when we add errors at the red dots. The errors create interest in an otherwise simple pattern. In fact, the more errors we make, the more interesting it gets—up to a point, of course.

number of errors in the middle, and just a few errors near the bottom. You can see the errors immediately after a line of either color ends, moving from the top down. At those points, the minority loses rather than wins.

Figure 3: Minority Wins with errors and color shading

If you study the photos of beadwork in this book closely, you will find many errors, some of which were made on purpose. Many were made by accident. We think that random errors can add character to artwork. If you use cellular automata to make art, we encourage you to enjoy the process, and don't fret over choosing the right color every single time.

Minority Wins has a property we call a *balanced color distribution*. By this, we mean that if you swapped the light and dark colors, the design would have the same general appearance. The dark stripes are the same kind of shapes as the light stripes. In contrast, *Triangle Party* does not have a balanced color distribution. One color is triangles and the other color is not triangles, or what we call the background. White triangles on a black background look different if reversed. With a balanced color distribution, the design has no foreground or background. We can also see that the colors are balanced in the rule itself. If we swap **0** and **1** everywhere in the number form of the rule, we get the same four parts of the rule, given in the opposite order. This swapping is called an *automorphism*, which means that the swapping of **0** and **1** is a way to map the rule onto itself, while, at the same time, preserving all of its structure. We write more about balanced color distributions in the next chapter.

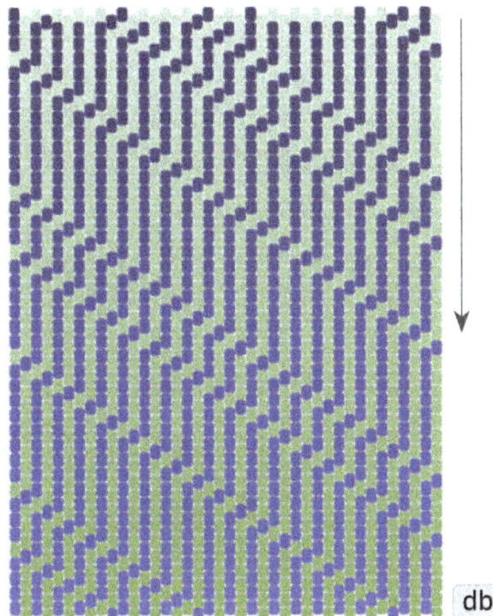

Figure 1: Minority Wins without errors

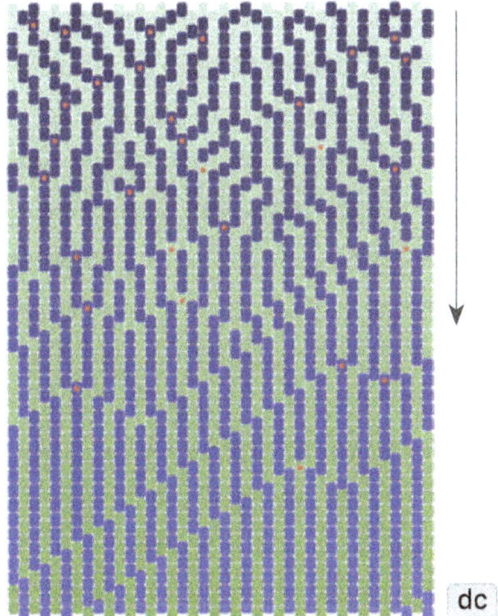

Figure 2: Minority Wins with errors

Figure 1 has no errors, whereas Figures 2 and 3 have many. With errors, the stripes stop and start and change direction. Figure 2 has a lot of errors near the top, a moderate

Minority Wins Pill Pouch

The photos below show the back and front of a tiny beaded pill pouch made with size 15° seed beads, and a button and loop clasp. The rule is *Minority Wins* with a lot of errors.

Start beading the pouch at its base with all black beads. After a few rounds of black, let the last row of black be the first row of the initial state. For the second row of the initial state, randomly choose black (dark) and pink (light) beads.

Use color shading as described in the first chapter, dividing the beads into dark and light colors. In the center is matte black with shiny white, the highest contrast we can get with beads. The colors toward the top and bottom have less contrast, making the design more subtle and difficult to see. More details on how to weave beaded pouches and clasps are in the chapter on peyote stitch.

A Hexagonal Beaded Bead

Minority Wins Hexagonal Beaded Bead
22 mm in diameter with 11° Delica beads

A hexagonal beaded bead is a really fun and easy project to stitch with cellular automata, and this chapter includes several examples. The beaded bead here uses a rainbow-colored hexagon at each end, and to make the barrel, we used the rule for *Minority Wins*, with a lot of errors. The figure above shows how to weave that rainbow hexagon, starting from the center and working outwards. The rainbow of dots on top of the thread indicates where to step up to start each new round. The pairs of green dots identify the increases, which occur in every third round. An increase is where you pick up two beads on a stitch, instead of one. After stitching a hexagon, weave a tube of beads as long as you want.

To keep the tube from collapsing, line the tube with plastic transparency film. Just before you stitch the second end of the beaded bead, cut a rectangle of film about three times the

circumference of the beaded bead by the length of the beaded bead. Roll the film into a tube, insert it into the beaded bead, stretch, and smooth the tube. Stitch another hexagon, in reverse, to finish the second end. Fortunately, the thread path for the hexagon works the same in both directions, so when the hexagon is stitched from the outside into the center, the green dots indicate the decreases, just as we would expect. To give the beaded bead a larger hole, omit (or pick out) the first circle of thread and possibly remove the six green beads in the center before securing the tail.

Multiset Rules

As we have seen, *Minority Wins* is an example of a multiset rule that we can describe with the following bead diagram.

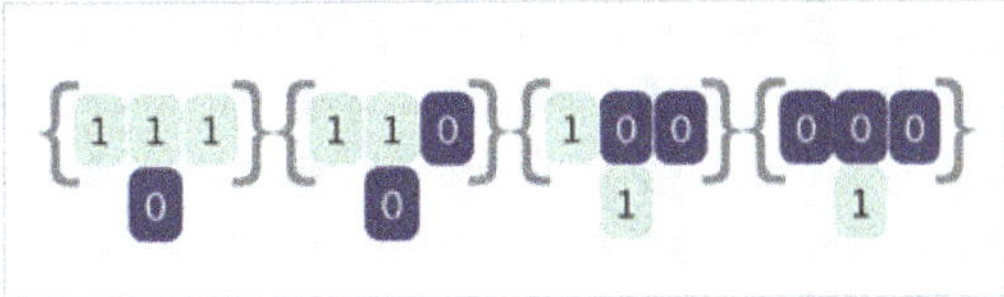

Sometimes, it is easier to refer to a rule by a shorthand code. The top "inputs" row is all possible multiset combinations and we fix the order, which results in a unique "output" code. In the case of *Minority Wins*, the outputs give us the code **0011**. More generally, this code has four digits, each of which has two alternatives: **0** or **1**. This is a four-digit binary code. The fundamental counting principle* tells us that there are $2^4 = 16$ such codes. Consequently, there are exactly 16 different multiset rules with two colors on three beads.

0000 0001 0010 0011
0100 0101 0110 0111
1000 1001 1010 1011
1100 1101 1110 1111

***NOTE:** The fundamental counting principle calculates the number of possible outcomes in a situation. It states that if there are n ways to do one thing and m ways to do another thing, then there are n × m ways to do both.*

The code below each patch identifies a two-color multiset rule that generates the patch. All 16 patches start with the same two rows for the initial state.

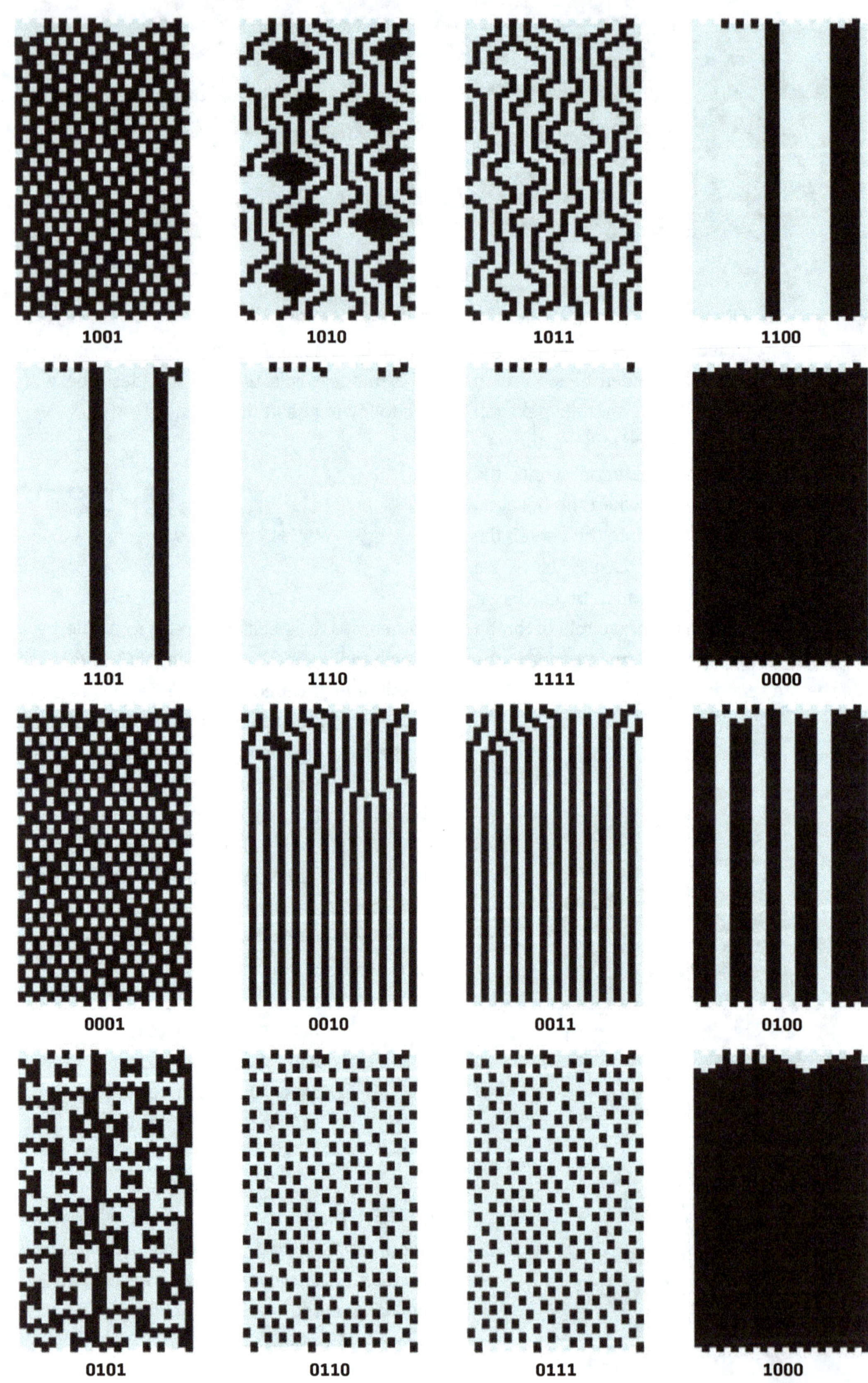

Some of these designs are very interesting:

0010/1011	Buds and Vines
0101	Picket Fence
1010	Groovy Checkers
0001/0111/1001/0110	Dot Arrays

Some of these designs are less interesting:

0011	Minority Wins
1100	Majority Wins
0000/1111	Mono
1000/1110	Boring
0100/1101	Scant

NAME OF RULE	CODE	RULE IN WORDS
Buds & Vines	**0010/1011**	Go with A if there is exactly **one** A; otherwise B.
Picket Fence	**0101**	Go with the color that appears an **even** number of times.
Groovy Checkers	**1010**	Go with the color that appears an **odd** number of times.
Dot Arrays	**0001/0111**	Go with A if there are exactly **three** Bs; otherwise B.
Minority Wins	**0011**	Go with the color that appears the **least** number of times.
Majority Wins	**1100**	Go with the color that appears the **most** number of times.

We now explore all of the interesting cases…

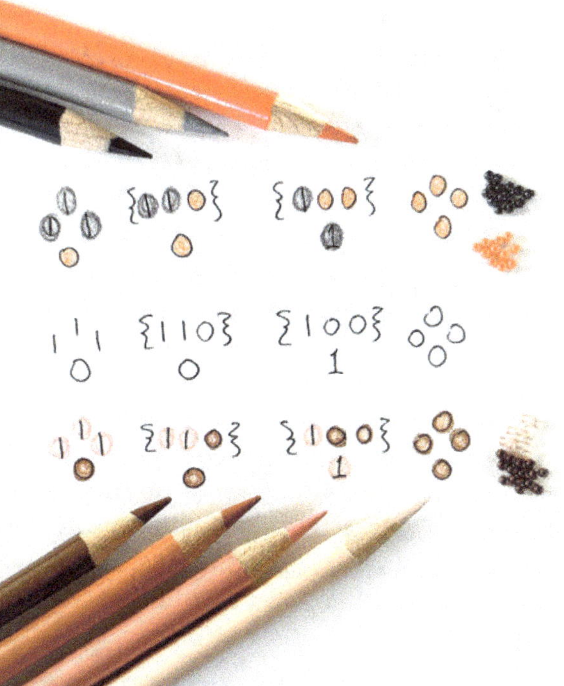

Numbers and Colors

The rules in this book are given in terms of numbers or colors or both. Before you use a rule with your own color palette, you can convert the rule to colors that match your beads. A good way to do this is to copy the arrangement of numbers; then color directly on top of the numbers with colored pencils, matching the colors to your actual beads as closely as possible. Color all of the **0**s one color, then color **1**s another color, and so forth. When we convert the colors of a rule, we usually convert them to numbers first. Then we convert the numbers into the new colors.

Buds & Vines
0010/1011

We think of *Buds & Vines* as vines with buds in one color, drawn on a background of a second color. The rule can be stated as follows: "If exactly one of the three inputs is the background color, then the output is the background color. Otherwise, the output is the buds' color." *Buds & Vines* is a family of two different rules given by two different codes: **0010** and **1011**. The first of these creates buds and vines with color **0** on a background of color **1**, and the second does the opposite. We say these two rules are isomorphic to each other, because we renamed the colors, yet they still have the same structure. To see this, swap all the **0**s and **1**s in one of these rules, and you will get the other (with the four parts in the opposite order). Here is an example:

A. Start with code for a rule, say **0010**.

B. Use the code to write out all of the parts of the rule with numbers. The parts are ordered by their inputs.

C. Swap **0** and **1** everywhere in the rule.

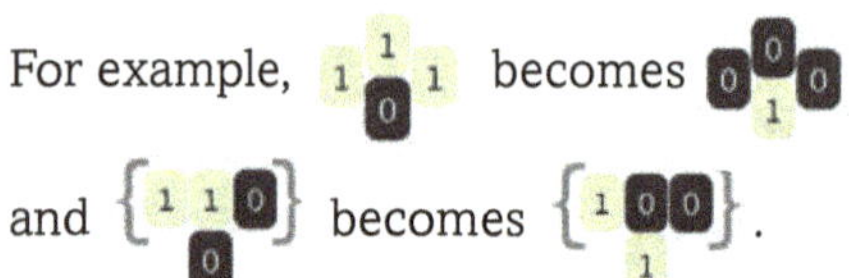

D. Reorder the parts using the inputs.

E. Look at the outputs to find the code for the rule **1011**.

This process shows that the two rules with codes **0010** and **1011** are isomorphic. They are part of the same family.

Notice the two parts without brackets around the **111** and **000** groups. Of course, the order of those does not matter. Therefore, we can write them either with or without brackets.

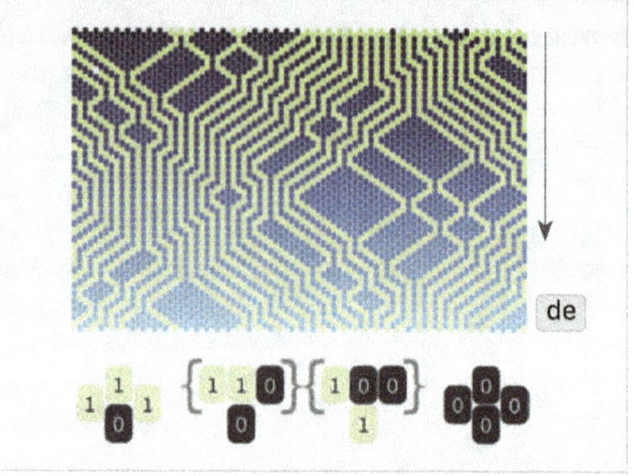

0010 *Buds & Vines*

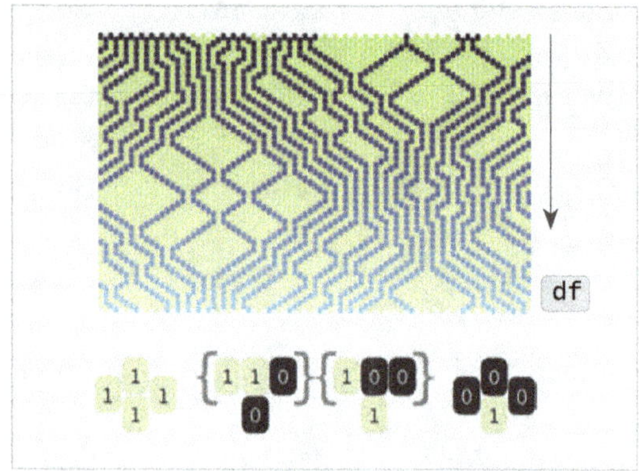

1011 *Buds & Vines*

The pendant shown here uses the multiset rule for *Buds & Vines*.

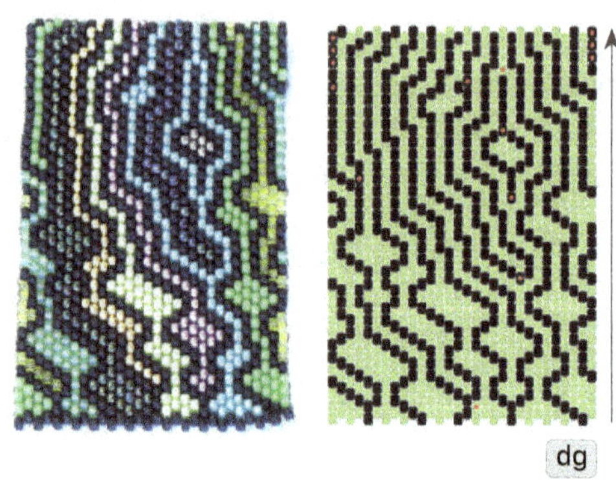

This pendant uses black for color **1** (the background), and ten different colors of beads for color **0**, including green, blue, gold, lavender, and silver. On the right above is a computer-generated version of the same patch in only two colors.

Start rows 1 and 2 at the bottom with all black. For row 3, add up to three sequential beads in one vine color, placing a single black bead between color blocks. For row 4, choose colors to keep the vines separated by one black bead. For all subsequent rows, follow the rule for *Buds & Vines*.

Buds & Vines is a fun rule to use with strategically placed errors. You can see our errors marked with red dots on the computer-generated patch above. Notice how the errors can be used to start new vines, terminate them, split vines in two, or join two vines together.

Next is another example of *Buds & Vines*, this time using burgundy-bronze beads for the background (color **1**) and 12 different colors of beads for the buds and vines (color **0**). The first two rows of the initial state create a design with narrow stripes and little buds. The errors are shown with red dots. Although *Buds & Vines* is not technically reversible, this rule works well to generate pretty designs in both directions, so you can start in the center of a patch and add rows of beads to both ends.

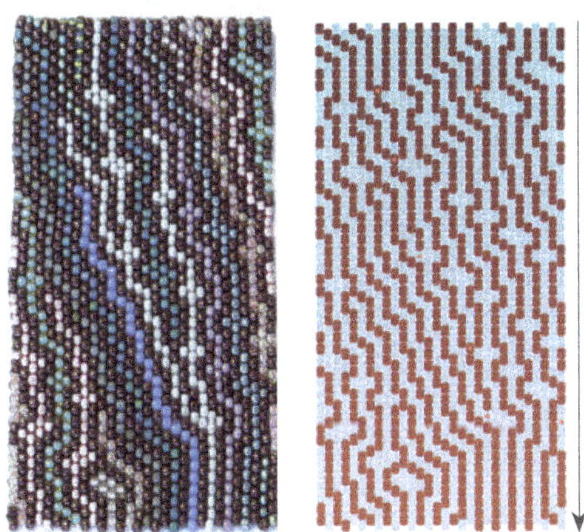

Picket Fence
0101

The rule for *Picket Fence* can be stated in words as: "Majority wins. Unanimous loses."

Like all multiset rules with two colors on three beads, it has four parts, and the inputs are taken in any order. We can also think about this rule in terms of the *parity* of the inputs. Parity is the evenness or oddness of a number. In this case, look for the even input color, and use that for the output color. In particular, if the input contains zero or two black beads, then the output is black. If the input contains an even number of light beads, then the output is light. In short, the parity rule for *Picket Fence* is "Go with even."

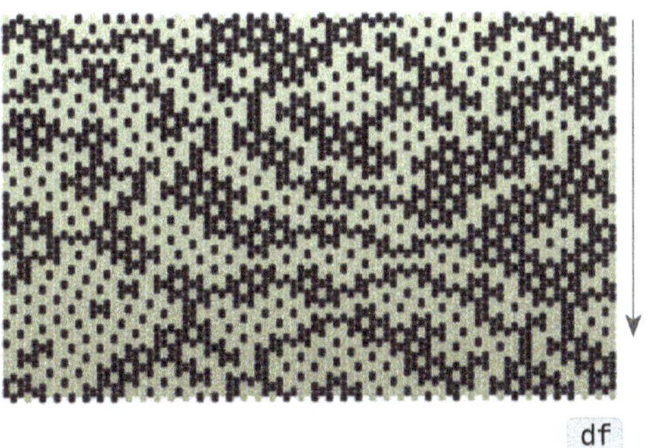

df

Picket Fence has many of the nice mathematical properties that we have seen before. Like all multiset rules on three beads, the rule for *Picket Fence* is symmetric, meaning you can flip the beadwork over after every row of peyote stitch. Like *Triangle Party*, *Picket Fence* is reversible, meaning we can use the rule to add new beads on both the top and bottom. Like *Minority Wins*, *Picket Fence* has a balanced color distribution, meaning we can swap **0** and **1** to get the same rule back again. In other words, the family of rules for *Picket Fence* only has one rule, code **0101**. (We discuss balanced color distributions in more detail in the next chapter.) All of these properties make *Picket*

Fence a very special rule. It makes designs with no front or back, no top or bottom, and no background or foreground.

Picket Fence produced the design for the beaded earrings and matching beaded bead. We used a short, repeating sequence for the initial state. The repeating pattern of dots and **x**s reminds us of expensive signature fashion fabrics commonly used for handbags and silk scarves. The patch of beadwork right below uses the rule for *Picket Fence* in dark and light, shading both in a range of colors. (Find details about color shading in Chapter 1.) The initial state was random.

Our next experiment with *Picket Fence* uses the same rule in different colors: silver, black, and bright orange in various tints.

Waste beads are the first rows of beads that we use to start a new patch of beadwork, knowing that we will pick them out after we have the pattern established and something to hold onto. String waste beads for rows 1 and 2. For the initial state, randomly chose orange and black for row 3, and randomly chose orange or silver for row 4.

This piece includes four different colors of orange beads. The sizes and shapes of the blocks of different oranges were made

randomly and intuitively. In contrast, the black and silver stripes were made algorithmically. In particular, we alternate the silver beads with the black beads, switching every row: All of

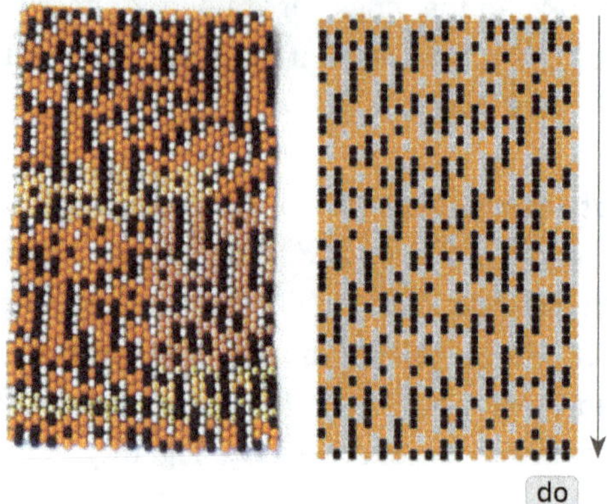

the even rows use silver and orange, whereas all of the odd rows use black and orange. The fact that color **1** (black and silver) alternates row by row means that color **1** has a color cycle with a period of length two.

Many one-stitch embroidery patterns, called hitomezashi sashiko, can be generated with the rule for *Picket Fence* when the tiles are diamonds (squares on point). The patches are rotated 45° from how they are classically presented.

Next is a patch of *Picket Fence* with color cycling for both colors **0** and **1**. Each color cycles with a period of length two, so we use four colors altogether: light purple and black on the odd rows and white and dark purple on the even rows, as shown in the table.

COLOR	ODD ROWS	EVEN ROWS
0	Light Purple	White
1	Black	Dark Purple

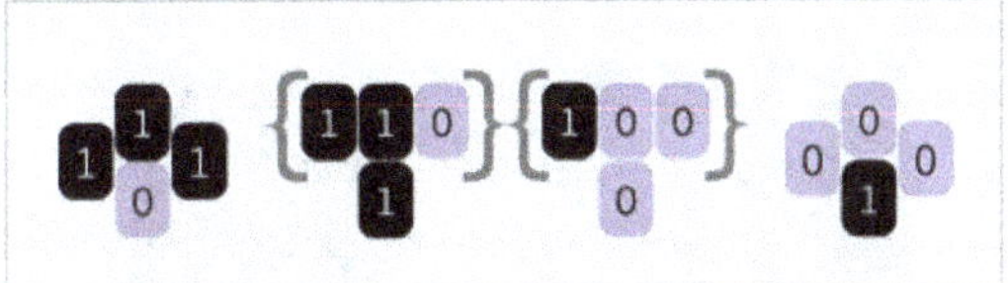

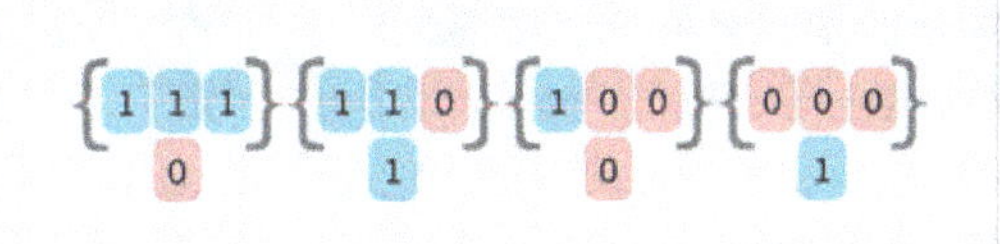

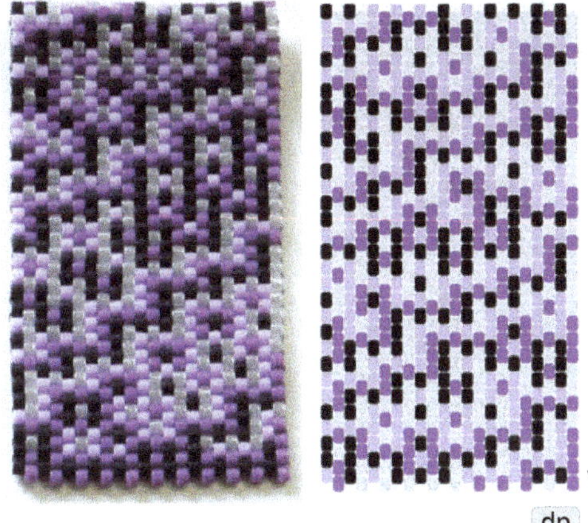

dp

This purple patch of *Picket Fence* shows something interesting when you look at the columns of beads. See how each column contains exactly two different colors? In fact, this happens for every rule with two colors where either (or both) of the colors cycle with two colors.

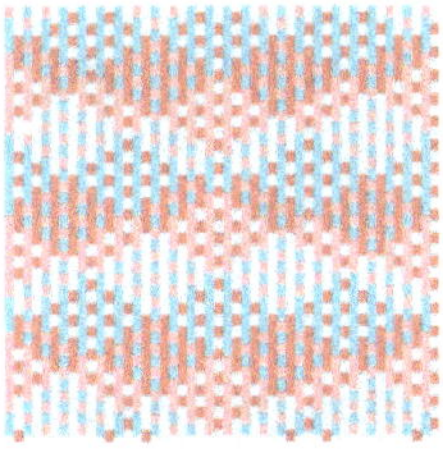

These three patches show how *Picket Fence* can look with a repeating initial state. In all three patches, the length of the period of the initial state is not a factor of the number of columns; still, the rows eventually repeat. These three patches are each 48 columns wide and have a period of 14 columns. In fact, the period is just seven columns, if you think of the first two rows as one staggered row, and you eliminate the color cycles, meaning you use the same two colors on every row. For example, in the first patch, if you read the top two rows straight across as if they were one long row that zig-zags, the sequence is **0111011**, repeating all the way across the 48 columns. In the second patch, the sequence is **1100110**, repeating, and in the third patch, the sequence is **1111000**, repeating.

dr   ds

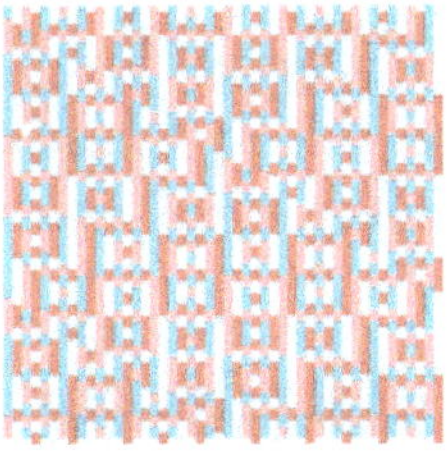

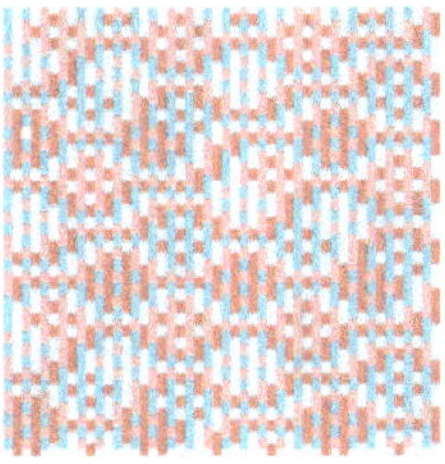

dt

The three patches above show *Picket Fence* with color cycling for both colors. The colors are as follows.

COLOR	ODD ROWS	EVEN ROW
0	Gold	Brown
1	Blue	White

Groovy Checkers

1010

While the name *Groovy Checkers* nicely describes the visual feel of this design, the rule can be stated simply as "Unanimous wins, and minority wins." As with all multiset rules, the inputs are taken in any order.

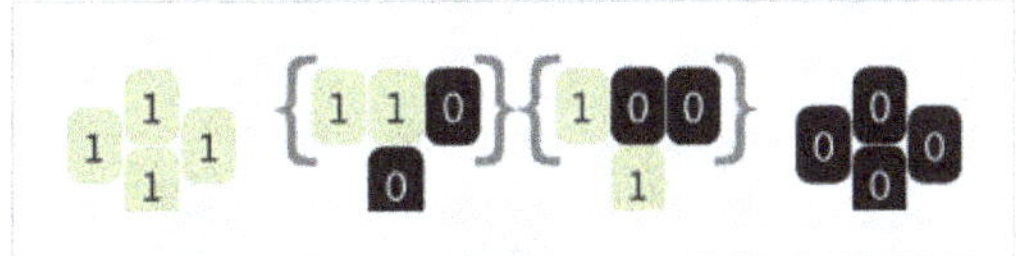

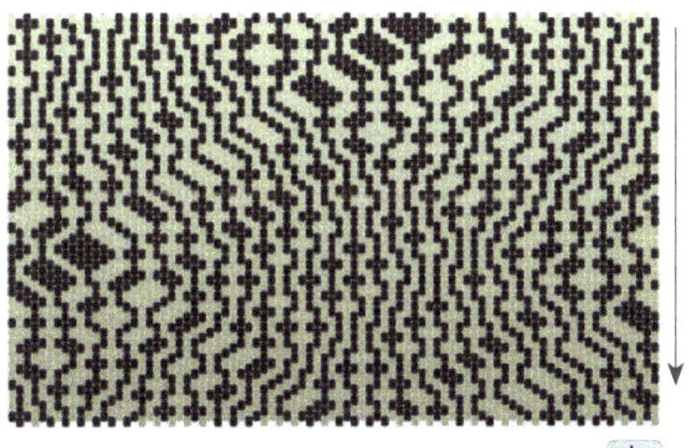

du

As with *Picket Fence*, we can think about *Groovy Checkers* using the parity of the inputs. In this case, look for the odd input color. In particular, if the number of black inputs is odd, one or three, then the output is black. If the number of light inputs is odd, then the output is light. In short: Go with odd.

In *Groovy Checkers*, if you start with long zigzagged strings of the same color in the two zigzagged rows of your initial state, you will make large checkers. If you start with a jumbled state of short color strings in the two zigzagged rows of your initial state, you will create thin lines and smaller checkers.

Like *Picket Fence*, the rule for *Groovy Checkers* is symmetric left to right, reversible top to bottom, and has a balanced color distribution between the two colors. This is true for both the two-color version and the three-color version, which we will look at next. Amazingly, you can make *Groovy Checkers* with as many colors as you want, and the parity rule still applies.

With three colors, these nine parts follow directly from parity: Go with odd.

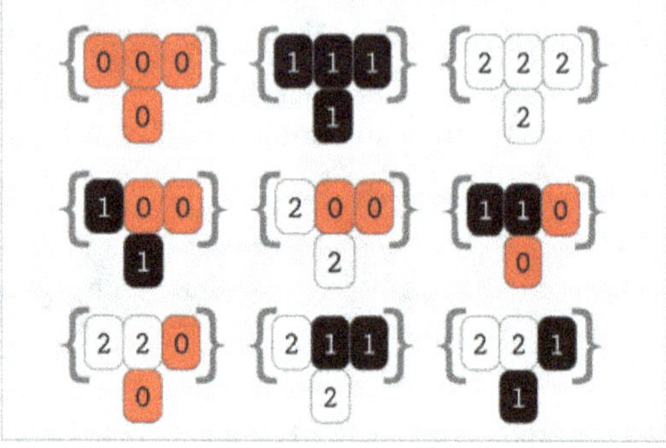

The parity rule is not sufficient when the three input beads are all different colors. In this case, choose the output to be the color of the *above* bead. The input beads for each of the next six parts are shown in order below. We indicate this by the staggered arrangement of the dots and no brackets.

Like *Buds & Vines*, *Groovy Checkers* makes wiggling vertical stripes. To make the stripes more than two colors, start your initial state with the colors in the order that you want them to stripe. Every time we change color in the initial state, we start a new stripe. In the beaded bracelet below, every other color in the initial state is black, creating the illusion that black is the background color, and that red and silver are in the foreground. Careful use of errors allows us to manipulate the stripes that end or reverse direction.

Are you sitting down? Because we have amazing news! We can use *Groovy Checkers* with as many colors as we want, and that means we can make groovy rainbows! Even with lots of colors, the parity rule still applies. So, "Go with odd." When all three input beads are different colors, choose the color of the *above* bead as the output.

The pendant above uses one repeat of a rainbow gradient across the width of the panel. The bracelet uses two repeats of a rainbow gradient.

On the rainbow bracelet, we broke the rule several times to keep the design from repeating. The rule breaks are on the borders, so they are deliberately hard to see.

Dot Arrays

0001/1001/0110/0111

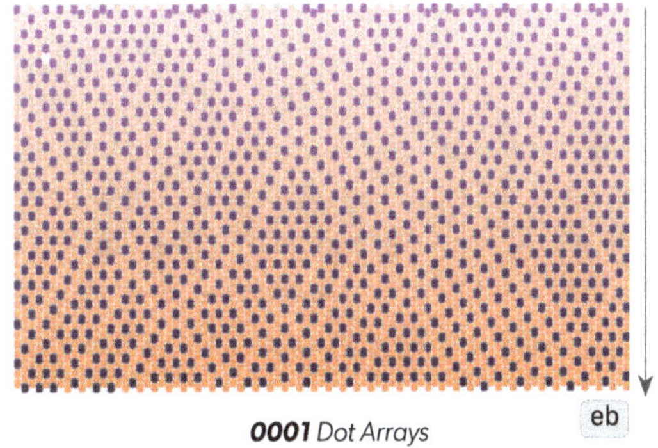

***0001** Dot Arrays* `eb`

One of the codes for *Dot Arrays* is **0001**, which gives this multiset rule:

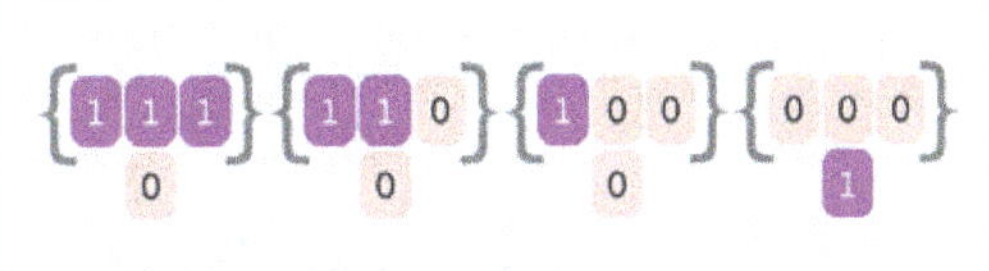

In words, the rule for *Dot Arrays* is as follows: "If the three input beads are the background color, then add a contrasting dot. Otherwise, add a bead in the background color." This rule is reversible, meaning we can add new rows of beads on both the top and bottom. Like all multiset rules on three beads, it is symmetric left to right.

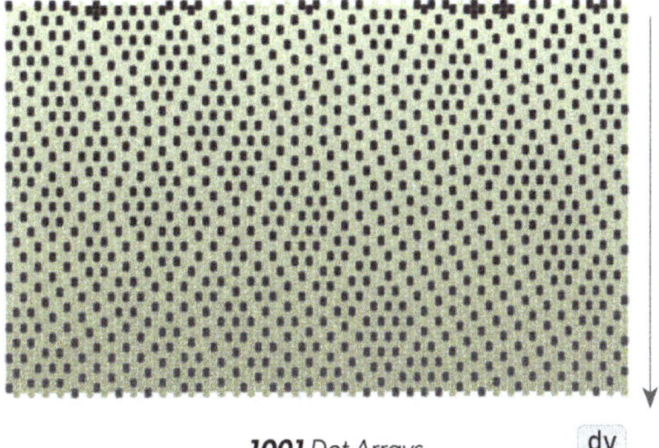

***1001** Dot Arrays* `dy`

Rule **1001** looks nearly identical to rule **0001**, both in terms of their codes and the patches they generate. In both cases, the background is color **0** and the dots are color **1**. Their

Learn to make the button and loop clasp in the chapter on peyote stitch.

codes, **0001** and **1001**, only differ by the first digit, the output for the input **111**, where **1** is the dot color. Looking at the patches, you can see that if the dots do not touch each other in the initial state, then the dots will never touch each other; so as long as your initial state does not have adjacent dots, then the rules **0001** and **1001** generate identical patches. Similarly, **0111** and **0110** can both be used to make all of the same designs with the background in color **1** and the dots in color **0**. The rules for *Dot Arrays* serve as a simple example of how two different rules can be similar enough to produce identical designs as long as specific initial states are met, while still producing different designs under other initial states. This kind of similarity is not unique to *Dot Arrays*.

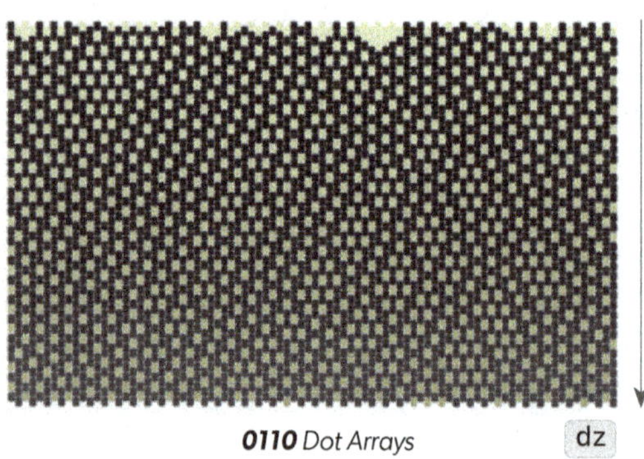

0110 Dot Arrays dz

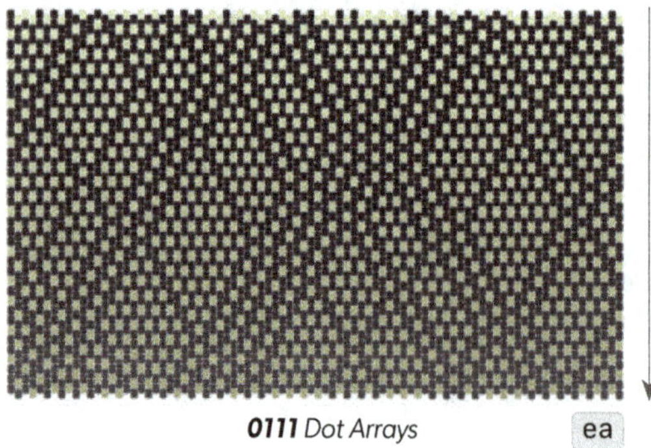

0111 Dot Arrays ea

This beaded patch of *Dot Arrays* uses color shading for the dots, and the background employs a color cycle with two colors. The illustration uses a color cycle with two colors each for the dots and background.

ea

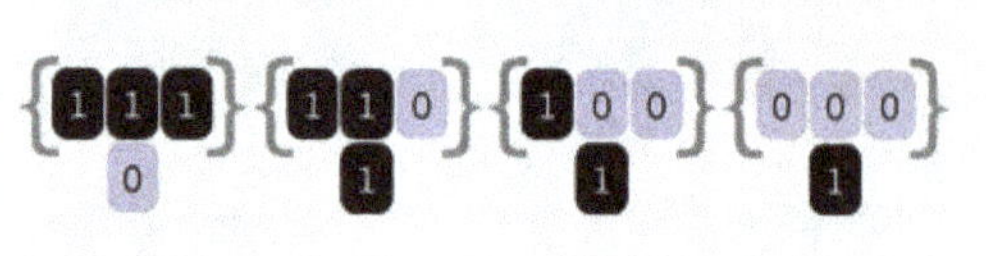

Both patches above have black beads in the odd columns and gray beads in the even columns. Black and gray are the two colors that cycle for the background color, color **1**. To bead the dots (color **0**), use color shading, starting with bronze at the bottom, then olive, gold, orange, red, burgundy, purple, pink, periwinkle, and a large section of silver at the top.

Dot Arrays is a natural choice to use with color cycling with three colors because of the way the colors separate into diamond-shaped regions. You can cycle the dots or the background or both. This beaded patch cycles the dots but not the background, using these dot colors: black (**1a**), burgundy (**1b**), and pumpkin (**1c**). The yellow background (**0**) is represented by three colors in the sketch.

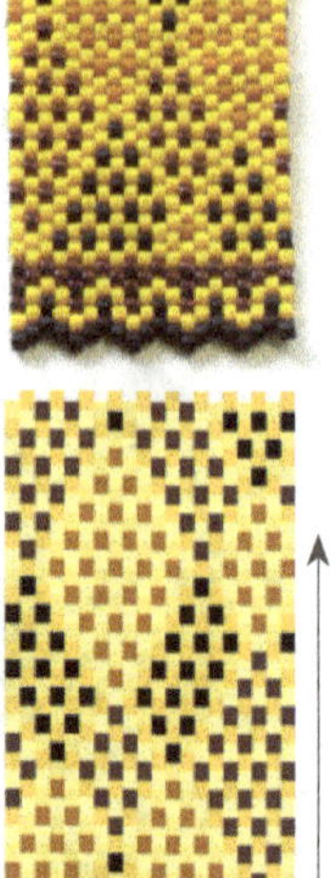

ed

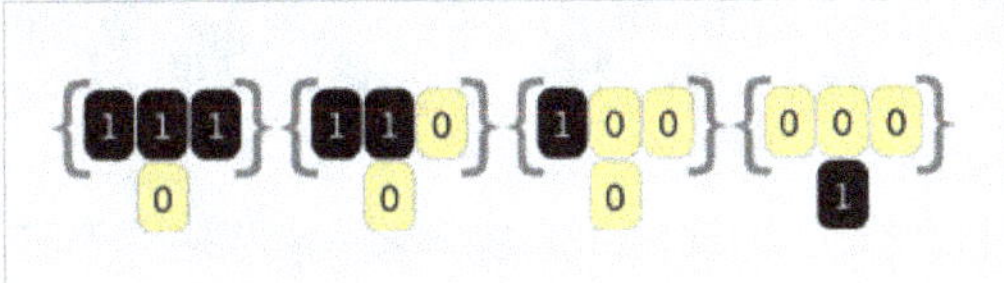

The color cycling for the dots is as follows:
For rows 1, 4, 7, ..., use dot color **1a**.
For rows 2, 5, 8, ..., use dot color **1b**.
For rows 3, 6, 9, ..., use dot color **1c**.

Design Tip: After beading the top of the pendant with the rule, finish the bottom edge with a fancy, repeating border design.

The next two patches use the rule for *Dot Arrays*, with a color cycle of length three for both colors, for a total of six colors. Both patches use the same six colors of beads. In the patch to the left, all of the background beads are light, and all of the dots are dark. The patch on the right doesn't have this easy visual distinction of light versus dark, so it was more challenging to weave. It helps to keep your piles of beads separate and labeled.

DOTS	BACKGROUND	ROWS	
Burgundy	Gold	1, 4, 7, ...	LEFT PATCH
Gray	Peach	2, 5, 8, ...	
Black	Salmon	3, 6, 9, ...	

DOTS	BACKGROUND	ROWS	
Burgundy	Gold	1, 4, 7, ...	RIGHT PATCH
Salmon	Black	2, 5, 8, ...	
Peach	Silver	3, 6, 9, ...	

Non-Multiset Rules

We now consider all rules with two colors on three beads, with a focus on inputs that are not multisets. In other words, we take the three input beads (left, above, and right) in order. For example, the outputs for **001**, **010**, and **100** can all be different without the multiset **{001}**. Such a rule requires eight parts, given in reverse numerical order of the inputs (like 111, 110, 101, ...). In fact, all of the two-color rules we have presented so far can be represented with an eight-digit code that corresponds to the eight different parts of the rule. For example, *Roots*, the subject of Chapter 1, has this presentation.

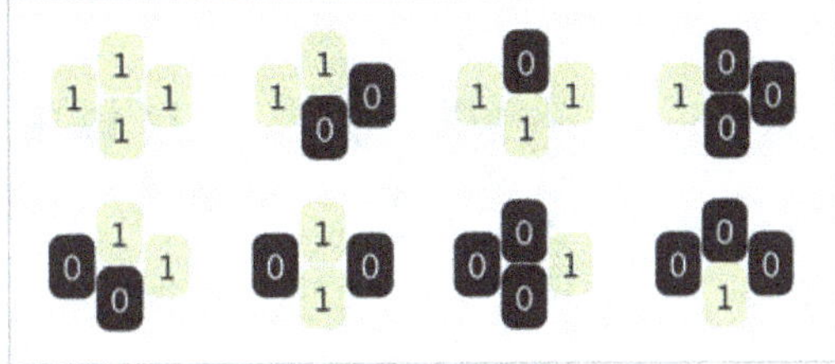

Convince yourself that this is really *Roots*, that is, the same-different rule on the left and right beads. Thus, *Roots* is given by the code **10100101**, and also by the code **01011010** with the colors swapped. There are also two codes for the same-different rule using the left and above beads (that is, *Triangle Party*, the subject of Chapter 2), **11000011** and **00111100**. Likewise, the two right-above codes for *Triangle Party* are **10011001** and **01100110**.

For each rule, the eight inputs are the eight numbers from seven to zero, written in base two. Base two gives these parts a natural ordering. How many eight-digit codes of **0**s and **1**s are there? There are $2^8 = 256$, giving us 256 different rules to consider for two colors on three beads. The complete set is shown on the next two pages. Of these 256, we have already shown you all of the easiest ones that make pretty designs. These are akin to the well-known 256 "elementary cellular automata" rules but applied to the staggered grid rather than the traditional square grid.

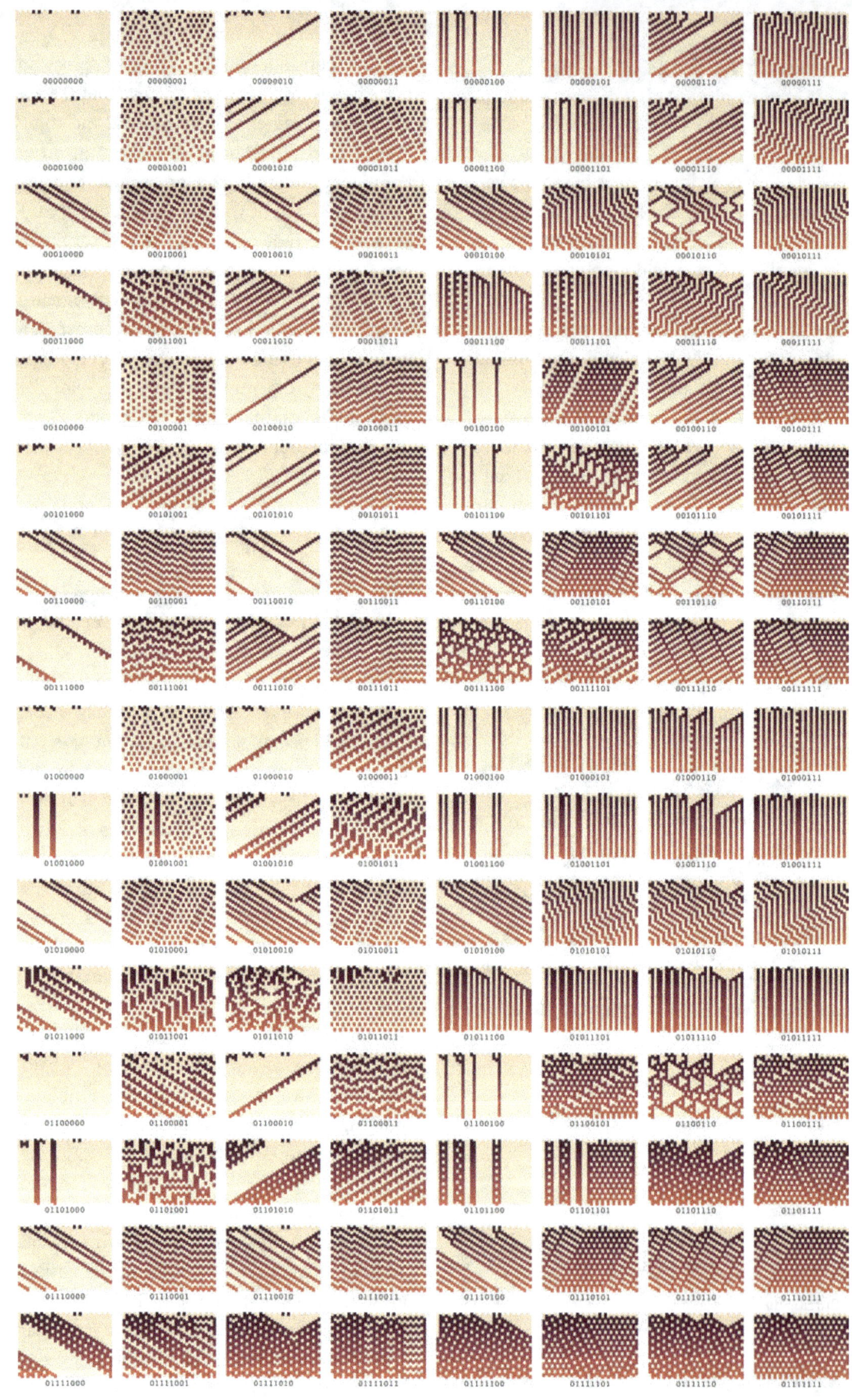

00000000
00000001
00000010
00000011
00000100
00000101
00000110
00000111
00001000
00001001
00001010
00001011
00001100
00001101
00001110
00001111
00010000
00010001
00010010
00010011
00010100
00010101
00010110
00010111
00011000
00011001
00011010
00011011
00011100
00011101
00011110
00011111
00100000
00100001
00100010
00100011
00100100
00100101
00100110
00100111
00101000
00101001
00101010
00101011
00101100
00101101
00101110
00101111
00110000
00110001
00110010
00110011
00110100
00110101
00110110
00110111
00111000
00111001
00111010
00111011
00111100
00111101
00111110
00111111
01000000
01000001
01000010
01000011
01000100
01000101
01000110
01000111
01001000
01001001
01001010
01001011
01001100
01001101
01001110
01001111
01010000
01010001
01010010
01010011
01010100
01010101
01010110
01010111
01011000
01011001
01011010
01011011
01011100
01011101
01011110
01011111
01100000
01100001
01100010
01100011
01100100
01100101
01100110
01100111
01101000
01101001
01101010
01101011
01101100
01101101
01101110
01101111
01110000
01110001
01110010
01110011
01110100
01110101
01110110
01110111
01111000
01111001
01111010
01111011
01111100
01111101
01111110
01111111

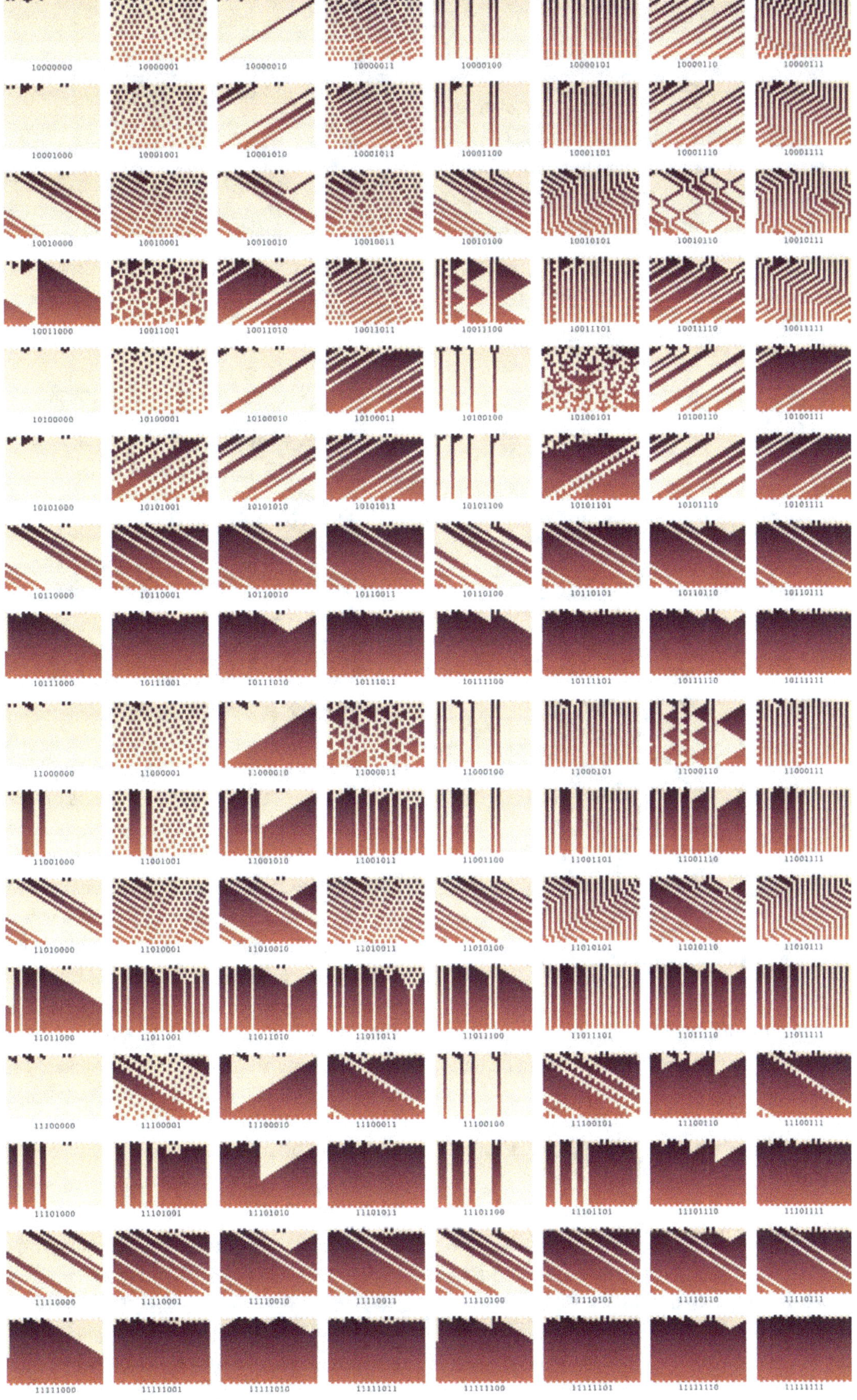

Feather Stitch Stripe

00111001

Feather Stitch Stripe is special because it is reversible and has a balanced color distribution. At the same time, this rule fails to be symmetric. However, if you flip the beadwork left to right and swap **0** and **1** everywhere in the rule's inputs and outputs, then the rule still works to produce the same designs.

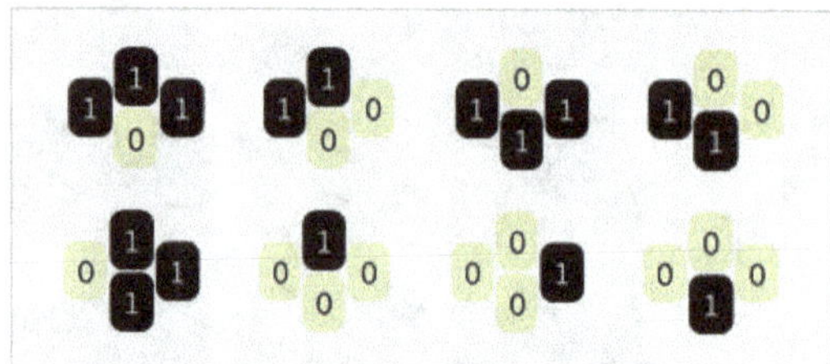

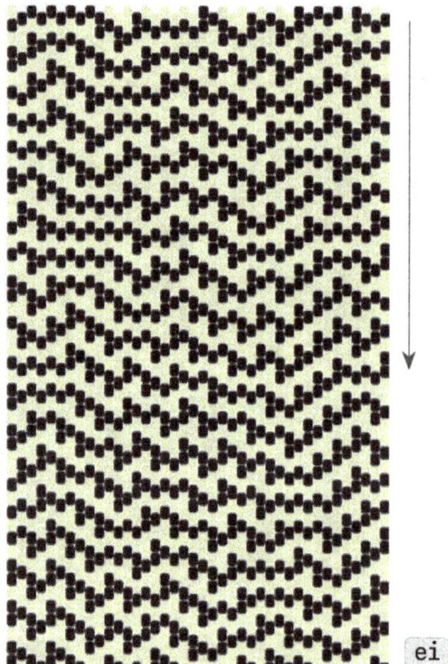

The name *Feather Stitch Stripe* comes from the classic hand-sewing stitch called feather stitch.

The complex beaded bead here uses the rule for *Feather Stitch Stripe* with color splitting. Color **0** is split into **0**, **2**, and **3**. Color **1** is split into **1**, **4**, and **5**. The six colors are peach (**0**), black (**1**), pink (**2**), gold (**3**), blue (**4**), and bronze (**5**).

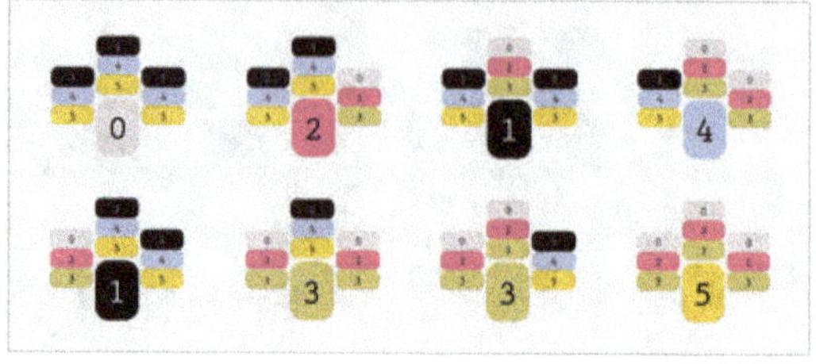

The color split destroys the reversibility of *Feather Stitch Stripe*. Also, the six colors do not have a balanced color distribution.

Design Tips: The tube was beaded with tubular peyote stitch, using 36 columns of size 11° cylinder seed beads. Starting with a tube (rather than with the flat hexagonal end) allows us to begin with two rows of waste beads, and then two rows for the initial state. When stitching complex patterns with color splits, we like to make the first four rows with waste beads that will be removed later. For clarity, we like to make row 1 one color and row 2 another color, stringing the two colors alternately on the beading thread. Then we make rows 3 and 4 the initial state, using just two colors.

For example, use colors **0** and **1** for rows 3 and 4. On row 5, start using the rule with its color split. When the tube is long enough to be structural and the pattern is well established, remove the first four rows of beads. Stitch both ends of the beaded bead with mostly size 11° cylinder seed beads, with size 15° round seed beads added two rounds before the decreases (as explained in the table below). The ends of the tube are stitched into hexagons as described earlier in this chapter, following the thread path from the outside into the center. Looking at the rainbow diagram (the hexagon), omit the last two rounds (yellow and green). In particular, use the following rounds for the hexagonal ends:

ROUND	COLOR	COMMENTS
1	Black	
2	Black	Bronze 15° every third stitch
3	Bronze	
4	Orange	Decrease over 15°
5	Pink	Bronze 15° every third stitch
6	Pink	
7	Peach	Decrease over 15°
8	Gold	

Omit the final loop of thread through the last six beads so that the beaded bead has a larger hole. The finished beaded bead measures 17 mm in diameter and 53 mm long.

ej

Like all of the previous cylindrical beaded beads, this one contains a rectangle of plastic transparency film curled into a cylinder to help it keep its shape.

Stained Glass

10010011/00110110

The two codes for *Stained Glass* generate the same design with its colors reversed. The second version produces a stained glass effect of light windows (parallelograms) in color **0** framed with black lines in color **1**. *Stained Glass* is both symmetric and reversible.

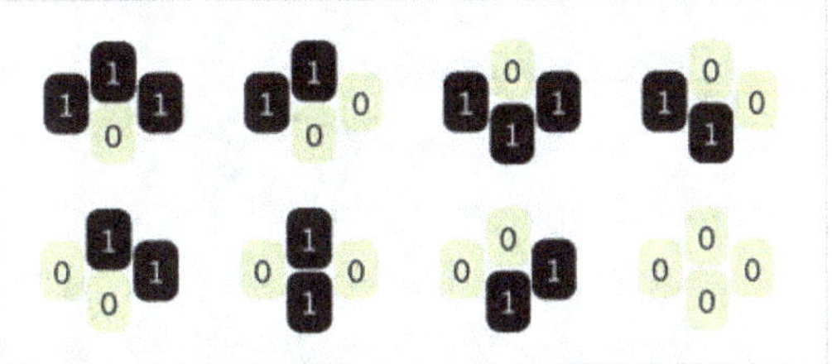

em

The beaded patch of *Stained Glass* uses both color cycling and color shading. For the windows (color **0**), shade with bronze, gold, yellow, white, olive, blue, and lime. For the outlines (color **1**), alternate gray and black beads with every other row.

Another possibility for *Stained Glass* is to make the windows different colors using color blocking. To do this, split the windows into different colors: Call them **0a**, **0b**, **0c**, ... You could make each window a different color, noting that each new window starts with **111** → **0**. The next piece takes this idea one step further by adding color blends in the windows. The patch below shows a combination of *color blocking* and *color shading* within each block. Put all of your window-colored beads in order, and slowly step through the colors for each new window as you add more and more rows.

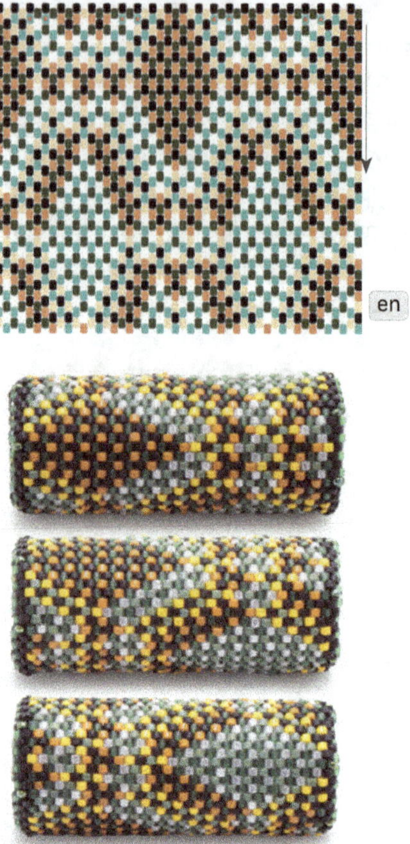

The green and orange hexagonal beaded bead below uses the rule for *Stained Glass* with color cycling for the output of both colors. Use a total of six colors of beads.

Color **0** cycles with three colors: **0a** (white), **0b** (yellow), and **0c** (persimmon).

Color **1** cycles with three colors: **1a** (black), **1b** (forest), and **1c** (green).

Use **0a** and **1a** for rows 1, 4, 7,...
Use **0b** and **1b** for rows 2, 5, 8,...
Use **0c** and **1c** for rows 3, 6, 9,...

This large hexagonal beaded bead uses 6 × 8 = 48 columns around. Use two repeats around the circumference as the initial state, giving the bead design four vertical lines of reflection symmetry.

Made with size 11° cylinder seed beads, this large beaded bead measures 21 mm in diameter and 53 mm long. The thread path for the hexagonal ends is given in the rainbow bead chart, shown earlier in this chapter.

The next beaded bead uses the rule for *Stained Glass* with a full color split, meaning that every part of the rule yields a different color. Since the rule has eight parts, we used a total of eight colors of beads. Color **0** is gold, beige, white, and silver. Color **1** is blue, black, purple, and dark metallic green.

111	**0a**	Gold
110	**0b**	Beige
101	**1w**	Blue
100	**1x**	Black
011	**0c**	White
010	**1y**	Purple
001	**1z**	Green
000	**0d**	Silver

This full color split destroys the reversibility and symmetry of *Stained Glass.*

The next beaded bead also uses the rule for *Stained Glass* with full color splitting. Hence, we used a total of eight bead colors. Color **0** is orange, flamingo, coral, and pale pink, while color **1** is purple, blue, gray, and bronze.

111	**0a**	Orange
110	**0b**	Flamingo
101	**1w**	Purple
100	**1x**	Blue
011	**0c**	Coral
010	**1y**	Gray
001	**1z**	Bronze
000	**0d**	Pale Pink

Vertical Stripes with Triangles

10011100/11000110

Does this design look familiar to you? The designs generated by *Vertical Stripes with Triangles* resemble native art from all over the world, art in all kinds of media, like mosaics, clay pots, patchwork quilts, bead weaving, and fiber weaving. A design like this is truly a celebration of the human mind! People across the globe have a shared human experience in this design, a mathematical-artistic experience that transcends culture.

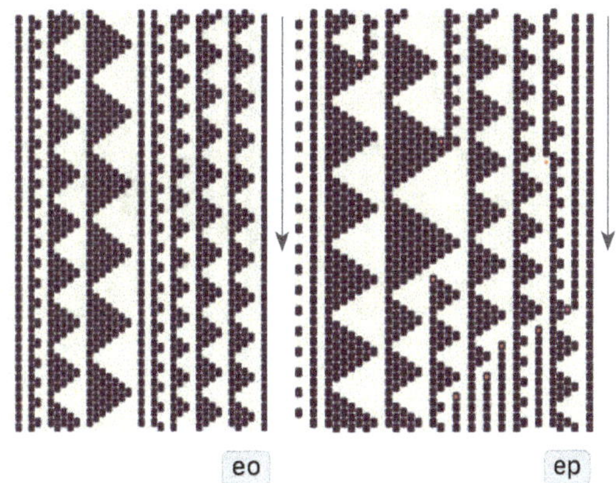

The stripes in *Vertical Stripes with Triangles* come in symmetric pairs of black and white. The stripes can be any width. This rule is reversible and has a balanced color distribution. At the same time, this rule fails to be symmetric. However, if you flip the beadwork left to right and swap **0** and **1** everywhere in the rule's inputs and outputs, then the rule still works to produce the same designs.

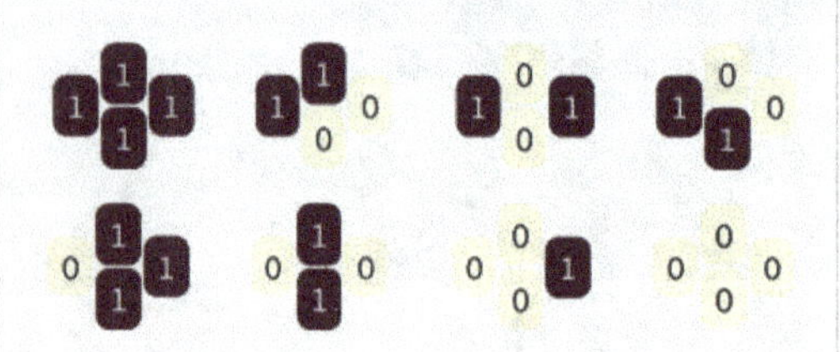

The patterns generated by this rule are very regular and repeat quickly. You might think it is an especially good choice for adding errors, but we found the results are difficult to control without the use of software. In the patch below, the colors alternate with a period of 2. Color **1** alternates between cream and dark brown, and color **0** alternates between light and dark pink. *Vertical Stripes with Triangles* is what we call a *find-same* rule that can be described with just the following four parts.

INPUT	OUTPUT
Left = Right	Above
Left = Above	White (**0**)
Right = Above	Black (**1**)
All Same	Same

We discuss find-same rules more deeply later in this book.

Praying Mantis

Every rule with two colors that we have presented thus far has some special property worth mentioning. Here is an example of a rule, called *Praying Mantis*, with two colors on three beads but no special properties. It is not symmetric or reversible, and it does not have a balanced color distribution.

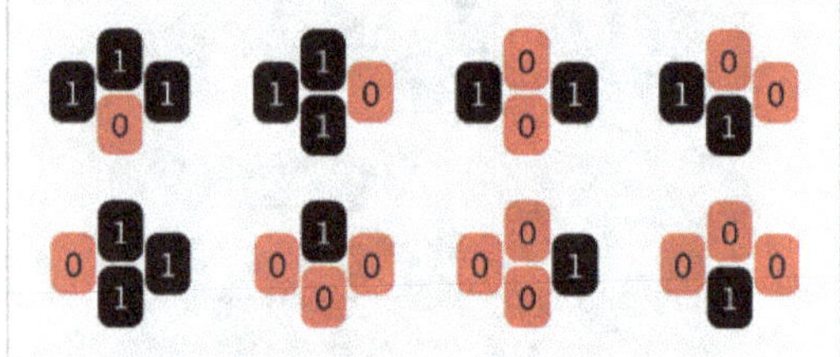

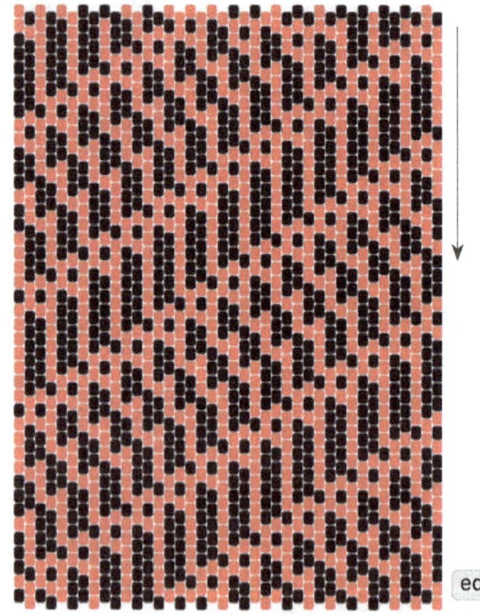

There are a handful of rules that create designs like *Praying Mantis*, but with subtle differences. Can you find a different one?

Chapter Four
THREE COLORS
ON TWO BEADS

Easy Triads

We now turn our attention to rules that require three colors. In this chapter, we consider rules that have only two input beads, like the above-right rule for *Triangle Party* or the left-right rule for *Roots*, but in this chapter, we use three colors to define our rule instead of just two colors. With three color choices for the first input bead and three color choices for the second input bead, rules on two beads can have as many as nine parts, like the above-right rule shown below.

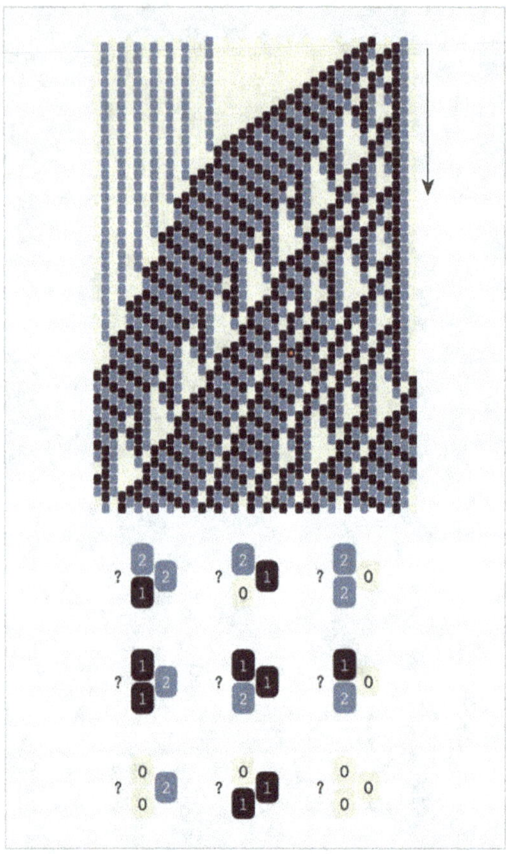

Because the output of each of those parts can be assigned any of the three colors, there are

3^9 or 19,683 such rules that are above-right, and another 19,683 rules that are left-right. That is a lot, and we will show a few of them at the end of this chapter. For most of this chapter, however, we narrow our search by simplifying our rules by using multisets. With multiset rules, the two input beads are taken in any order. So multiset rules with three colors on two beads have just six parts, like the one on the next page. There are only 3^6 or 729 multiset rules with three colors on two beads. Most of these 729 rules are repeats or near-repeats of each other, or not very interesting. But there are many gems, and we include all of our favorites.

In selecting rules, we looked for designs that are both complex and beautiful, and we were challenged to determine exactly what those terms mean. We found that complicated designs typically do not have short repeats, like solids or stripes. So, we favor designs that go on for many rows before repeating. Many of the most beautiful designs have at least one color that makes large connected regions separated by areas of more detail. We also found rules with beautiful mathematical structure among their parts. These unusual rules have balanced color distributions and other symmetries. Their structure makes them particularly easy to memorize and follow when making art.

In this chapter, we see more examples of color splitting following the *same-different* rule from Chapters 1 and 2. We look at some near misses of the *same-different* rule. We also show some ways to split three-color rules into rules with more colors.

Multiset Rules on Two Beads

Here are the six multisets with three colors on two beads. We use these six multisets as the inputs for the six parts of a rule.

As before, we denote multiset rules with brackets around the input beads. This means that the input beads can be taken in any order. The space in each set indicates that the multisets here are given in their left-right form, but we can also write them as left-above or above-right multisets, as shown on the next page. As we know from Chapter 2, left-above and above-right rules can be proven to be identical by merely flipping over a patch of beadwork. As we know from the end of Chapter 3, left-right and above-right rules give us two different ways to follow the same rule, and the patches they generate look different. So for each left-right rule we show in this chapter, we will also show the corresponding above-right rule. You get two designs for the price of one rule. As one might expect, many of the left-right rules resemble *Roots*, whereas many of the above-right rules resemble *Triangle Party*.

An important advantage of left-right multiset rules is that they are symmetric, so you can flip your beadwork over after every row. They can also be easily used to create symmetric designs. On the other hand, all non-trivial above-right rules fail to be symmetric, so you cannot flip your beadwork after every row. Another difference is that left-right rules only use a single row for the initial state, whereas above-right rules require two rows for the initial state.

Cloth of Gold

011102/021112/100210/102200/212021/220021

A left-right multiset rule with three colors has the six possible inputs shown on the left.

A particular rule is therefore completely specified by the output values for each of these six neighborhoods. Let us pick some concrete output values, say **0**, **1**, **1**, **1**, **0**, and **2**, in that order. We represent this choice with the three-color multiset code **011102**.

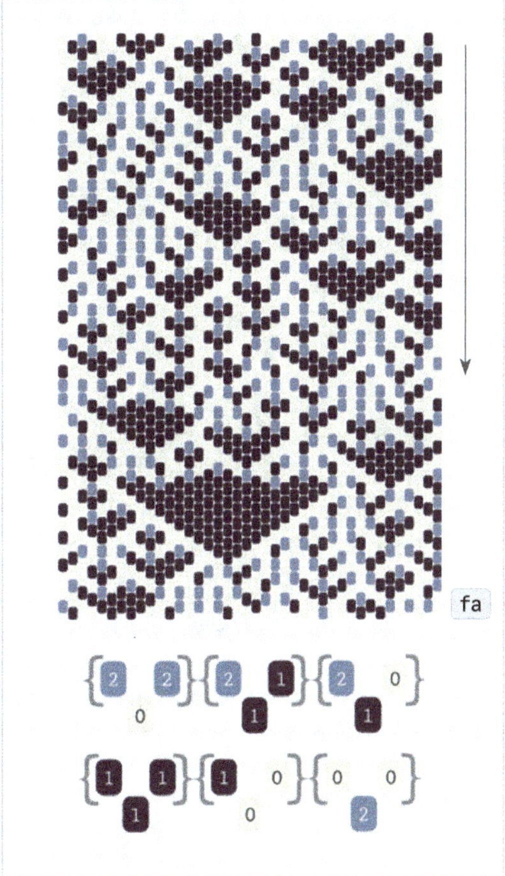

If we employ the above-right version of **011102**, we obtain the following.

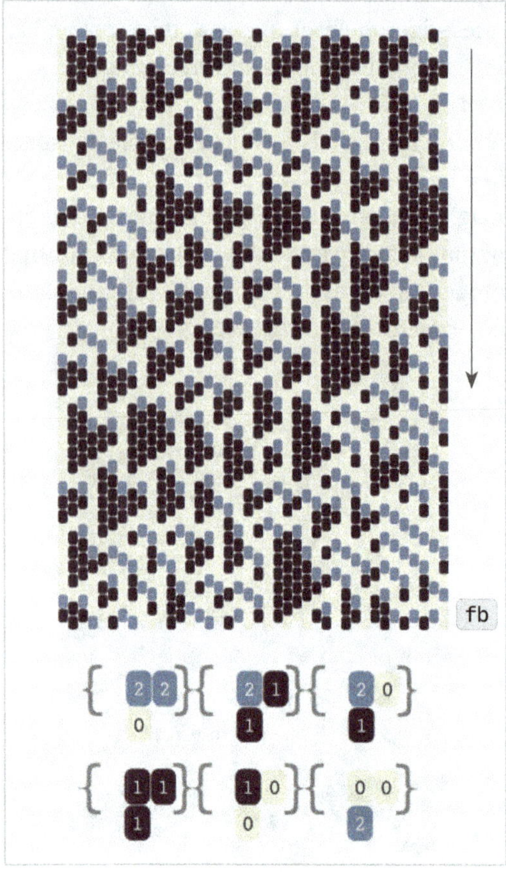

fb

Notice how the left-right version of *Cloth of Gold* looks a bit like *Roots*, and the above-right version looks a bit like *Triangle Party*.

Before we proceed, we should mention why we have six codes for one family of rules. Ultimately, these six codes correspond to the six different ways we could assign the colors black, blue, and white to the numbers **0**, **1**, and **2**. These six assignments also correspond to the six permutations of three objects.

Accordingly, the codes **011102**, **021112**, **100210**, **102200**, **212021**, and **220021** are all members of the same rule family, differing only in the way you assign the colors to the numbers. They can all produce exactly the same patterns. We say these six codes are isomorphic to each other. You can see six isomorphic colorings of the same patch made with this rule (as a left-right rule) at the bottom of the page.

Say we want to show the following two codes are isomorphic: **011102** and **220021**. To do this, make an input-output table for **011102** (shown left). Replace every **2** with a **1**, and vice versa. Then rearrange the parts to put them back in order (using their inputs), and you will find the rule for **220021** (shown below).

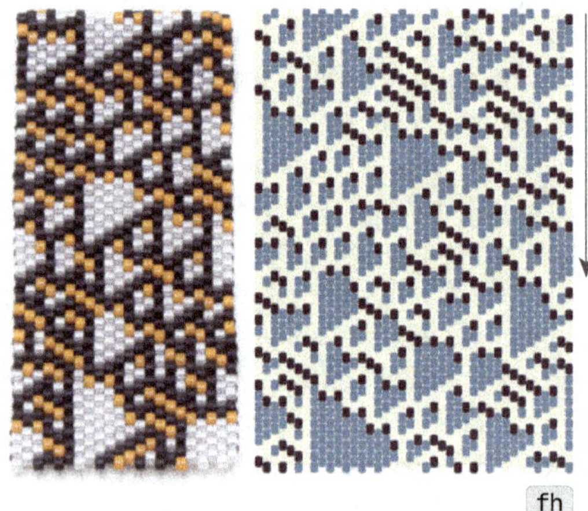

fh

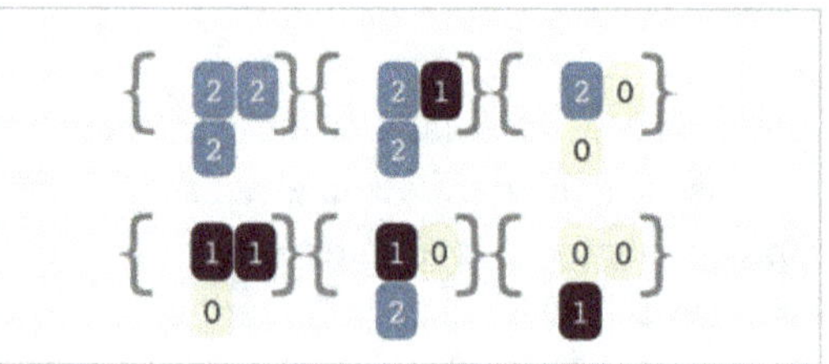

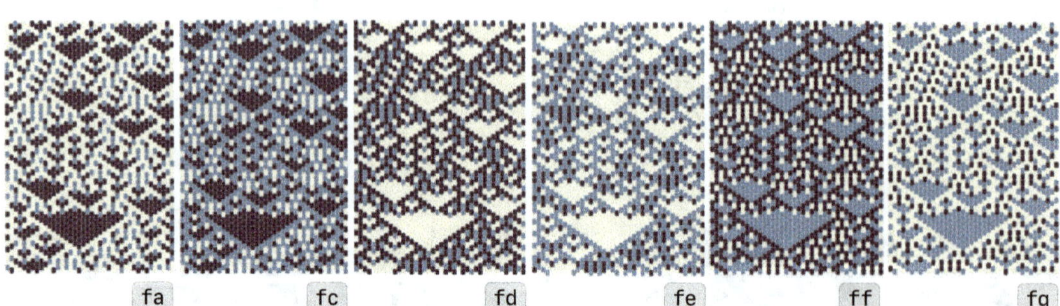

fa   fc   fd   fe   ff   fg

Lightning Strikes

002101/012220/120122/121010/200012/211201

Rather than choosing codes randomly, we can start with a two-color rule and then add a third color. For example, here we see the *same-different* rule in black and white, with three more parts added that explain how to use a third color, blue. Although the blue does not persist in *Lightning Strikes*, it still creates some beautiful designs. This rule includes a subrule in the last three parts of the rule, because the last three parts are all of the parts that use only the numbers **0** and **1** for the inputs, and the outputs are **0** and **1**. We discuss this idea in more detail when we talk about rules with three-bead inputs and the concept of extension in the next chapter.

When we start with three colors, sometimes, one or even two of the colors die out within a few rows of the patch. In this way, a rule that starts with three colors might essentially be equivalent to a rule with fewer colors. As such, we tend to favor rules that produce patterns that have colors that never die out, with a few notable exceptions. Informally, we say that a color *persists* if it never dies out of the pattern for almost all of the seeds. We can talk about color persistence locally, at the level of *rules*, or globally, at the level of *patterns*. *Local persistence* means that for any part of a rule, the output color is one of the input colors for that part. This implies that if a color appears in one row, it also appears in at least one of the next two rows. *Global persistence* means that if a color appears in one row, then it will necessarily appear in some subsequent row. It is easy to see that if you have local persistence, you must also have global persistence. But, it is possible to have global persistence without local persistence. This happens because of the interplay between the colors. It is often very hard to spot exactly what makes a rule globally persistent. For example, the patterns for *Lightning Strikes* and for *Percolation* have a long initial phase, called a *transient phase*, where interesting things happen before one color eventually dies out.

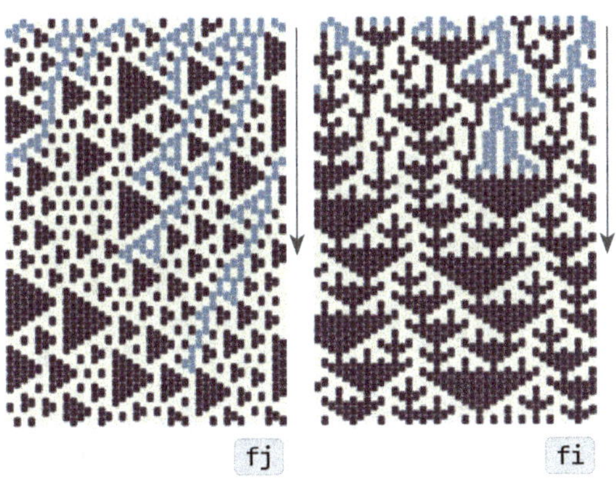

fj   fi

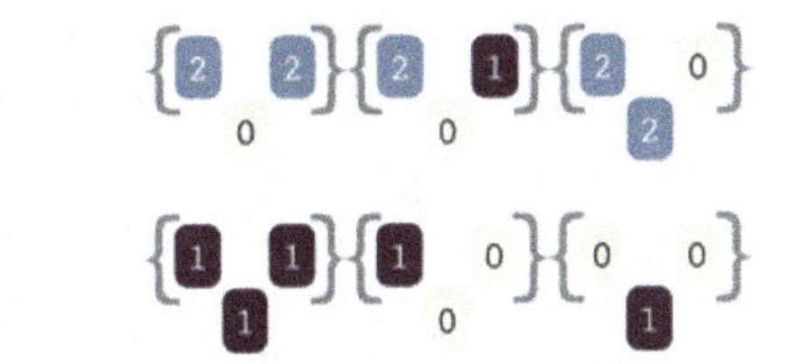

Used as an above-right rule, the code **220021** creates designs like those on the shells of the textile cone snail (conus textile). These venomous sea snails produce shells that are known as cloth of gold cones. *Can you find a rule that gives a better match?*

Percolation 101

012120/120120/200112/202101/211200/221010

Percolation includes all three parts for a complete rule on blue and cream, then adds three new parts that explain how to use black.

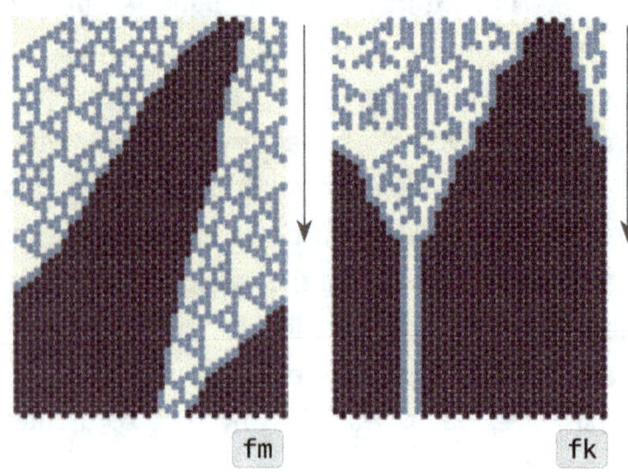

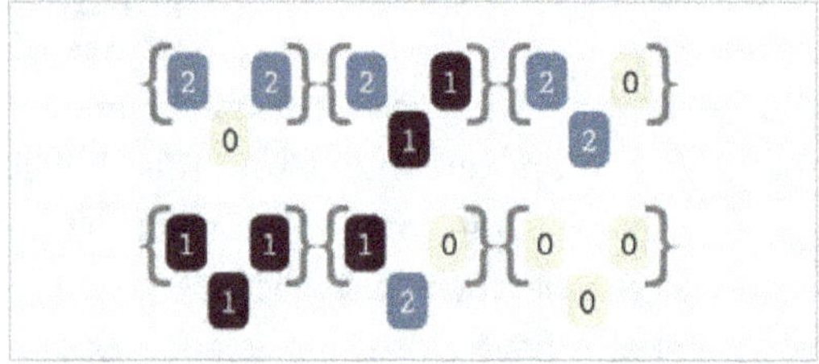

Ice Cream Cones

021110/102100/200210/211102/212020/220121

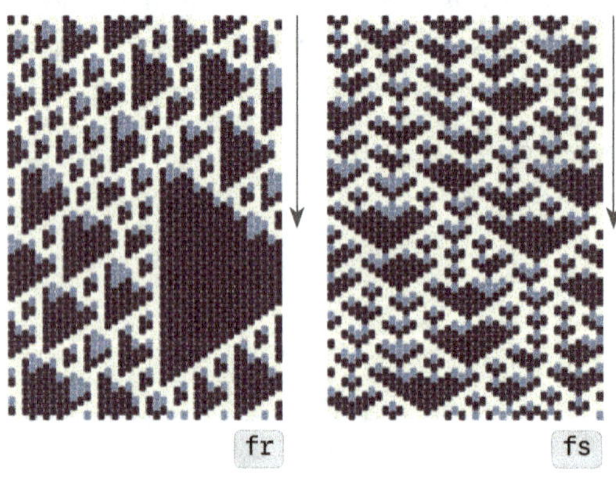

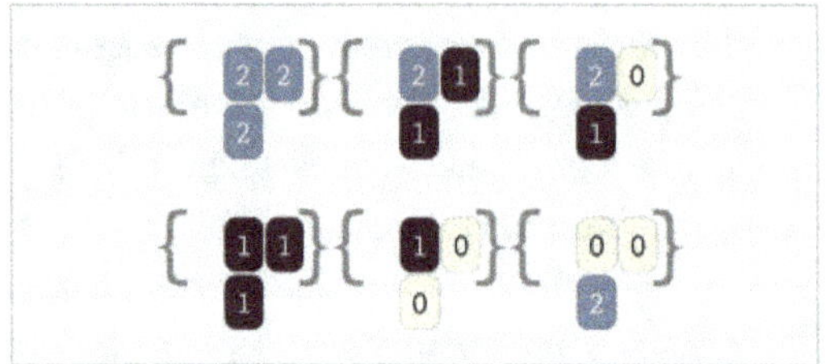

Nouveau Waterfall / Chrysler Building

011202/012021/021012/100212/102201/120021

This pair of rules generates some remarkable patterns. We call the above-right version, *Chrysler Building*, which generates designs with strong diagonals. The left-right version, *Nouveau Waterfall*, makes pretty vertical designs.

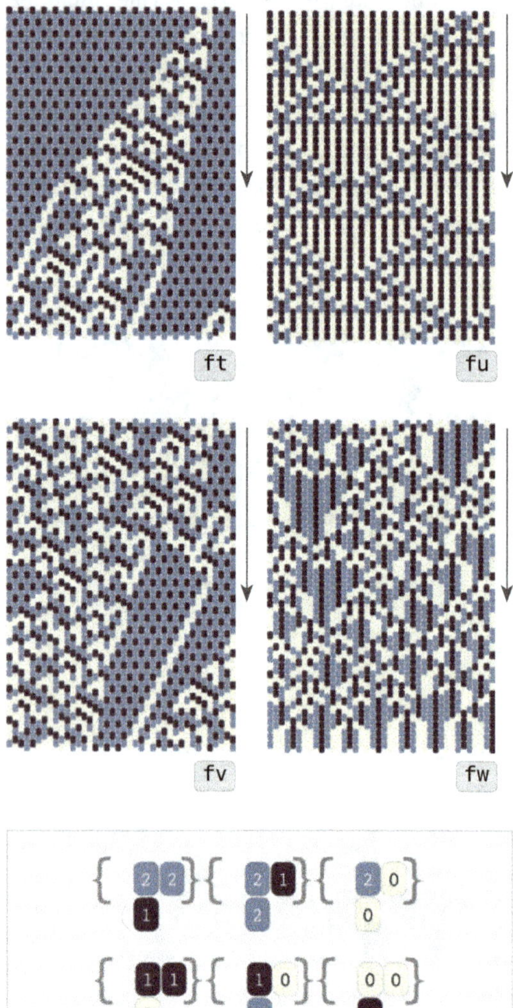

Baskets and Vines

001210/021121/101102/102020/200221/211022

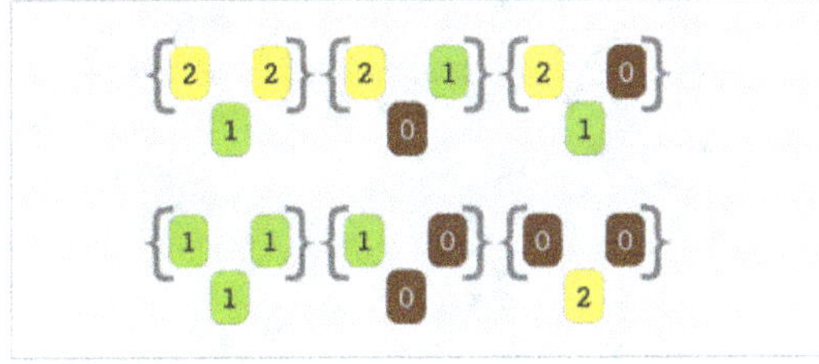

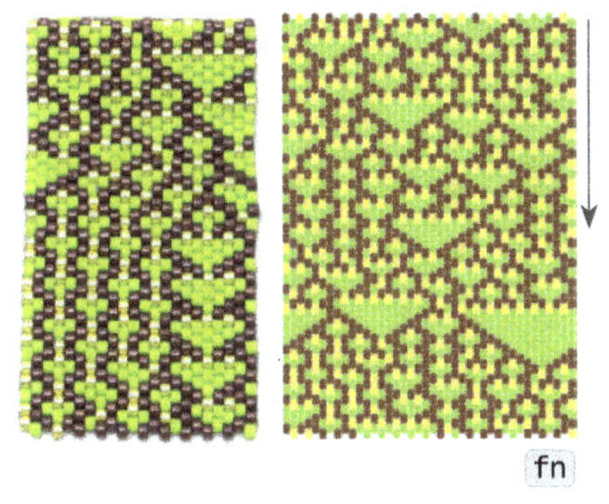

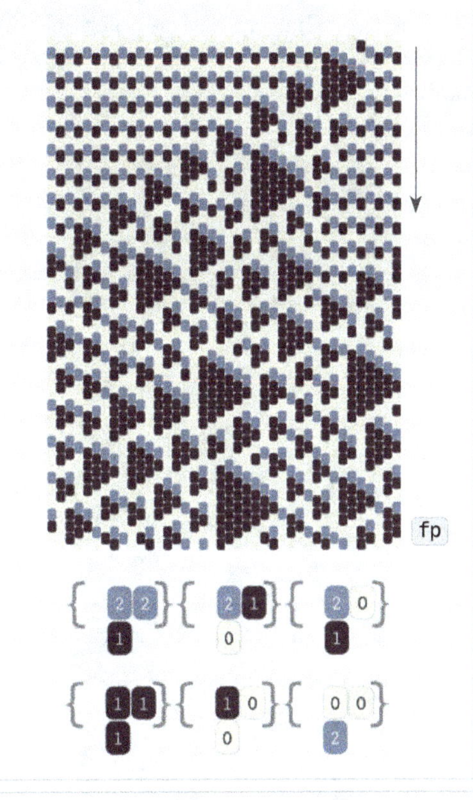

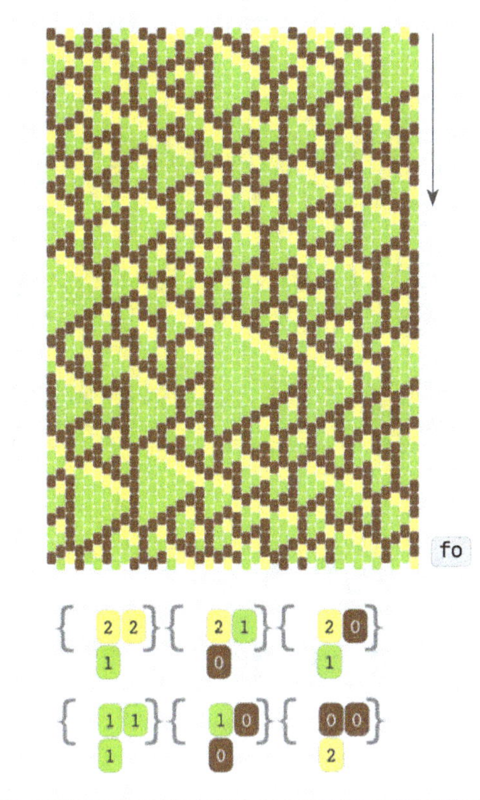

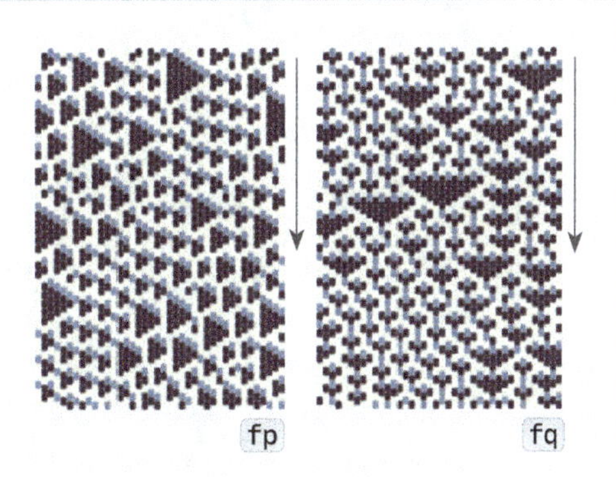

This tubular beaded bead uses the above-right version of *Basket and Vines* with a color split.

INPUT	OUTPUT	
?22	1	Gold
?21	0	Bronze
?20	1	Gold
?11	1	Gold
?10	0	Black
200	2	Dark orange
100	2	Peach
000	2	Light Peach

The beadwork below shows a color split. The bead colors are peach/yellow (**0**), black (**1**), and blue/silver (**2**).

ga

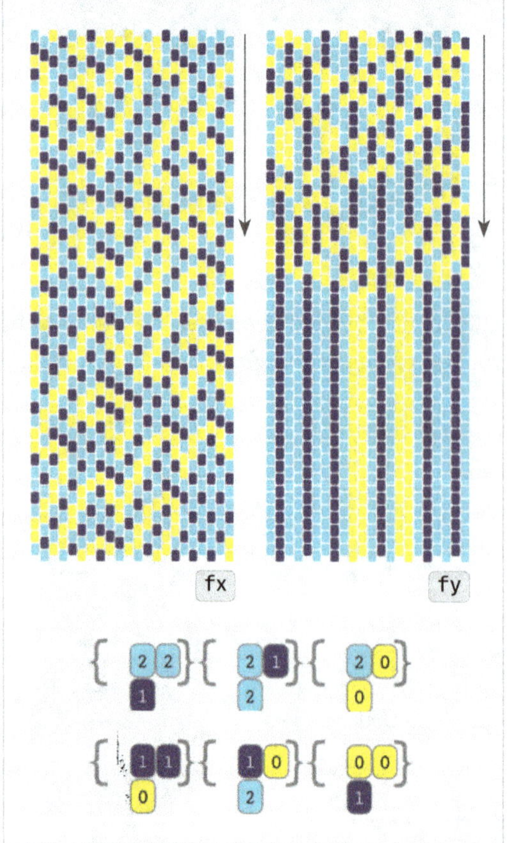

fx

fy

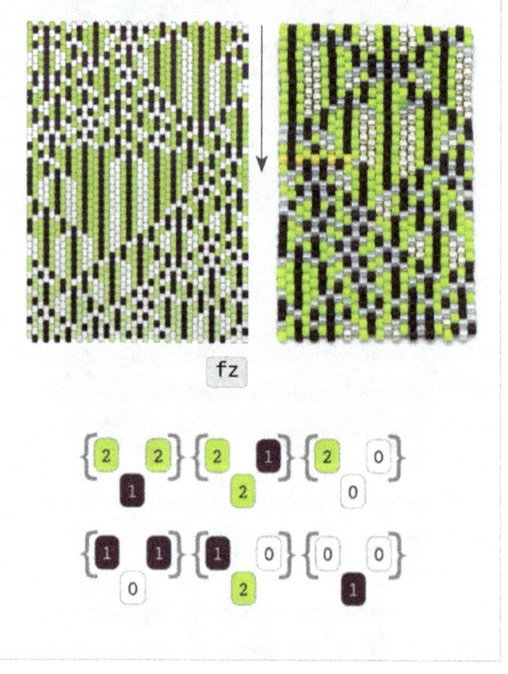

fz

The beadwork above shows a partial reboot of the pattern with five yellow beads. The design had started an obvious repeat, and the reboot interrupted that.

Diagonal War

001102/021122/101210/102220/200021/211021

The rule for *Diagonal War* creates beautiful designs when used as a left-right rule (below left). It is less interesting when used as an above-right rule (below right).

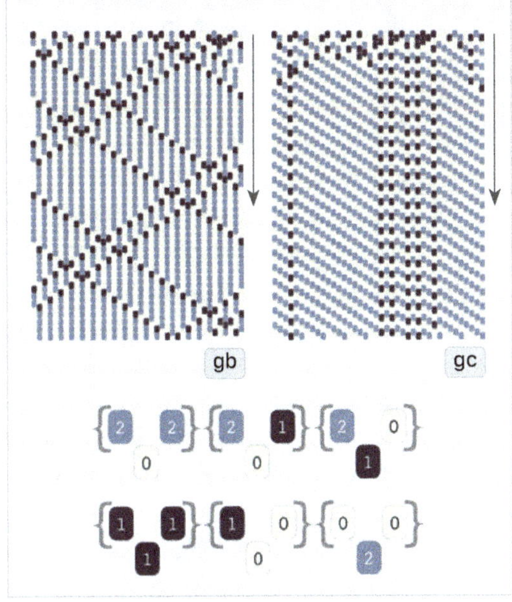

As a left-right rule, *Keith Haring* gives this:

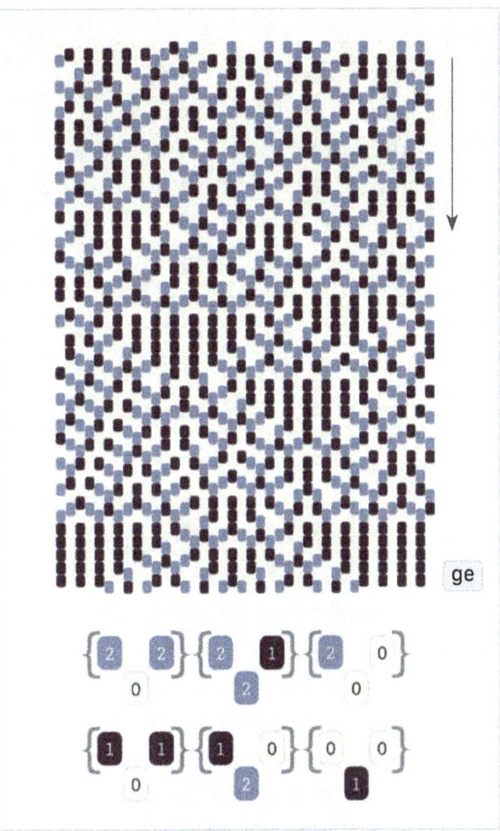

Keith Haring

011002/020021/021212/100211/102202/112021

As an above-right rule, *Keith Haring* yields this:

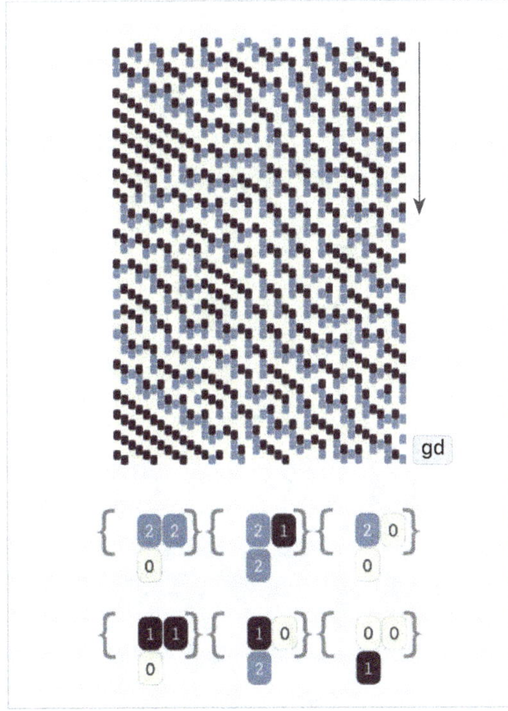

When a rule has six parts, we can use as many as six colors without adding any new parts by using a color split. The beadwork for *Keith Haring* below uses a color split with six colors. The six colors are shaded in a gradient. To make this color split, we used a different color for the output of each part of the rule in the following order: **0a** is pink, **2a** is orange, **0b** is dark yellow, **0c** is light yellow, **2b** is purple, and **1** is black. The gradient goes from light to dark, in order from **0a** to **0c**, **0b**, **2a**, **2b**, and ending with black for **1**. After we drew the rule with circles of color, we set our piles of beads in the same arrangement as the outputs in our drawing of the rule.

Color Splits of the Same-Different Rule

There are a variety of different ways to split colors in the *Same-Different* rule from Chapters 1 and 2, and we present a few in the examples below. To find the "same" color in the *Same-Different* rule, look at a patch of the above-right version (*Triangle Party*) and find the triangles. The triangles are the "same" color, and the background is the "different" color. Either the triangles or the background will be split into two colors. If we join those two colors back into one, then the *Same-Different* rule appears in the two remaining colors.

Color Split of the Same-Different Rule #1

012210/022101/120102/122010/210012/210201
010210/022111/110102/122000/212012/220201
011210/022121/100102/122020/211012/200201

This first color split of the *Same-Different* rule has 18 different codes given in three sets of six isomorphic codes each. The differences across the three sets are highlighted. These differences only matter for the first few rows, based entirely upon the initial states we choose. Once a pattern stabilizes, these differences no longer come into play because the part they identify eventually dies out.

The part that dies out has the input **{20}** in the rule below. This corresponds to the highlighted parts of the rules above. The result is that the 18 codes above all give essentially the

same designs, even though there are three non-isomorphic sets. We mention this phenomenon here to make the reader aware of its existence. It is common. However, we will not discuss it further. When we give multiple versions of a code, they are an isomorphic set.

Color Split of the Same-Different Rule #2

001020/101121/201222

This version has a striped background.

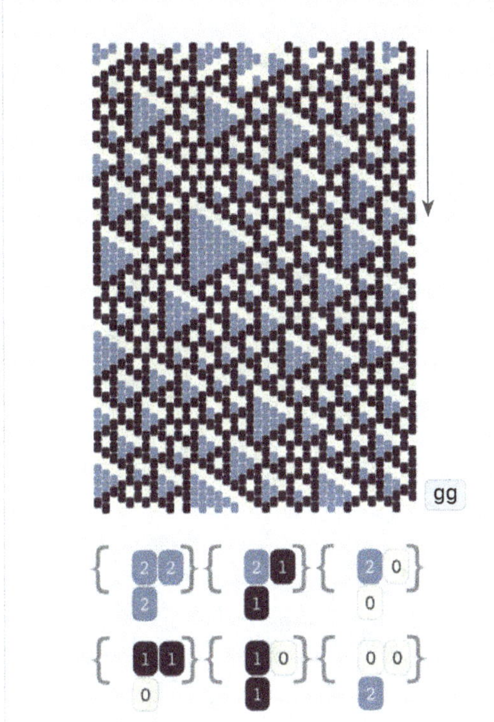

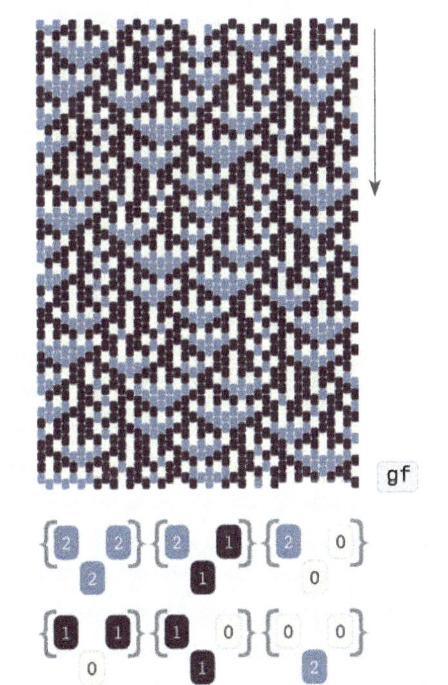

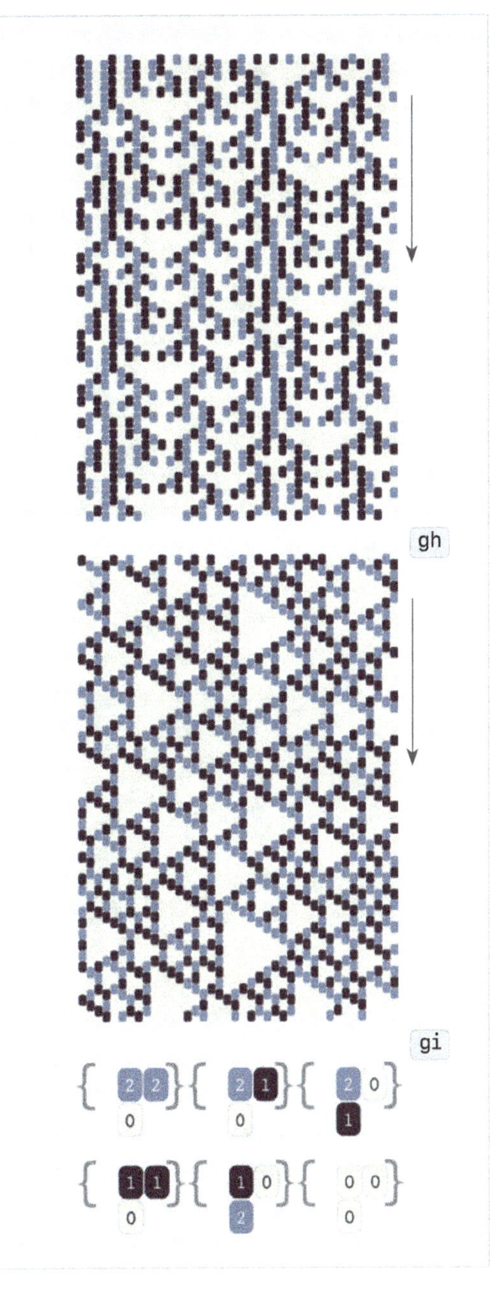

Color Split of the Same-Different Rule #3

010212/012012/022011/110202/120201/122001

This version has striped triangles.

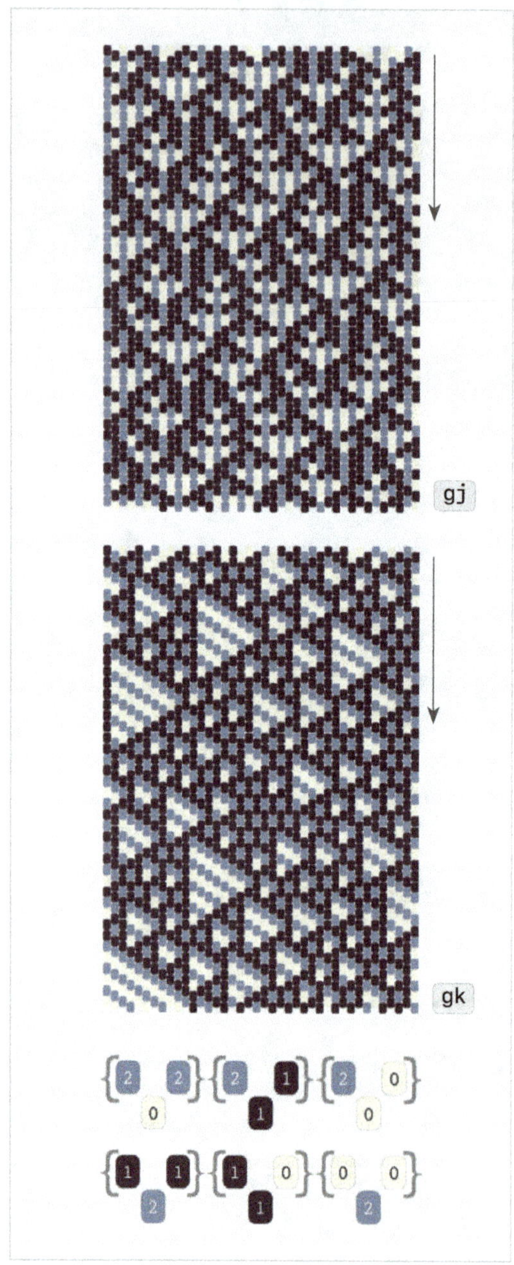

Color Split of the Same-Different Rule #4

002010/121101/210222

This version has the background split into large regions of color.

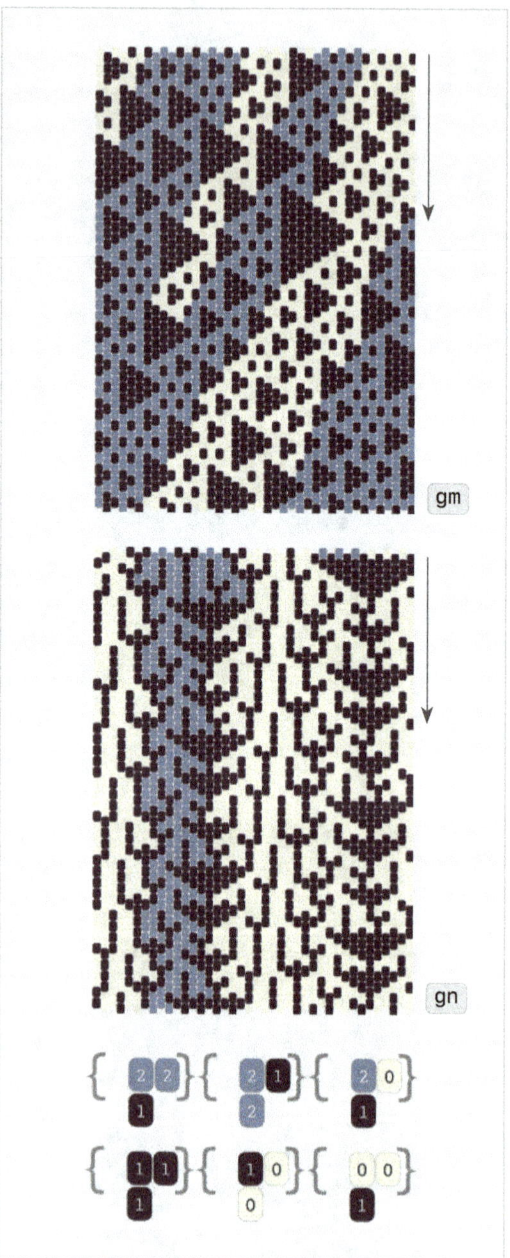

Near Misses

Same-Different Rule Near Miss #1

021120/102120/200121/201102/201210/211020

There are several *Near Miss* rules that appear to be a color split of the *Same-Different* rule, but they are not. Within the space of all possible 3-color rules, there are many *Near Miss* variations like this.

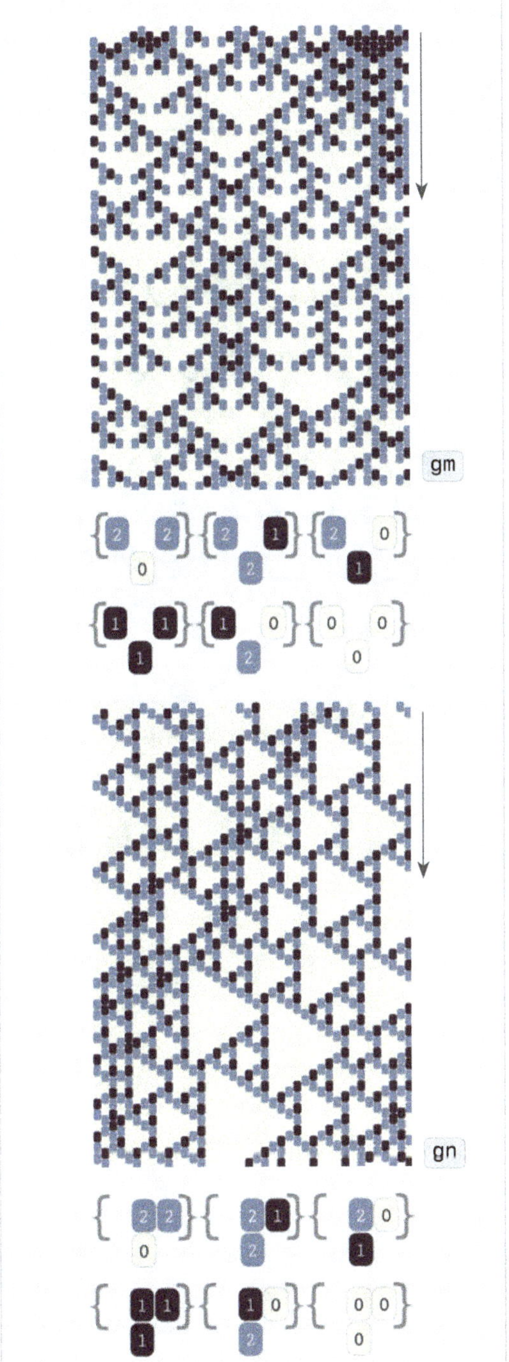

Same-Different Near Misses #2–6

011012/011212/022021/100201/100202/122021
001121/001220/101020/101122/201022/201221
011210/022121/100102/122020/200201/211012
000121/021220/102122/111020/201002/201211
011020/021020/100121/102121/201202/201212

Roots Near Miss

Here is a color split of *Roots*. If we make **1** and **2** the same color, we have *Roots*.

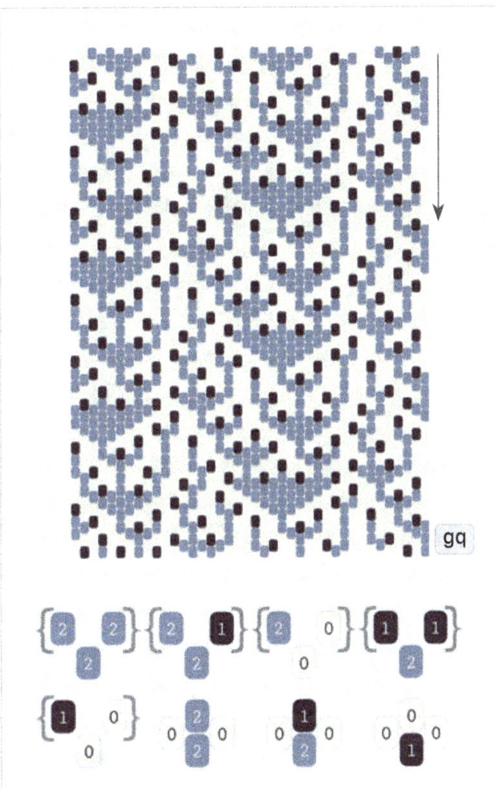

Roots Near Miss (continued)

The following rule is almost a color split of the *Roots* rule. The new rule was created from the *same-different* rule by splitting the part for **{0 0}** into three parts and introducing a new color. The difference between this and *Roots* is given in the last part of the rule, shown below. The difference in the design is that the vines are all one bead taller. Using three beads for the input of a three-color rule gives you a prelude for the next chapter.

Here is the rule for *Lightning Strikes*, shown earlier in this chapter.

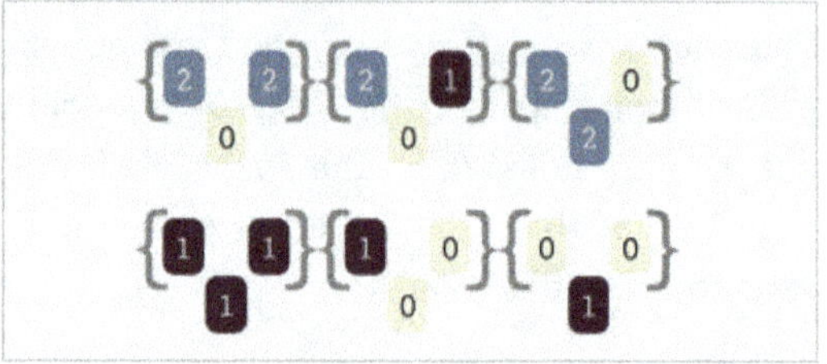

We can break the last part for **{0 0}** into three new parts to produce the following design that resembles *Lightning Strikes*. However, in this version, all three colors persist.

Balanced Rules

We now turn our attention to rules with a special type of symmetry in which two or more colors are balanced, meaning that they occur with roughly the same frequency and make the same kinds of shapes. This section contains a lot of mathematics. Know that if your primary goal is to make art, then you can safely skip all the text about balanced rules.

An *automorphism* of a rule is a permutation of the colors in that rule that leaves the rule otherwise unchanged. The *trivial permutation* maps every color to itself, thereby leaving a rule unchanged. All rules have a trivial automorphism that corresponds to the trivial permutation on their colors. *Picket Fence* **0101** is an example of a two-color rule with a non-trivial automorphism. *Groovy Checkers* **1010** is another example, whereas *Roots* does not have any non-trivial automorphism. To see a non-trivial automorphism in a patch, notice that the design motifs made by two or more colors are the same shapes. To see a non-trivial automorphism in a two-color rule:

A. Start with code for a rule; say **0101**, which is the code for *Picket Fence*.

B. Use the code to write out all of the parts of the rule with numbers. The parts are ordered by their inputs.

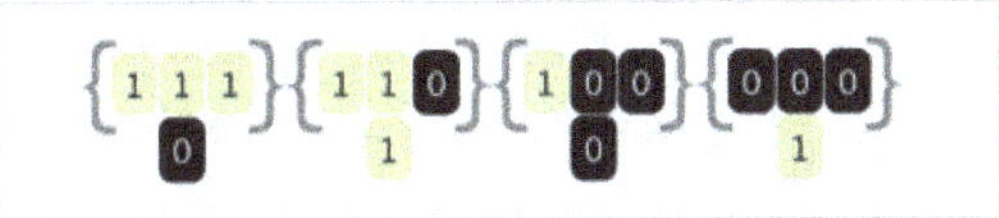

C. Swap **0** and **1** everywhere in the rule. For example, {1 1 1}/0 becomes {0 0 0}/1, and {1 1 0}/1 becomes {0 0 1}/0.

D. Reorder the parts using the inputs.

E. Find that the code for the rule is unchanged.

This process shows that one color plays the same role as the other color. For a rule with three colors, automorphisms include swapping a pair of colors, or cycling all three colors. The next example does both, which makes it special.

Balanced Roots and Balanced Triangles
201120

We can generalize the *Same-Different* rule to three colors on two beads. In words, "If the two input colors are the same, the output is that color. If the two inputs are different, then the output is the excluded color." When used as a left-right rule, we call this *Balanced Roots*. The above-right version is *Balanced Triangles*.

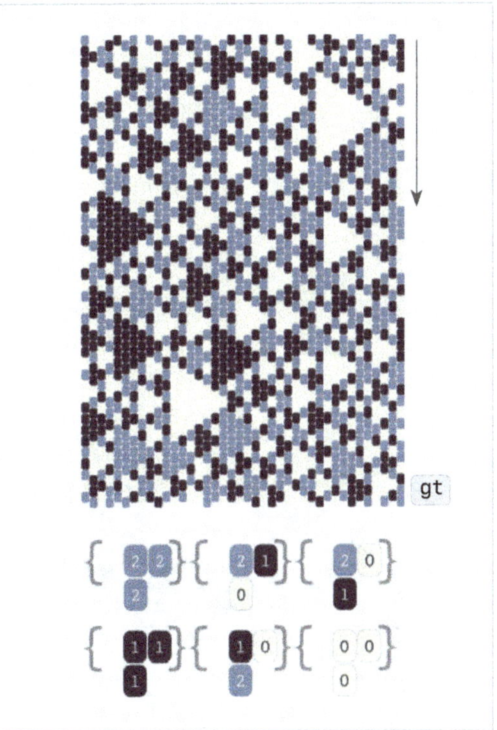

Using three colors rather than two, this generalization of the *Same-Different* rule does not produce a foreground color and a background color the way the two-color version does. Instead, the three colors are equally balanced, hence the names *Balanced Roots* and *Balanced Triangles*. The patches generated by these rules show how the three colors cluster into connected regions of the same few shapes, over and over. For example, in *Balanced Triangles*, every connected cluster of one color is either a single bead or a triangle of beads.

A rule is balanced when it has symmetry among the colors. To see the pairwise symmetry in **201120**, write out the six parts of the rule, swap any pair of numbers, reorder the parts, and find that we get the code **201120** back again. Moreover, we can see a different symmetry by cycling the three colors forward or back, such as **0** goes to **1**, **1** goes to **2**, and **2** goes back to **0**. Reorder the parts, and we get the code **201120** back again. This shows that every color in this balanced rule is playing the same role as every other color. In other words, every permutation of the three colors is an automorphism. As a consequence, the code for **201120** is unique. Special, indeed!

The rule for *Balanced Triangles* is reversible, meaning you can bead from both the top and bottom edges. However, changing this left-right rule into an above-right rule will destroy its reversibility. So although *Balanced Triangles* is reversible, *Balanced Roots* is not.

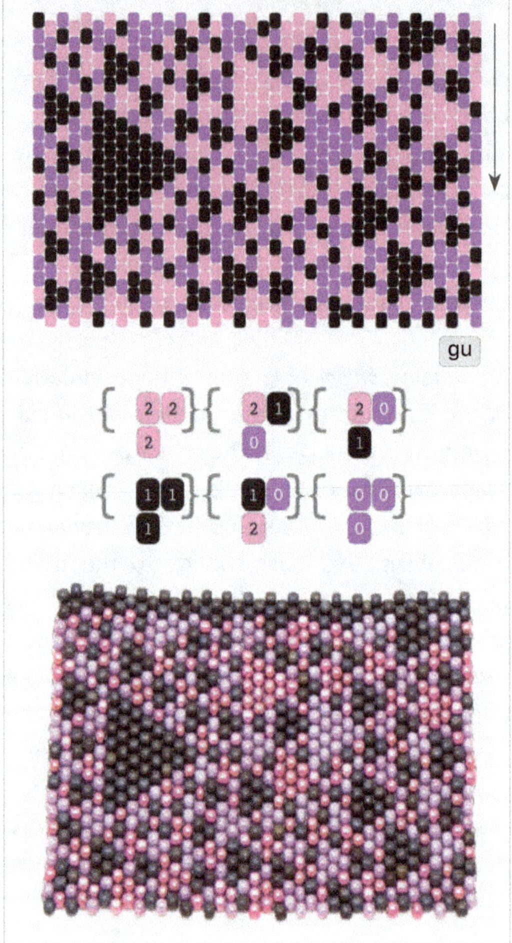

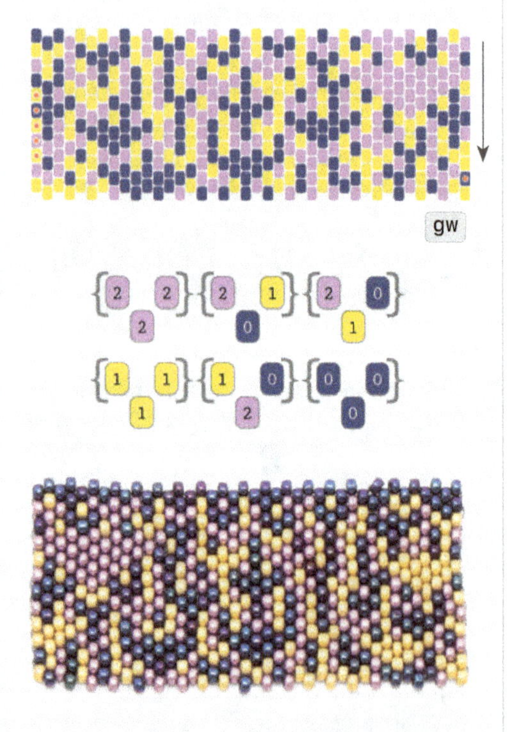

Partially Balanced Rules

A rule can be partially balanced in a number of different ways. When looking for balance, we look for automorphisms in the codes. Can we swap or cycle any of the colors to get the same code back again? If so, the rule has some kind of balance among the colors. If every permutation of the colors is an automorphism, then the rule is fully balanced. But if some permutations are automorphisms, and others are not, we say the rule is *partially balanced*. The length of the longest automorphic cycle gives the number n on the n-balance. The number n in the n-balance tells us how many colors in the patches are making the same kinds of shapes. That number n is the largest number of colors that can be permuted to result in an automorphism.

3-Balanced Shoes and Goggles

012201/120012

In *Shoes and Goggles*, we see shoes in the patches made by the left-right rule, and goggles in the patches made by the above-right version. The rule comes as a pair of codes. If we swap any two colors using one code, we get the other code. That is not an automorphism; instead, the two codes are an isomorphic pair. However, if we cycle the three colors, we get the same code we started with. That is an automorphism. If we cycle backwards, we get another automorphism. When we look at the patch, we can see that every color makes the same kinds of shapes as the other two. That is the visualization of the automorphism of the cycle of the three colors.

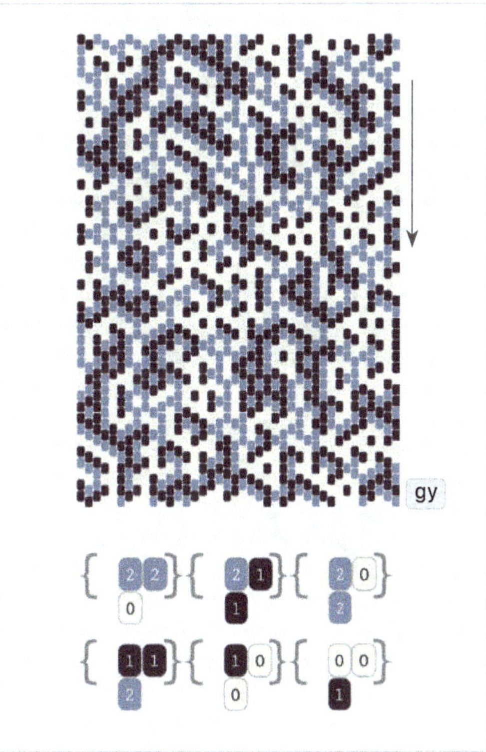

We identified two more 3-balanced rules, including *Balanced Stripes* **001221/101022** and *Balanced Zigzags* **020211/112002**, but we think the patterns they generate are a little boring, so they are not included.

2-Balanced Rule
021102/102210/210021

A rule can be balanced in exactly two colors, but not the third. In a *2-balanced* rule, swapping a particular pair of colors is an automorphism; it gives us the same code. However, any other permutation of the colors produces a different code in the isomorphic set. Cycling the three colors produces the three different codes because cycling is not an automorphism.

Notice below how the blue and cream beads make the same shapes, but the black shapes are different. This rule is 2-balanced in blue and cream.

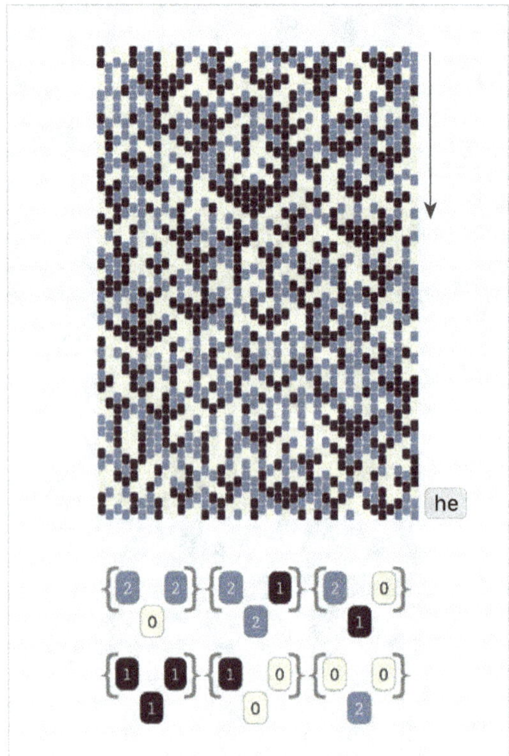

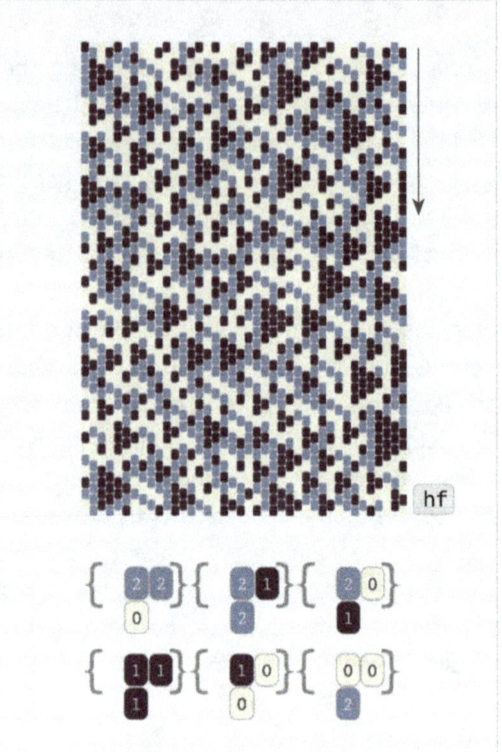

A few less-interesting examples of 2-balanced rules are given by the codes **001122**, **101220**, and **201021** (not shown here).

Local versus Global Balance

Our discussion about balanced rules so far has been all about local balance, in terms of the rules themselves. We can also think of global balance as a property of patches generated by a particular rule. A rule is *balanced globally* if, under most initial states, a large enough patch will have nearly the same number of beads for each color. Another way to think about global balance is that any random bead in a patch is equally likely to be any color. The rule above appears to be balanced globally, even though the black shapes are different from the others.

A rule can be locally balanced but not globally balanced, like the otherwise uninspiring rule **212100/220110**. This rule rarely produces patterns that are globally balanced, even though the rule itself is locally balanced. Cycling the three colors is an automorphism, but swapping is not. That is why there are two codes.

Counting Equivalent Patterns

The discussion above demonstrates a method for finding interesting patterns by counting how many non-equivalent codes one can get by permuting the colors. With three colors, there are six ways to permute the colors. We saw that sometimes these permutations yield the same code, and sometimes they don't. For example, in *Balanced Triangles*, all six permutations yield the code **201120**. The fact that there is only one such code for *Balanced Triangles* means there is some underlying symmetry there. Rules that have exactly two codes also exhibit more symmetry than those that have three or six codes. No pattern is generated by exactly four or five different codes. As we saw earlier, some patterns can be generated by as many as 18 different codes, as long as we choose the first row or two to avoid using some specific parts of the rules. We saw this kind of similarity across codes for the first time with *Dot Arrays* in Chapter 3. There, we saw that two different codes for *Dot Arrays* can generate identical designs after advancing past the first few rows.

Oscillators and Gliders

An *oscillator* is a localized pattern that repeats vertically. A *glider* is a localized pattern that repeats diagonally.

Three-Color Gliders

001202/011021/021022/100021/101212/102221

The above-right rule *Three-Color Gliders* generates multiple types of oscillators and gliders. Moreover, this example shows how diagonal gliders can repeat with different angles and different periods. We have found oscillators with periods four, eight, and 16. Gliders have periods two, three, and four. We wonder if the periods of all the oscillators are always powers of two. The left-right version of this rule generally produces less interesting designs.

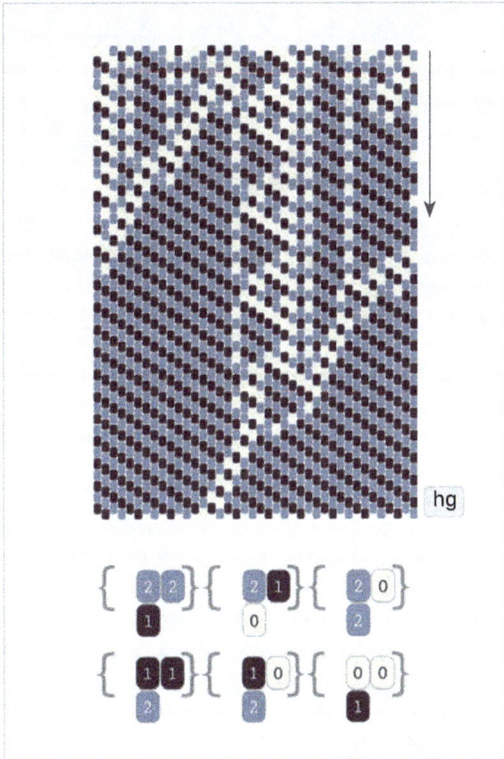

The rule for *Three-Color Gliders* generates some nice examples when started with periodic initial rows. Take the example that shows a long, beautiful glider; this patch has exactly one error, which is at the top of the Sierpiński-type triangle.

Non-Multiset Rules on Two Beads

We now turn our attention to rules with three colors on two beads, where the inputs are not multisets. Without multisets, we remove the brackets, and we take the input beads in the exact order they are given. In general, the left-above, left-right, and above-right versions of these rules produce different designs.

There are nine ways to choose two beads from three colors when the order matters. Therefore, each of these rules has nine parts, and the code for each rule has nine digits. Since these rules are not necessarily left-right symmetric, you cannot always flip your beadwork after every row. As with any above-right rule, you need two rows for the initial state.

Color Split of the Same-Different Rule #5

001001220/002002110/101212101/121010121/200122122/211022022

This rule splits the roots in *Roots* into two colors. We have blue on the left and black on the right.

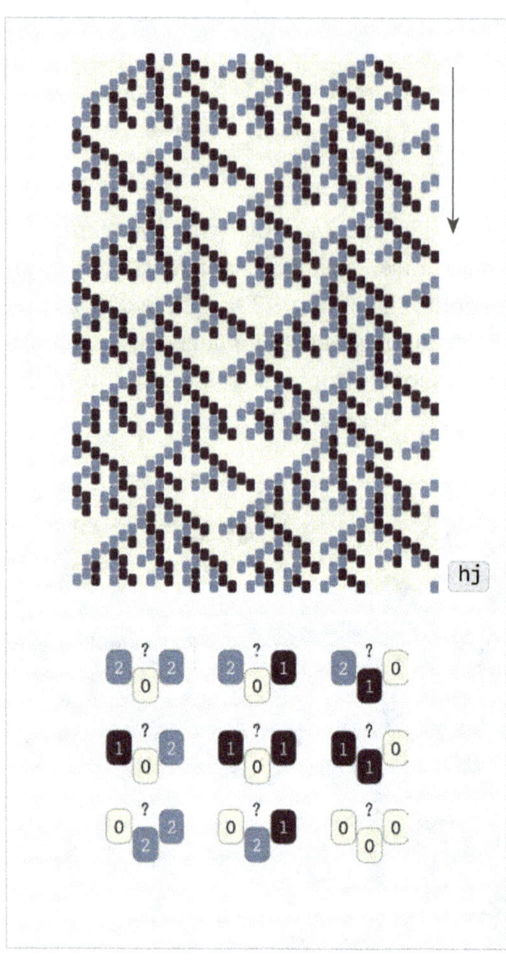

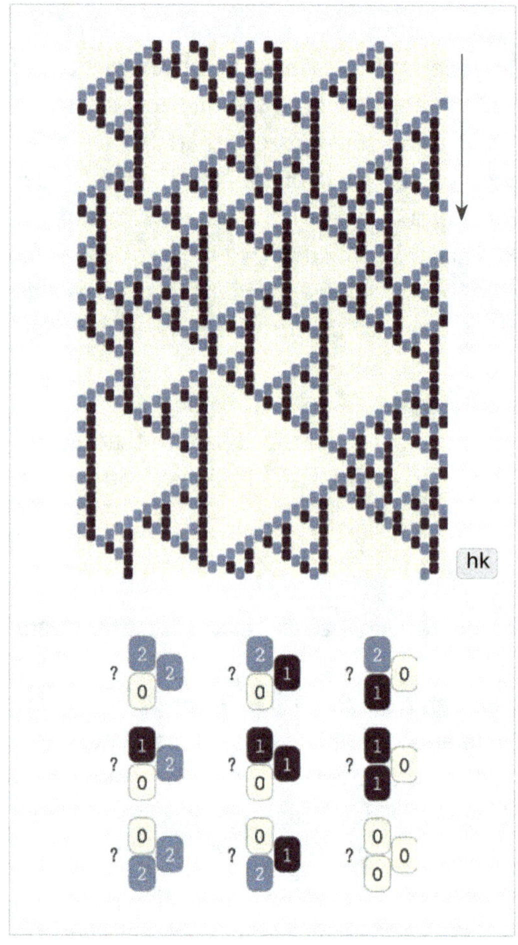

Taller Vines

011110002/022211112/100121010/122020200/212101221/220202001

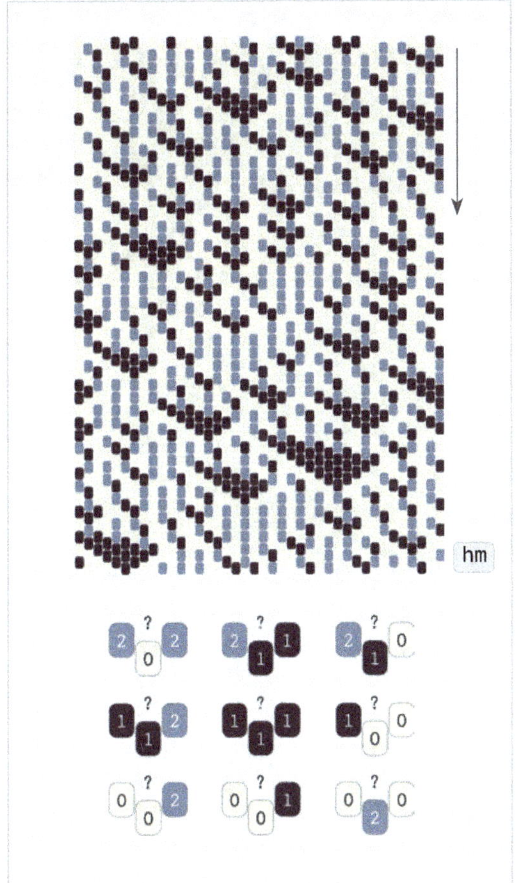

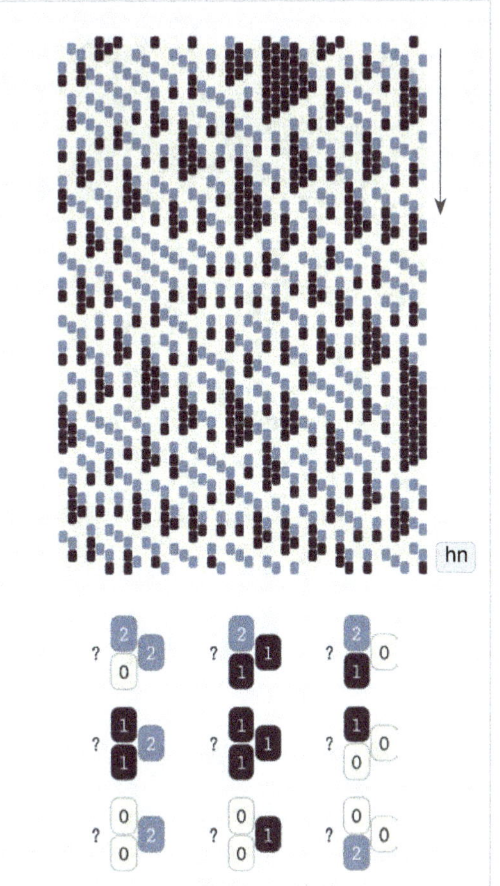

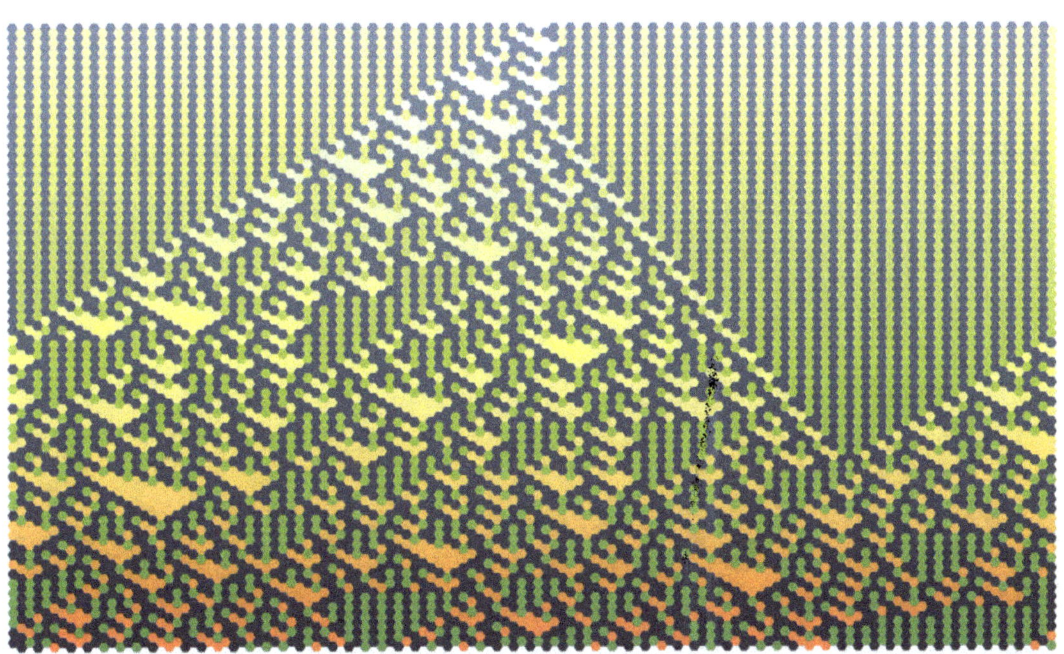

Icicles

002120010/012211101/120001200/121110012/212201022/220122201

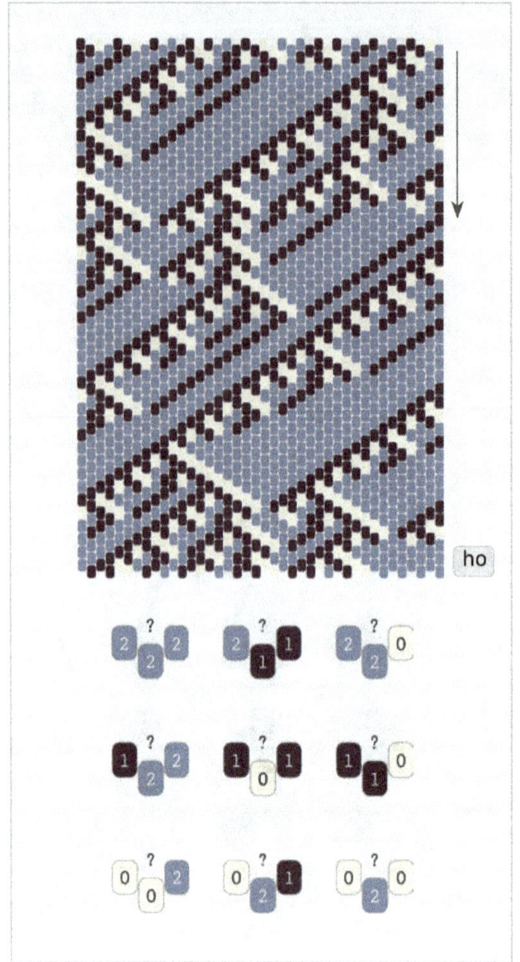

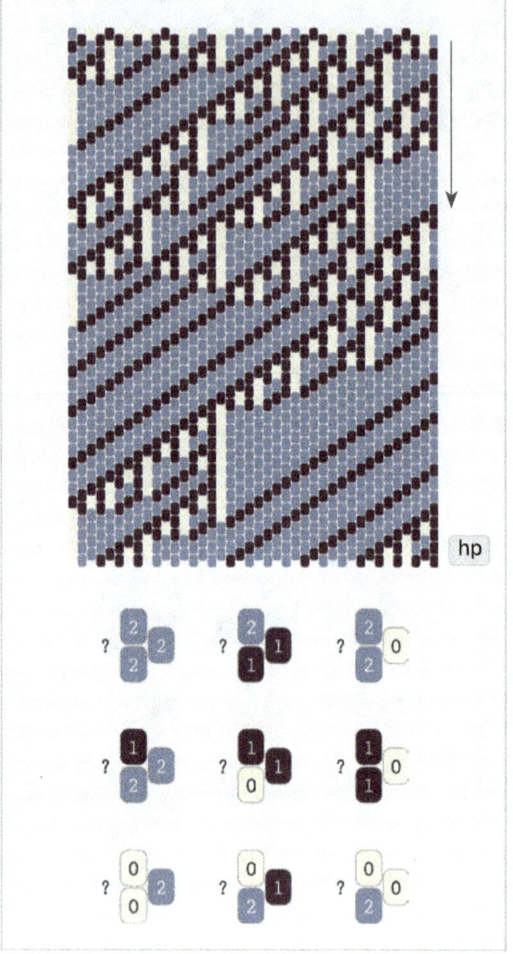

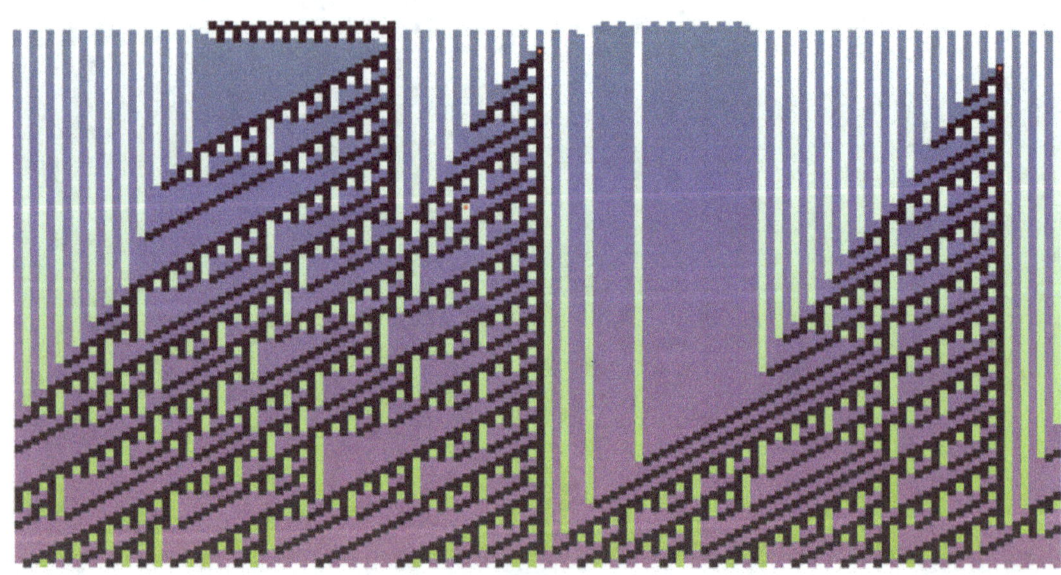

Let Them Eat Cake
121110012

Guillotine
002020010

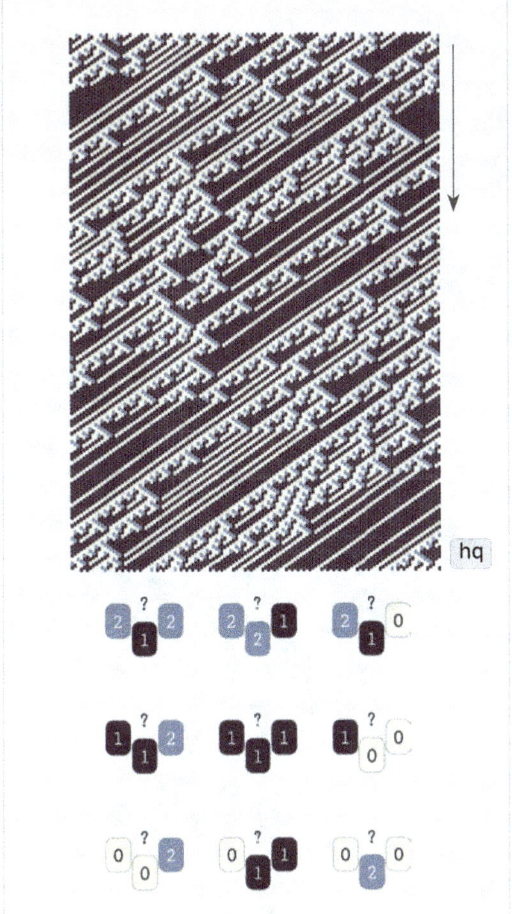

hq

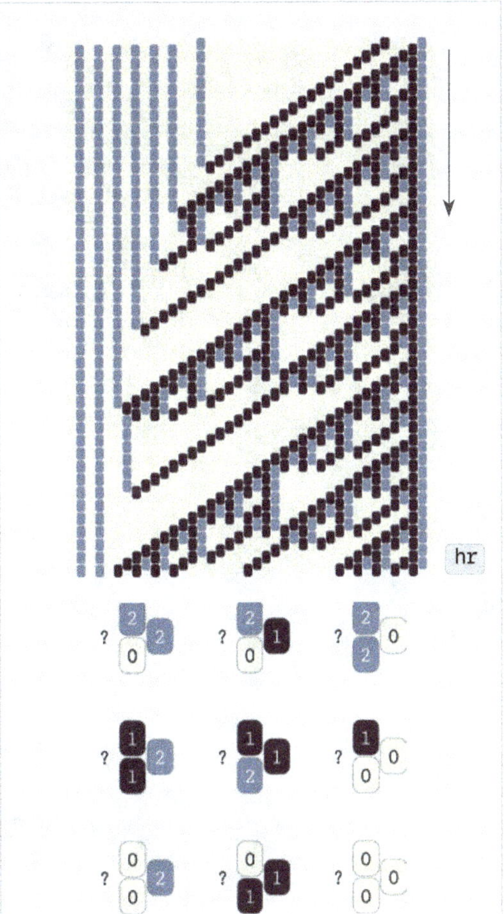

hr

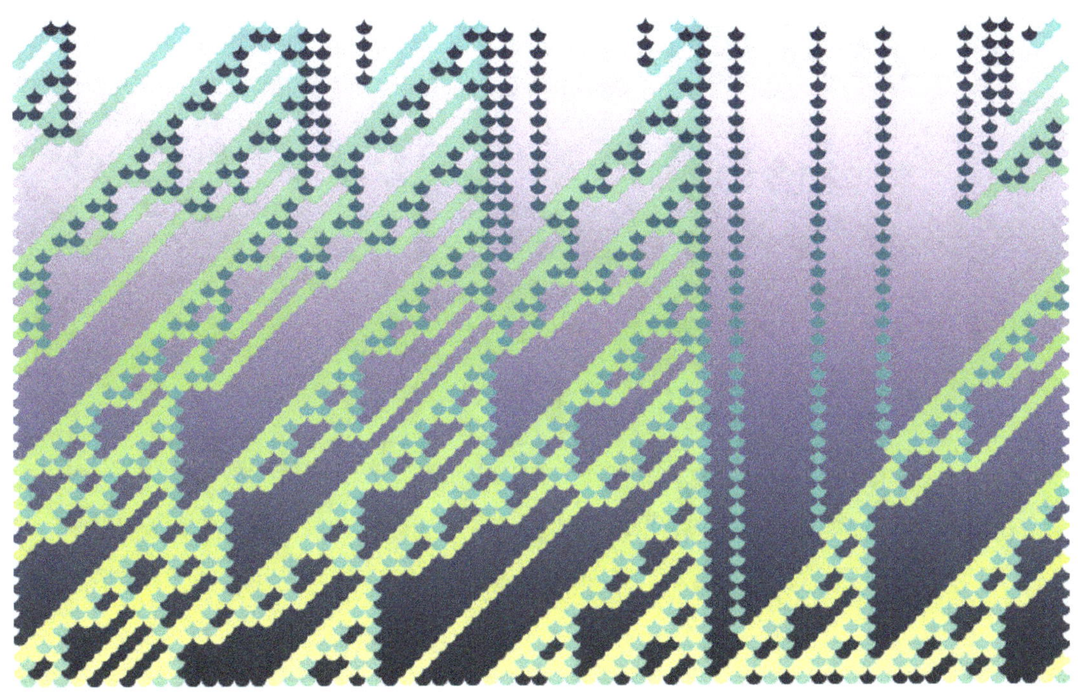

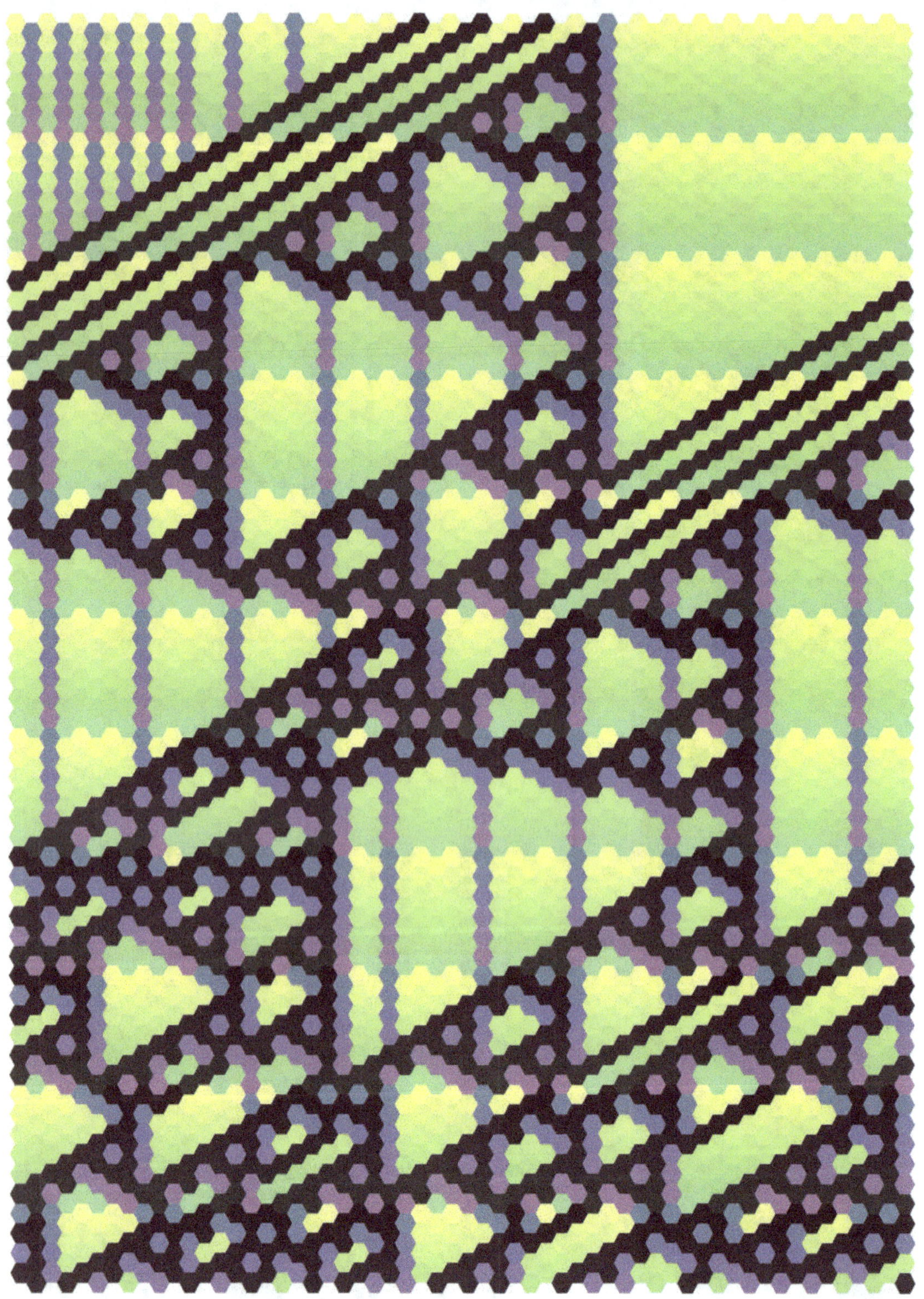

012120010

THREE COLORS ON THREE BEADS

Multiset Rules on Three Beads

The rules in this chapter use the three nearest neighbor beads for their inputs, namely, the left, above, and right beads. A rule with three colors and three input beads can have as many as 27 parts, which is a lot to follow when we make art by hand. Because each of those parts can be assigned any of the three colors, there are 3^{27} different rules to choose from. That is 7,625,597,484,987, or over seven trillion. If we looked at one of these rules every second, it would take about 241,806 years to see them all. These rules include all of the different two- and three-color rules we have seen so far. Up until now, we have sampled our favorites from about 20,000 of these, a mere drop in the bucket when compared with seven trillion. Fortunately, using multisets, we can simplify our search.

As a multiset, the colors for the left, above, and right beads are taken in any order. There are ten different multisets with three colors on three beads:

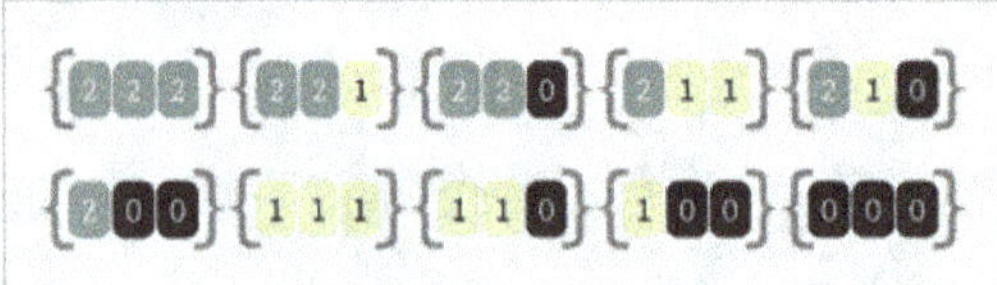

These ten possible multisets give us only 3^{10} rules (less than 60,000). We have ordered these using base three. The smallest value is placed bottom right, and the largest value is placed top left, where the smallest and largest refer to the numbers in base three. Notice, for example, that **200** is to the left of **111**. In other words, the inputs are ordered lexicographically, largest to smallest.

For each of these ten parts, we must choose an output value, for example, in the following way: A shorthand code for this rule is **2000222211**.

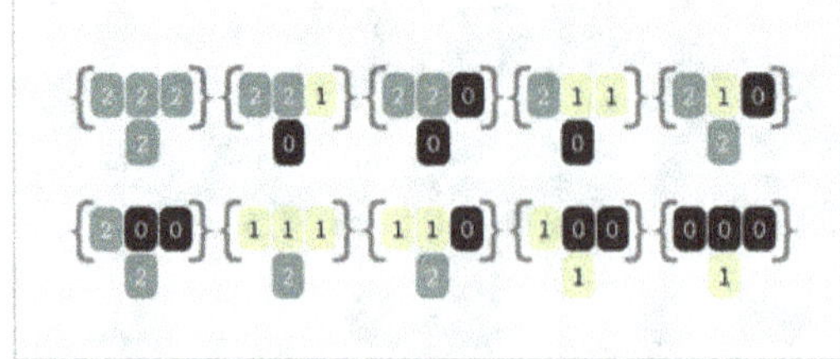

Whenever we use shorthand codes in this section, we are using this particular ordering.

Multiset rules on three beads are always symmetric, so you can flip your beadwork after every row. Since these multiset rules all use three beads for the input, we need two rows for the initial state.

We encourage you to experiment with different orderings when making your art. The following shows another way we like to order the parts for beadweaving. The first row contains the parts with mostly **2**s. The next row contains the parts with mostly **1**s, and the last row contains the parts with mostly **0**s and the multiset where the inputs are all different. This would be a *majority color ordering* of the ten parts of the rule, and this is a good choice when you are applying a rule by hand.

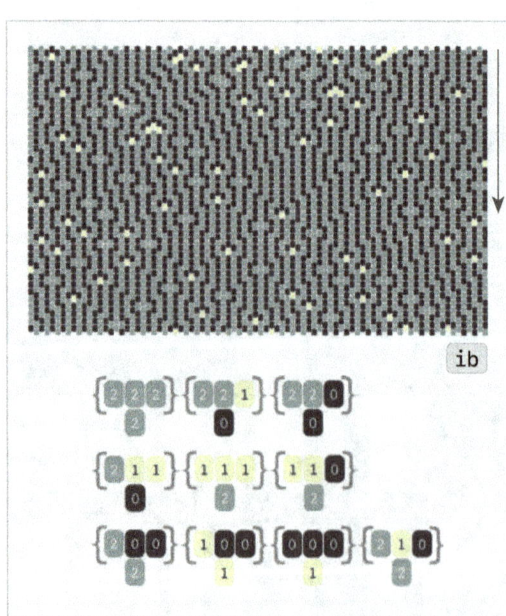
ib

We cannot possibly cover all 59,049 of these multiset rules, so instead, we will show you a sample of our favorites.

- *We start with rules that have two-color subrules.*
- *Then, we show rules that are color splits of two-color rules.*
- *Then, we look at rules that don't fall into these categories.*

Subrules and Extensions

Kintsugi: A Rule Within a Rule

0122201102/0221001012/1201222100/
1221102010/2122100101/2201020101

The following pattern is named for Kintsugi, the Japanese art of repairing broken pottery with lacquer and gold.

If you look at just the black and blue, you will see the pattern for *Picket Fence*. If we start a patch with only black and blue, the design would be the same for *Kinstugi* as for *Picket Fence*. We say that the two-color rule for *Picket Fence* is a subrule of the three-color rule for *Kintsugi*. Conversely, the three-color rule is an extension of the two-color rule. The patch shows how we can see the pattern of a *subrule* inside the pattern of an *extension*. We can also see a subrule inside an extension by looking at the parts of the rule.

For example, the rule for Kintsugi is this:

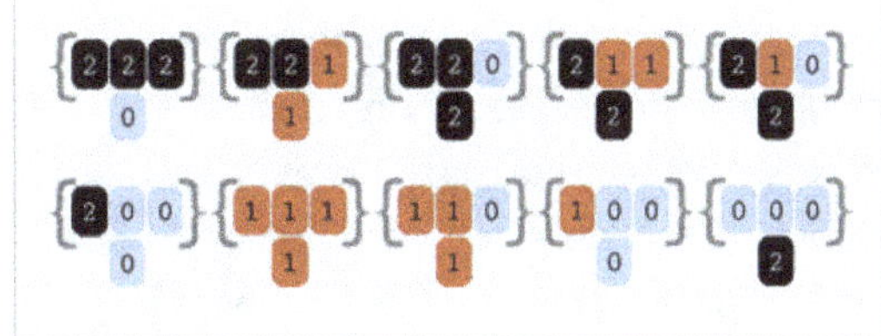

How can we identify a two-color subrule inside of this three-color extension? The first, third, sixth, and last components of this rule show that this rule is closed on the set {0,2}. The definition of *closed on {0,2}* is that if the input colors are all in {0,2}, then the output is also in {0,2}. In other words, if we eliminate color 1, we are left with all of the parts for a two-color rule on {0,2}, in this case, *Picket Fence*. This is what we mean when we say *Picket Fence* is a subrule of this three-color rule. Rules that are closed on a set of two elements are among our most favorites.

Here is an acrylic painting of *Kintsugi* on canvas, measuring 20 inches by 30 inches, where a fourth color has been used in a color split of gold.

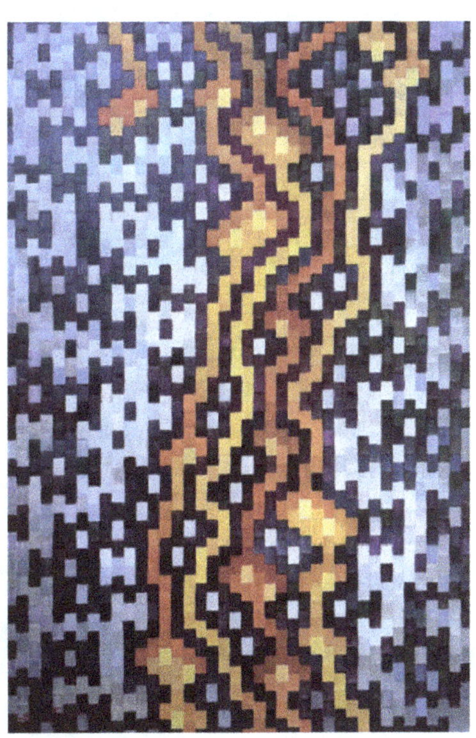

Kari's Rule

(Extension of Picket Fence)

0101020101/0122202002/0222000012/

1102100101/1201222112/1221122011

This is another rule with *Picket Fence* hidden within it; it can do exactly what *Picket Fence* can do, but more, because it has one more color.

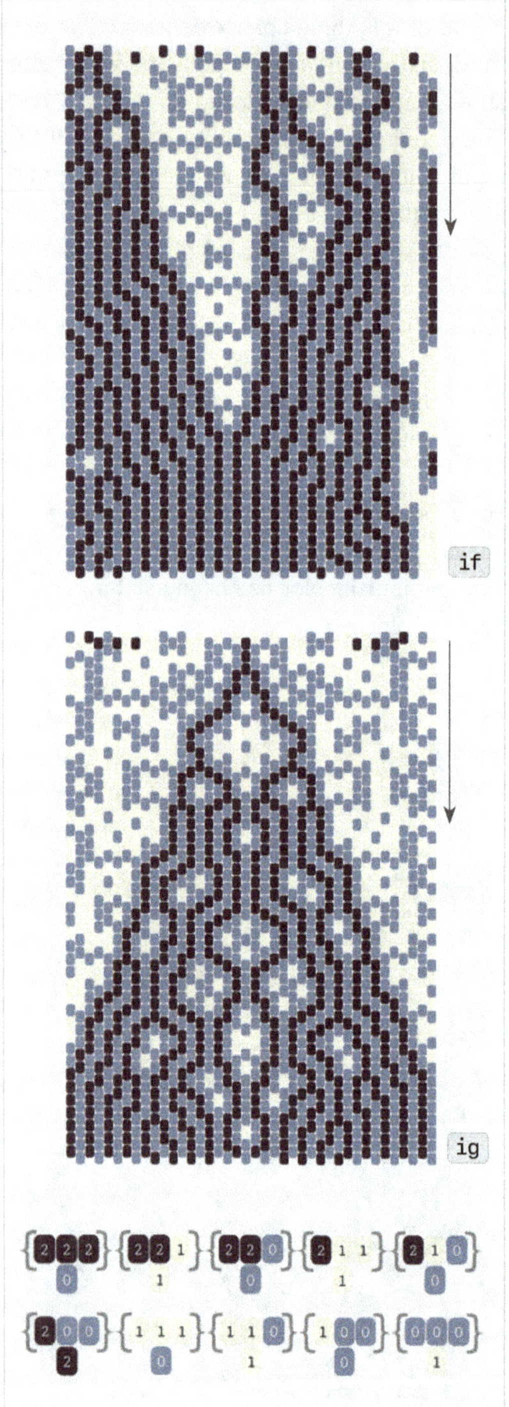

if

ig

ih

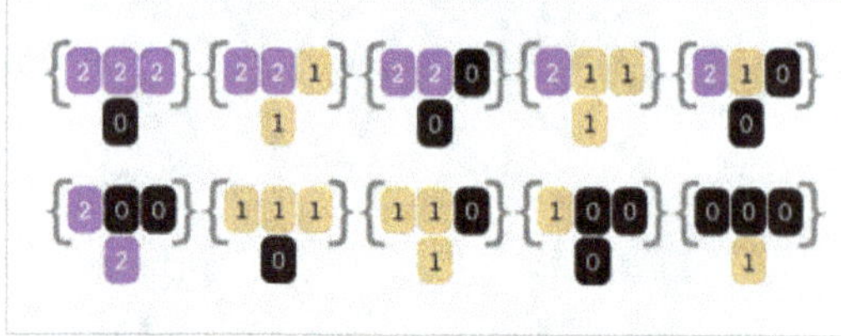

While *Kari's Rule* is not technically reversible, we treated it that way in this patch of beadwork. We beaded the first ten or twenty rows, ripped out the first three rows, and then continued beading from both ends, so the red dots that indicate errors are no longer errors if you flip the patch upside down.

🎨 Design Tips

*If you get too many stripes repeating in one place, break the rule to add two to five color **0** beads consecutively in a row. Kari's Rule is especially beautiful with a symmetric start.*

Groovy Picket Fence
(Extension of Picket Fence)

We call this *Groovy Picket Fence* because it has *Picket Fence* as a subrule in **{0,1}** and almost *Groovy Checkers* in **{0,2}**.

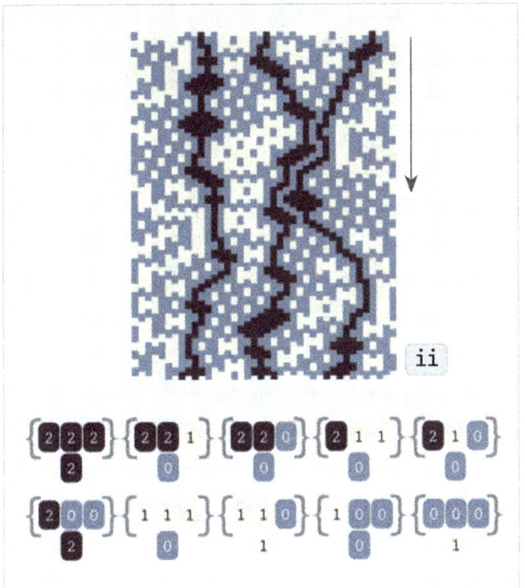

This is particularly interesting in large patches, because it takes a very long time to stabilize into a periodic pattern. In other words, it has a long transient phase.

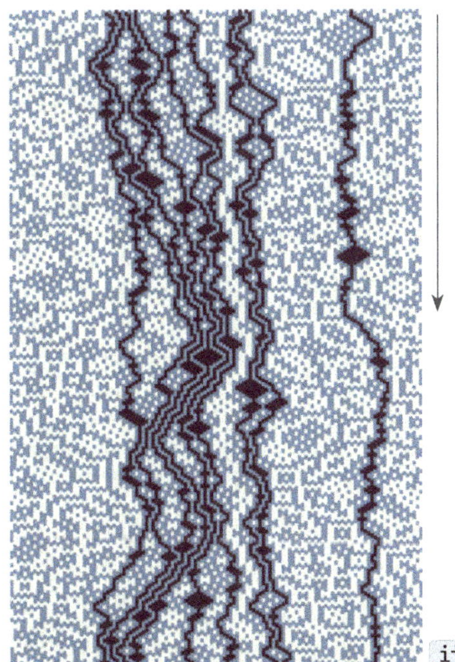

Next, we show samples of our favorite three-color extensions of two-color rules.

Percolating Picket Fence
(Extension of Picket Fence)

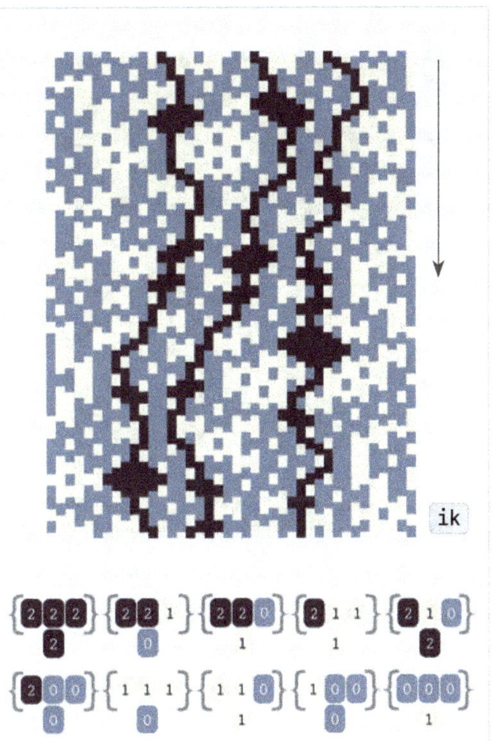

Switching Fence
(Extension of Picket Fence)

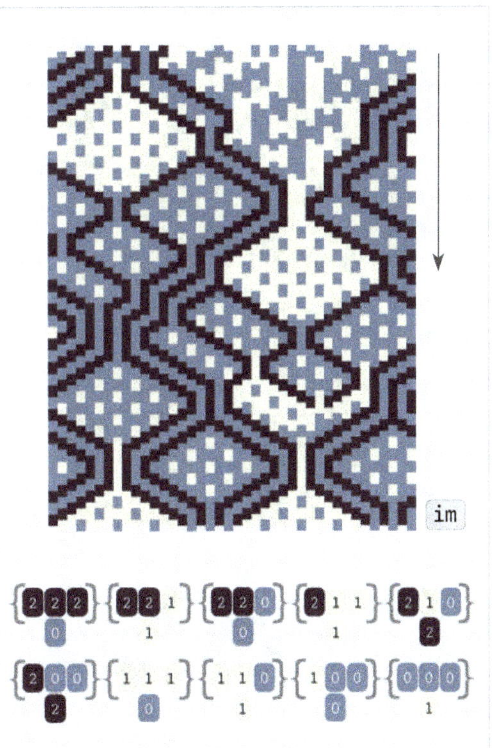

Framed Chevrons
(Extension of Minority Wins)

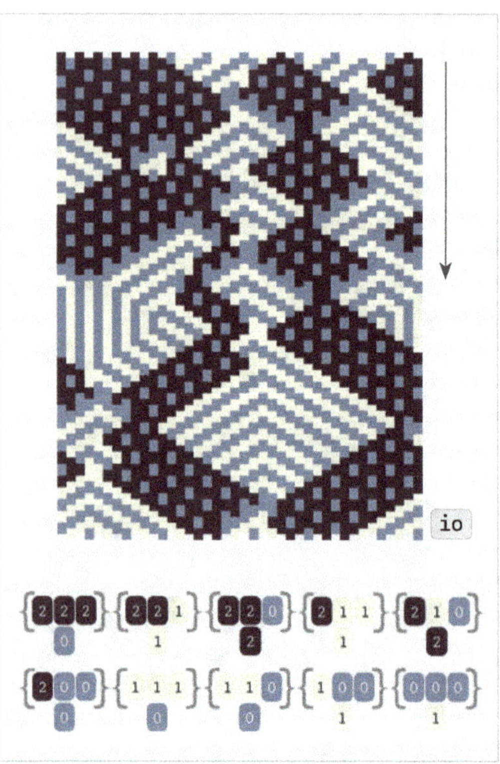

Jagged Minority
(Extension of Minority Wins)

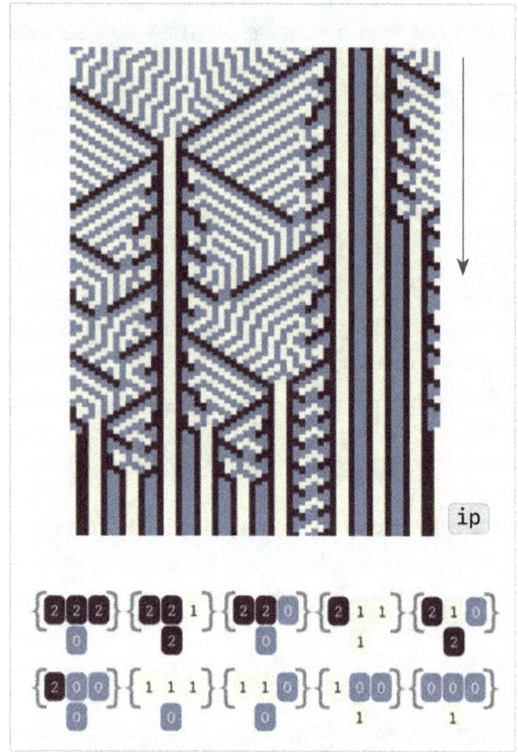

Rooftops
(Extension of Minority Wins)

Here is a version of *Jagged Minority* with color cycling of period 2. It uses a total of five colors.

Complicated Minority
(Extension of Minority Wins)

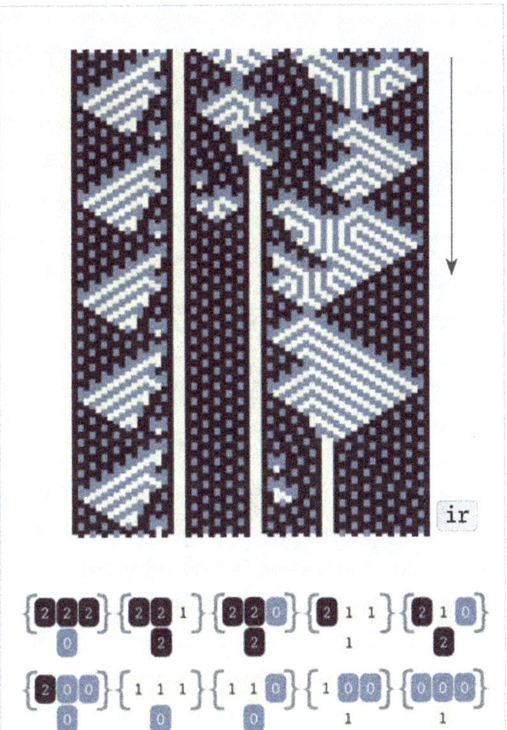

Scant Groovy
(Extension of Groovy Checkers and Scant)

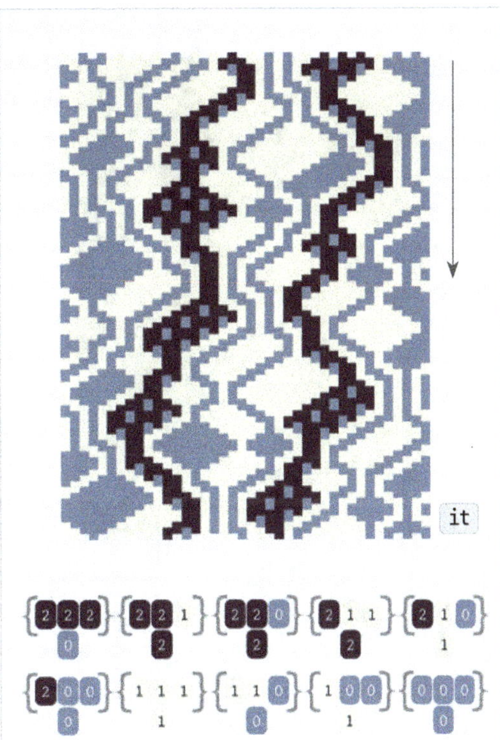

Paths Through Buds & Vines
(Extension of Buds & Vines)

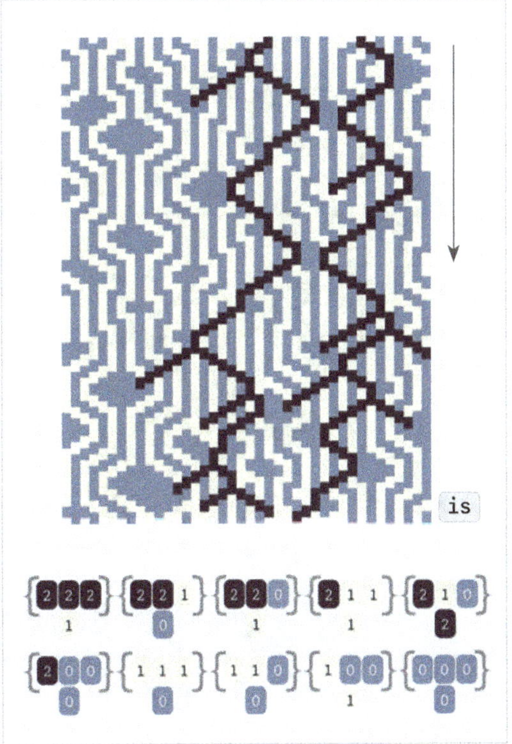

Groovy Buds & Vines
(Extension of Groovy Checkers and Buds & Vines)

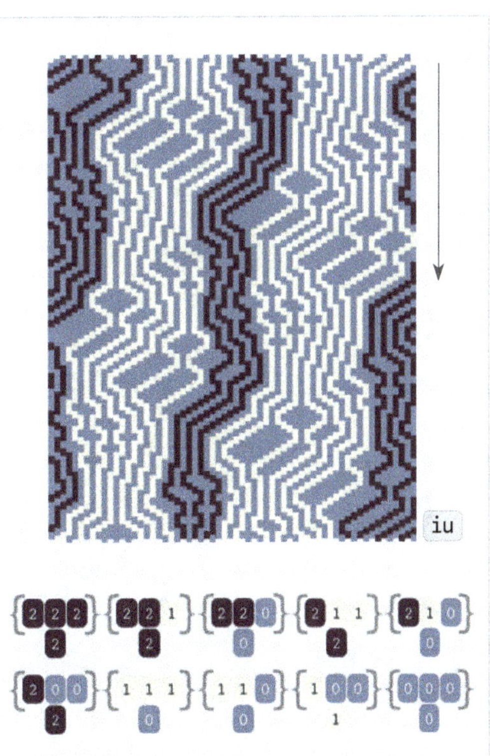

Confused Dot Arrays
(Extension of Dot Arrays)

Clean Mix
(Extension of Scant)

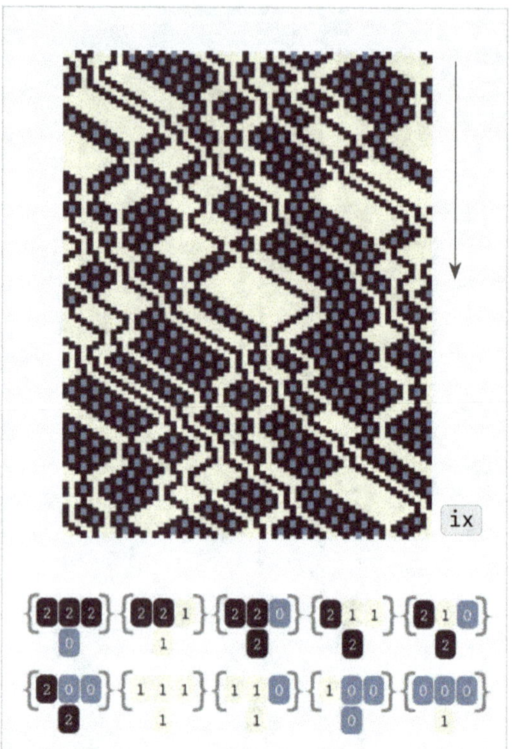

Paths Through Dot Arrays
(Extension of Dot Arrays)

Dirty Mix
(Extension of Scant)

Here is a version of *Dirty Mix* with color cycling of period 4, but all the **0**s are black. It uses a total of nine colors.

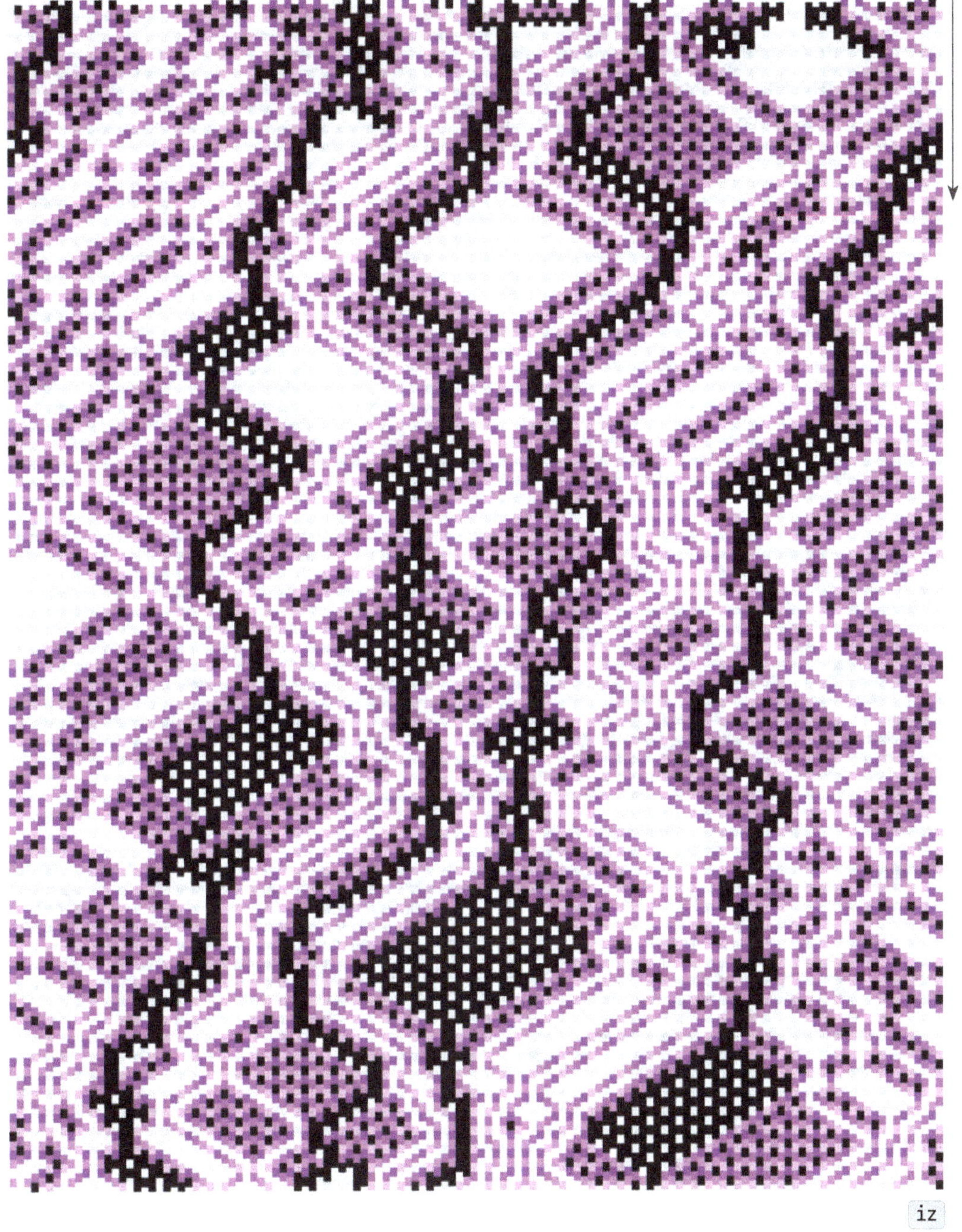

iz

Color Splits of Two-Color Rules

We now turn our attention to the three-color multiset rules on three beads that are color splits of two-color rules.

Color splits are the rules where two colors act as one color in a simpler rule with two colors. If the two colors were replaced with a single color, we would be left with a two-color rule. We say that the two colors act as one.

An interesting aspect of color splits is that they can highlight some of the underlying properties and hidden structures of two-color rules that one would not be able to see otherwise.

Color Splits of Groovy Checkers

Here is our familiar rule, *Groovy Checkers*.

ja

Many variants are possible when we color split *Groovy Checkers*. When we split color **0** into the two colors **0** and **2**, we get the following designs.

0100121012 jc

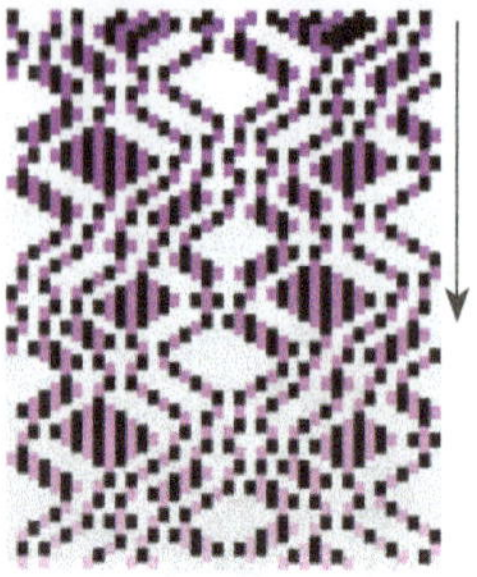

0100121210 jd

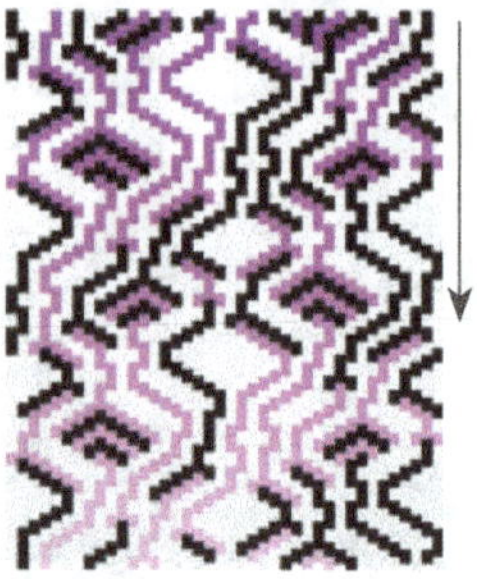

0102121012 je

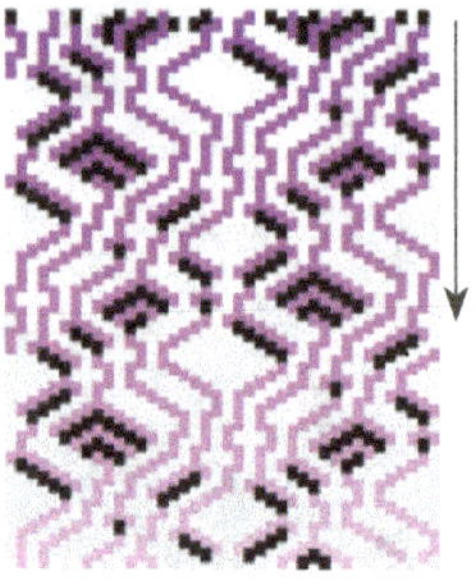

0102121212 jf

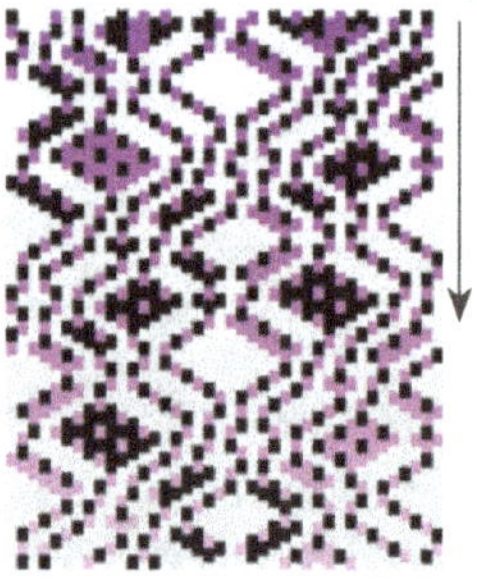

0120101212 jg

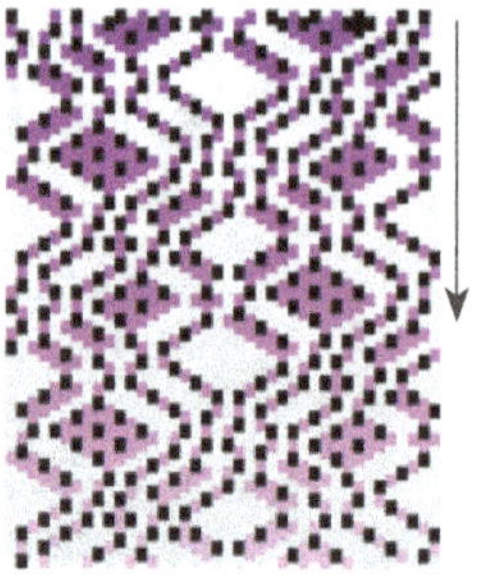

0120121210 jh

2102101010 ji

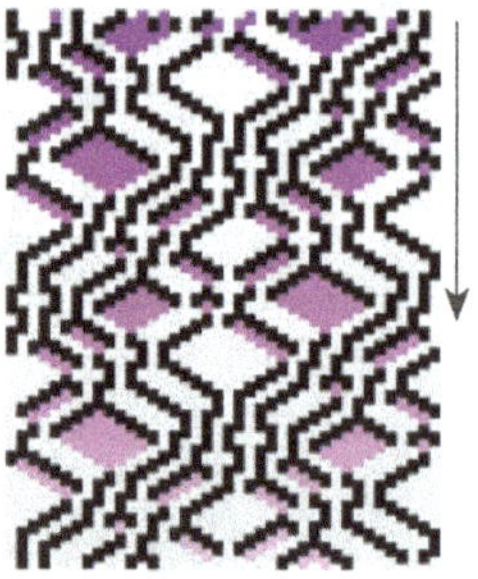

2120121012 jj

2122121212 jk

Color Splits of Dot Arrays

Dot Arrays can be a boring pattern, but it has a rich hidden structure right under its surface. The following designs are all color splits of *Dot Arrays*. The patch below shows *Dot Arrays* with initial red dots plus color shading in rainbow (color **1**) on a white background (color **0**).

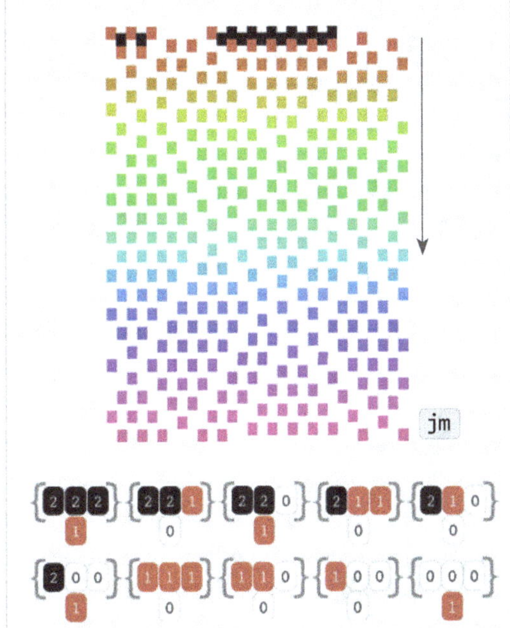

jm

js

We encourage the reader to explore repeating patterns made with these codes, especially for **1212010021** and **1012012221**. To make a repeating design, start with a repeating initial state using an odd number of columns for the repeat, like five, seven, or nine. If we make the number of columns a multiple of the repeat width, we get simpler repeating designs. If the number of columns is not a multiple of the repeat width, we can create designs like the one below.

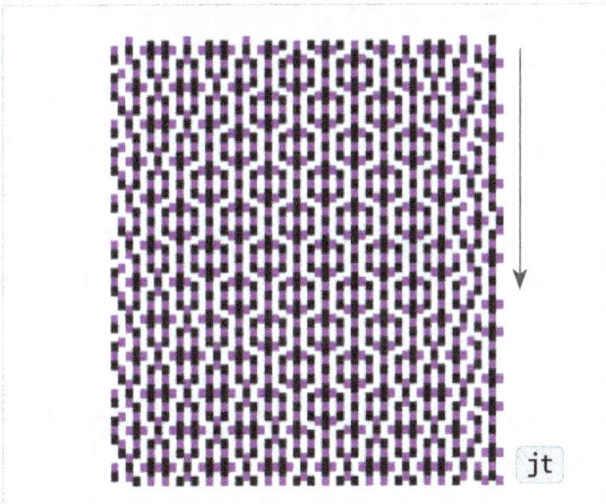

jt

The designs below all use the same initial state, but a subset of the white outputs is colored black (color **2**). See if you notice the similarities among the designs!

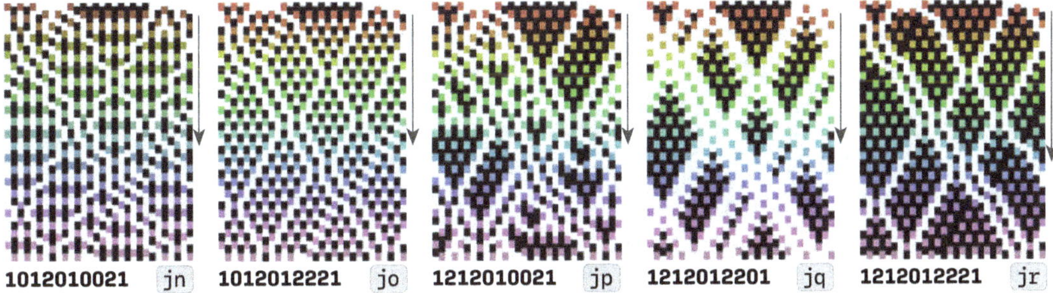

1012010021 jn   1012012221 jo   1212010021 jp   1212012201 jq   1212012221 jr

Color Splits of Picket Fence

In a similar way, we can explore color splits of *Picket Fence*. The first patch below shows *Picket Fence* in white (color **0**) and black (color **1**). In the following patches, a subset of the black outputs is colored with a gradient with teal (color **2**) at the top and gold at the bottom to make a color split of *Picket Fence*. Many variants are possible when we split colors on *Picket Fence*. In particular, when we split **0** into two colors, **0** and **2**, we get 64 new rules with three colors. You can see from the last example that one of them is just the two-color rule for *Picket Fence*, now using colors **2** and **0** as the outputs instead of colors **1** and **0**.

0010100201   jv

0010100202   jw

0010200201   jx

0010200202   jy

0020100102   jz

0020100202   ka

0020200201   kb

0020200202   kc

ju

kd

All of these patches use the same rule, a color split for *Picket Fence*. They all employ a color cycle with period 2, using the colors to the right, a periodic start, and squares on point for the cells.

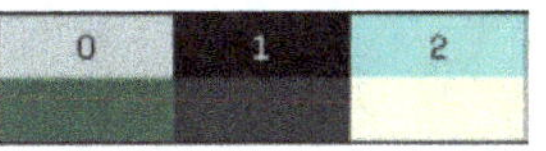

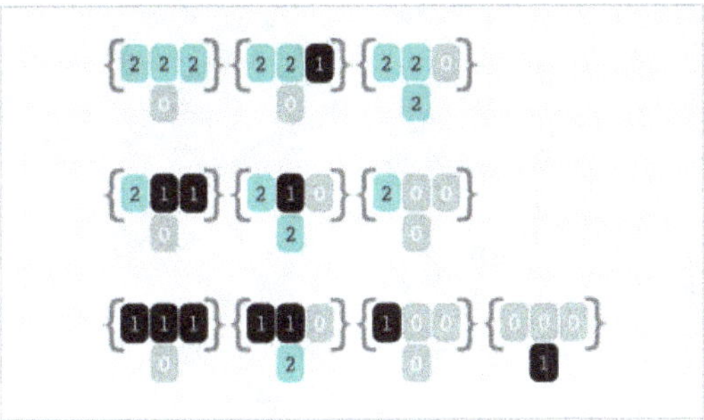

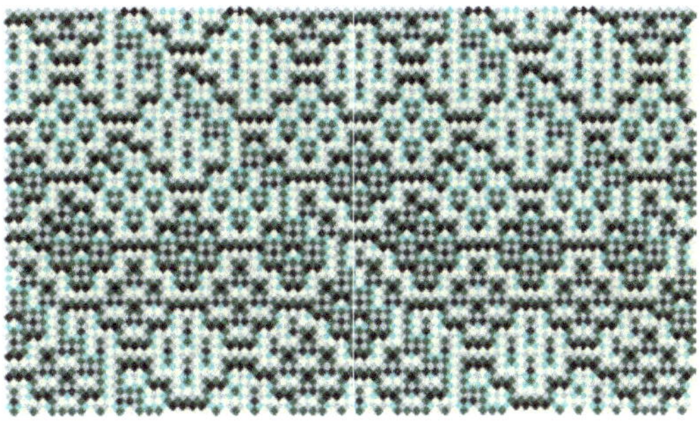

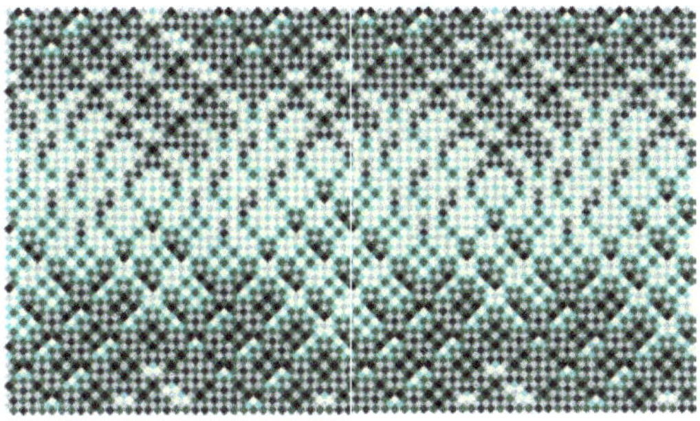

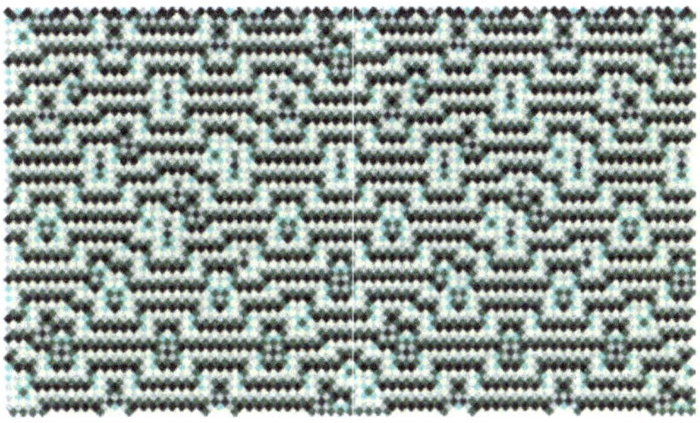

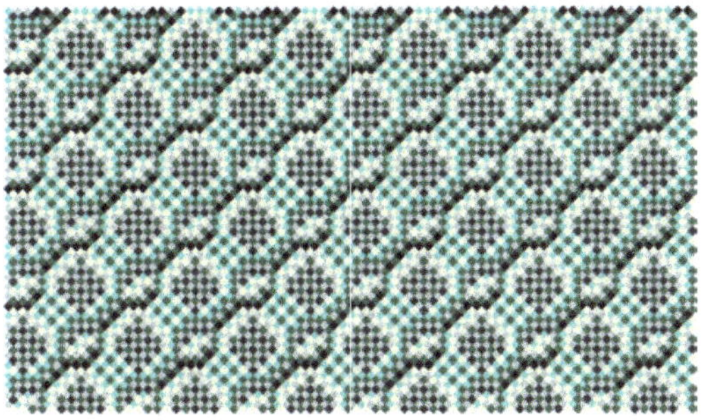

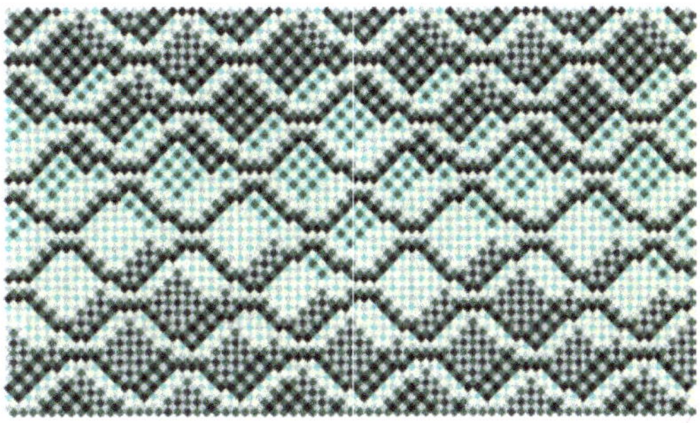

Color Splits of Buds & Vines

With *Buds & Vines*, we have more variants than with *Picket Fence*. The following small patches are all color splits of *Buds & Vines* with identical initial conditions.

0100100010   ke

0100100012   kf

0102102212   ki

0102120010   kj

0102120210   km

0102120212   kn

0102122212   ko

0122120012   kq

2100120012   kr

2100122212   ks

2102120010   kt

2120122212   ku

0122120012   kv

We now look at three-color multiset rules on three beads that are neither extensions nor color splits.

Snake Fence

Snake Fence is *almost* a color split of *Picket Fence*, which is one of the most special two-color rules.

For reference, here is the ordinary *Picket Fence*. If we split white (color **0**) into white (color **0**) and blue (color **2**), we obtain the following rule for *Picket Fence*:

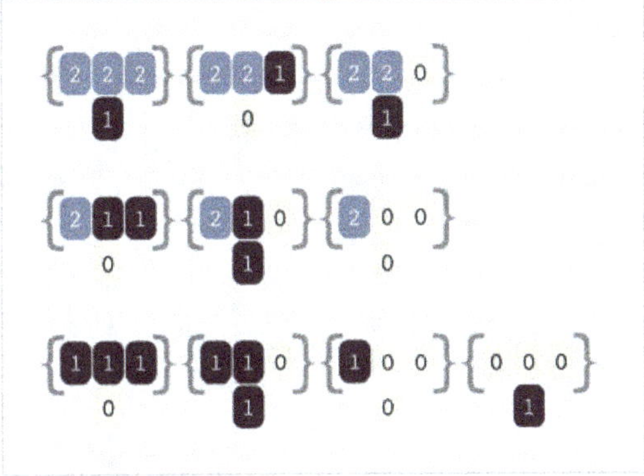

By changing any of these white outputs (color **0**) to blue (color **2**), we get a color split of *Picket Fence*. However, *Snake Fence* is obtained simply by changing the output for three whites (**000**) from **1** to **2**. This is no longer a simple color split of *Picket Fence*.

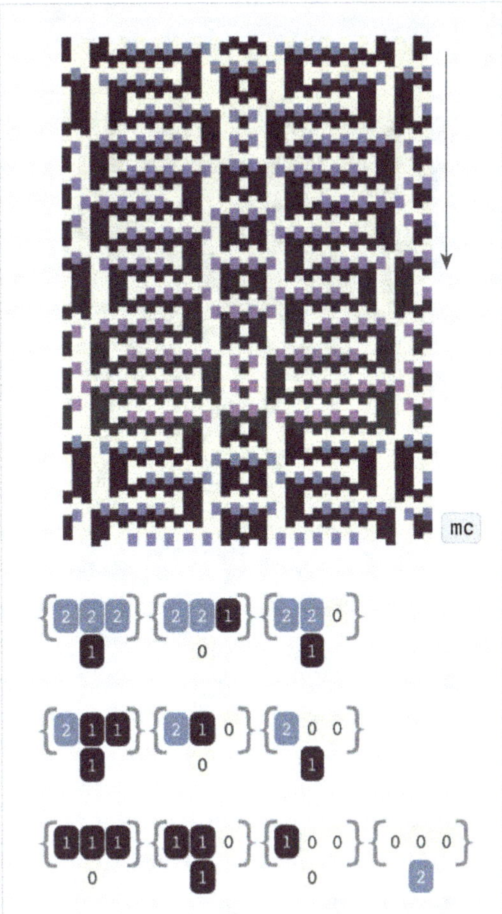

Here are a few more variants derived in this way. What all of these variants have in common is that one or more outputs of *Picket Fence* are switched from **1** to **2**.

Snake Fence Variant #1

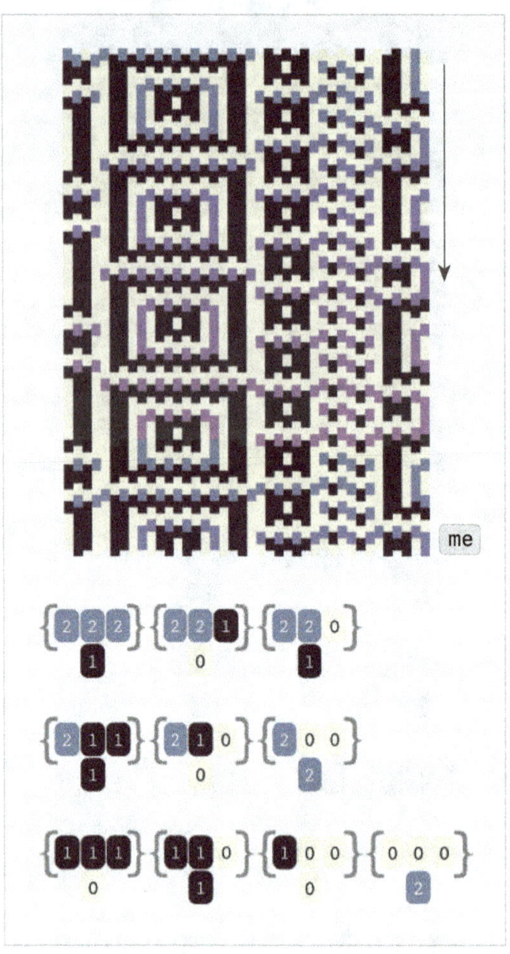

me

mf

Snake Fence Variant #2

mg

mh

Snake Fence Variant #3

mi

Snake Fence Variant #4

mk

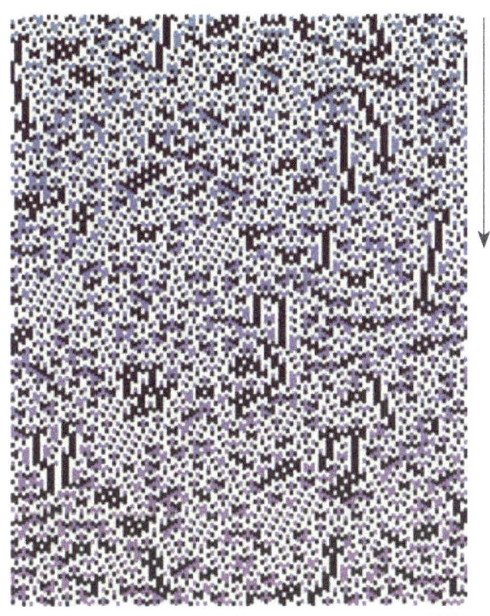

mj

mm

Oscillators and Gliders

A common area of interest in cellular automata is the study of oscillators and gliders.

Oscillators are repeating elements that cycle in place. Gliders are repeating elements that move. This rule creates both. The oscillators are visible in the vertical repeats. The gliders are visible in the diagonal repeats.

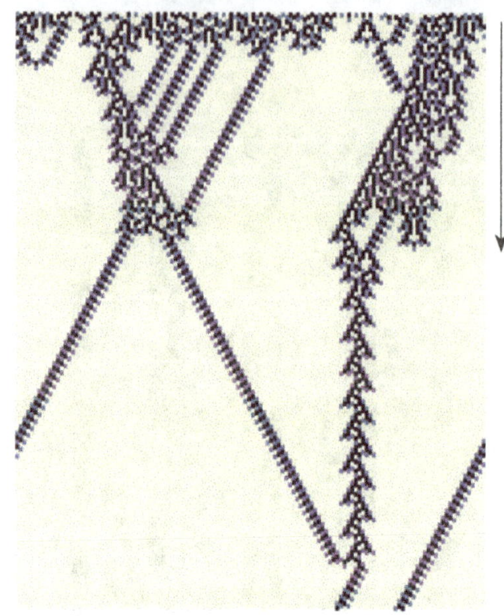

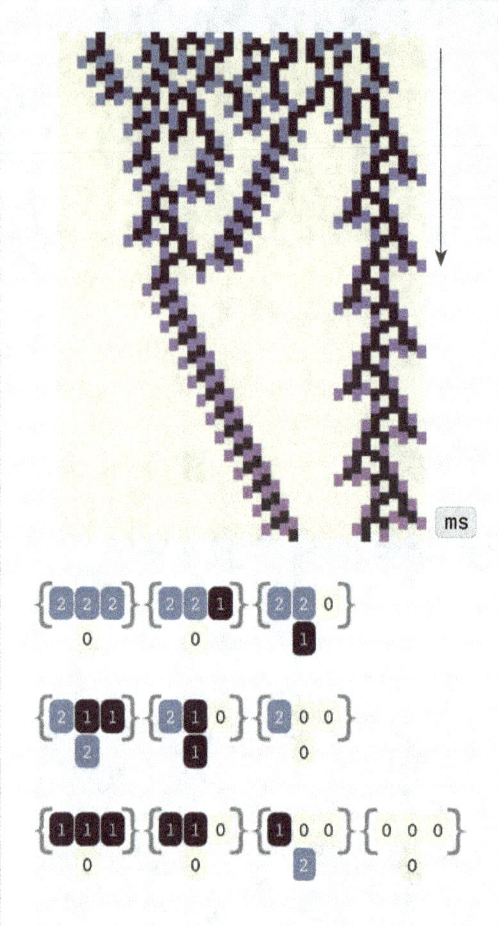

In the patch below, the colors alternate with a period of 2. Color **0** alternates between light and dark cream. Color **1** alternates between black and pink. Color **2** alternates between blue and aqua. The initial row has a period of 5 and the width of the patch is 70, which is a multiple of 5.

Roger's Shards: Interplay Between Symmetry and Asymmetry

This pattern is very special because it exhibits an organic and irregular form of symmetry. Notice that almost none of the triangle shapes is left-right symmetric, despite the fact that the rule itself is symmetric (because the input is a multiset).

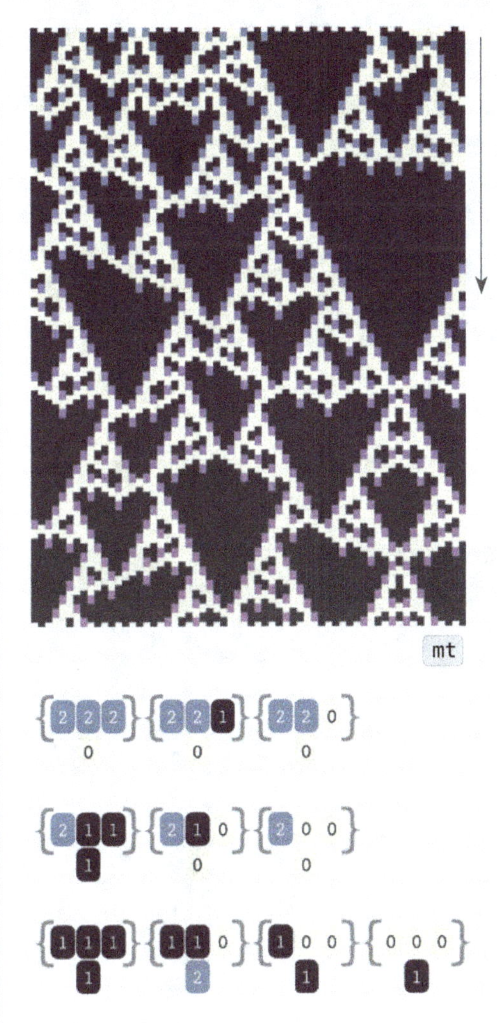

mt

mu

Here is a Sierpiński-like triangle. Notice that the triangles on the left shape are mirror images of the triangles on the right, and that no single triangle has left-right symmetry.

mv

Open question: Does the left-right symmetry eventually reveal itself in the overall pattern? How large a patch would be needed for that to happen?

Connected Shards

This is a variant of *Shards*, where some of the triangle shapes are vertically connected to each other.

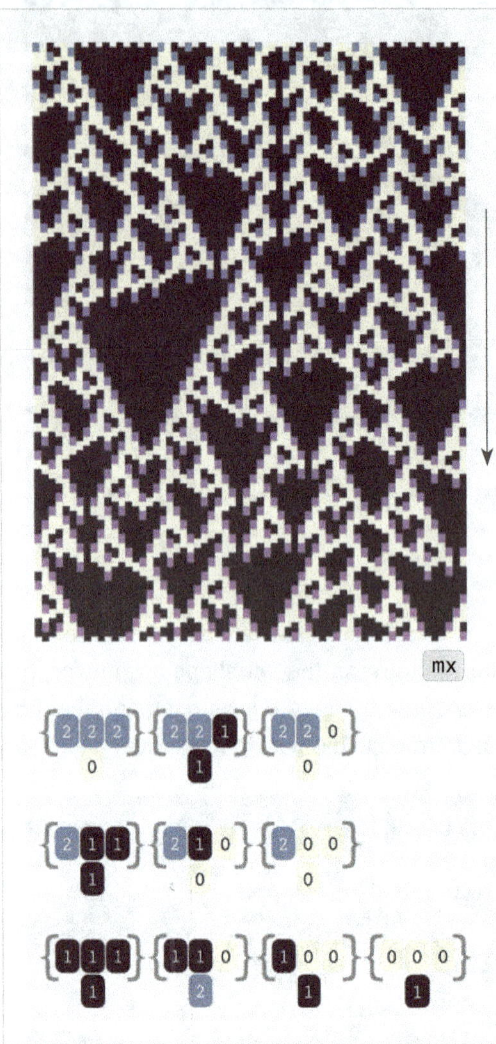

mx

my

The following triangle appears from a seed consisting of two single white cells.

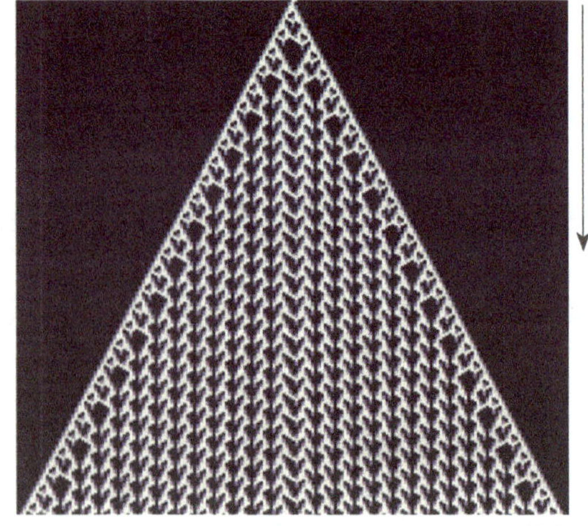

mz

Sharp Shards

This final variant of *Shards* has no triangle shape that is connected to another one, either vertically or horizontally. Consequently, if the black areas were left empty, then the remaining pixels could be held together like a piece of lace.

nb

nc

The following triangle appears from a seed consisting of two single white cells.

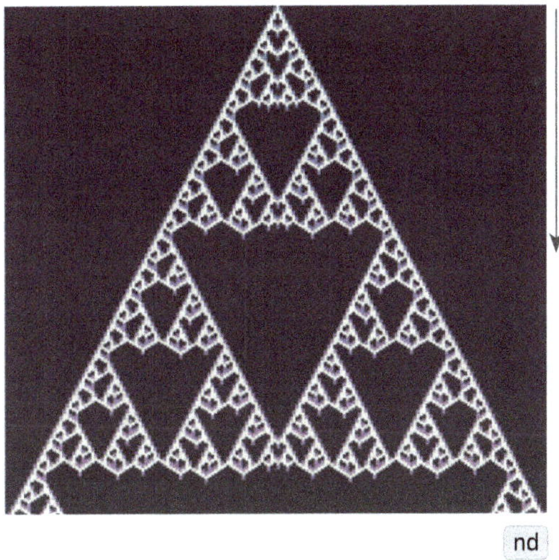

nd

In this variant of *Shards*, the seed start gives reflection symmetry to the triangles along the center axis.

Lightning Bugs

2100000021

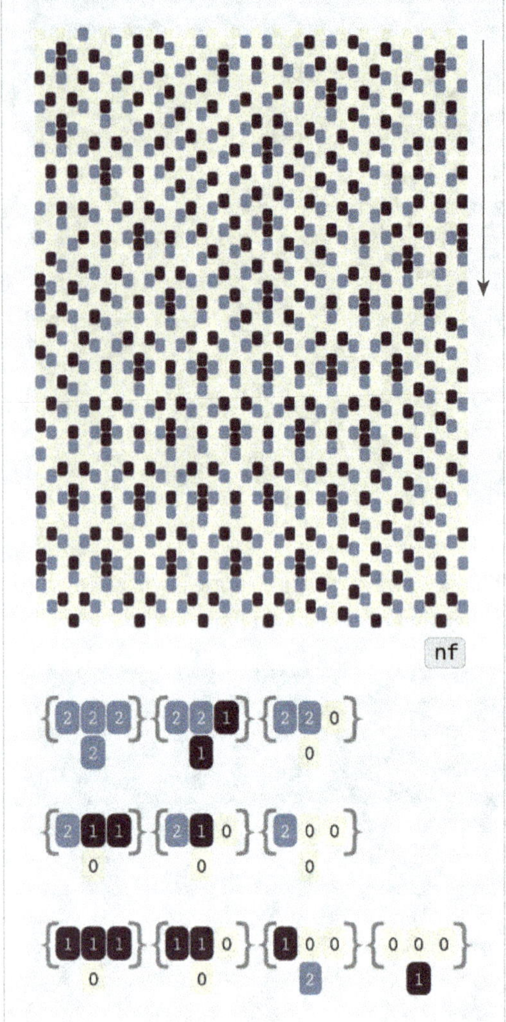

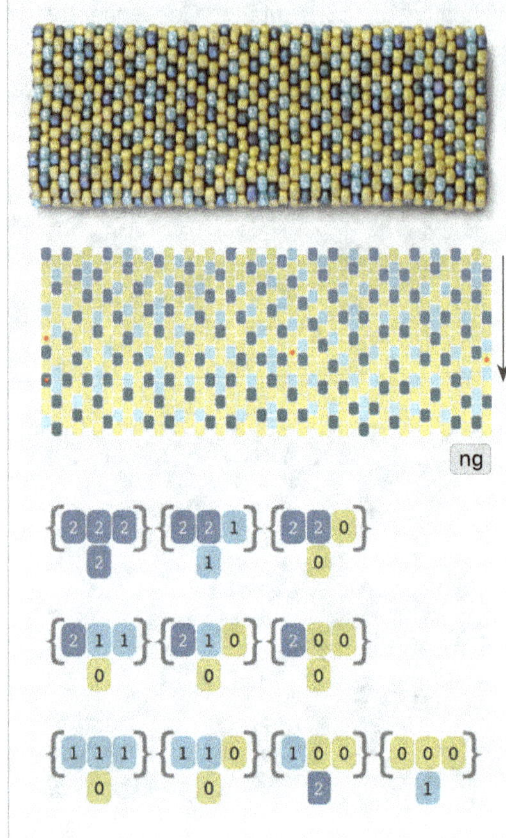

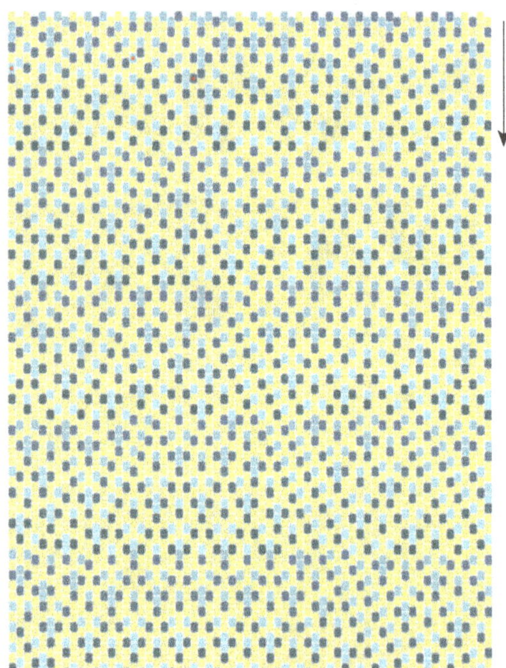

Water Lilies: Earrings

0012012010/0102111221/1010121012
100020220/2000222211/2112210022

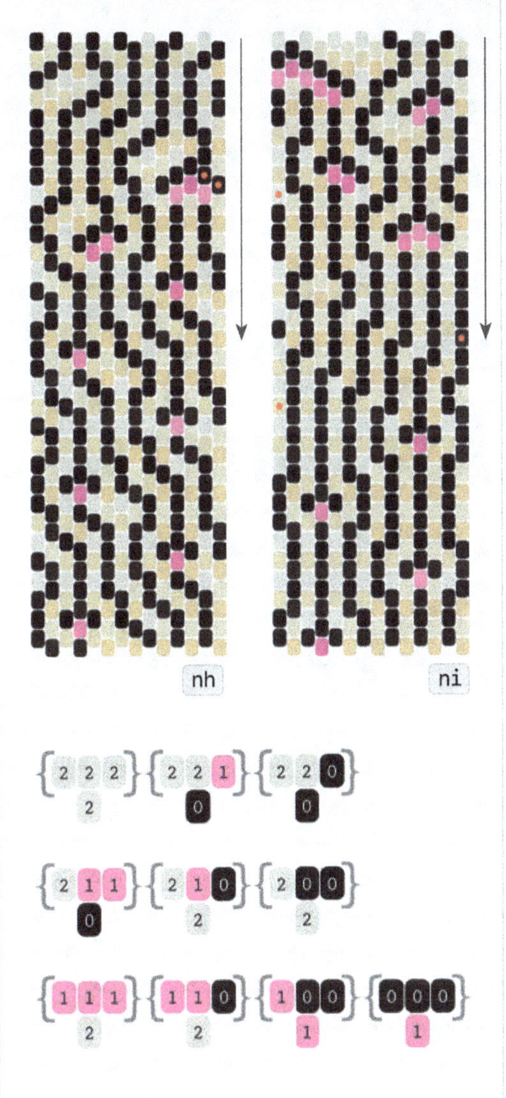

These earrings feature long thin strips of bead-work using the rule for *Water Lilies*.

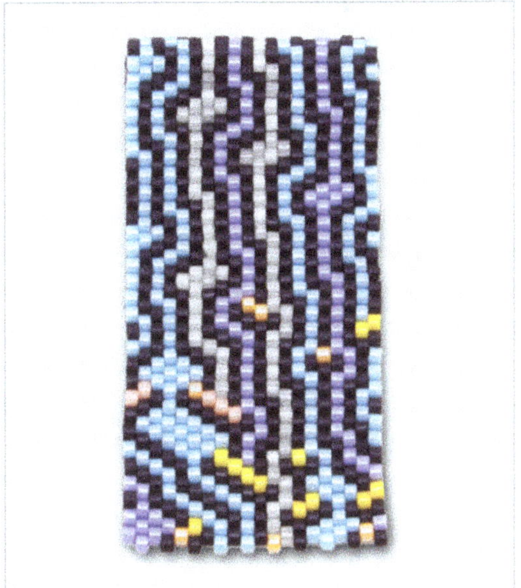

Design Tips

Each earring is a strip of peyote stitch using size 15° seed beads. Each strip is 12 columns wide, with a pendant loop stitched at one end to hold wire. The earrings also include a half-hard wire, head pins, a fine rolo chain, 6 mm open jump rings, 6 mm round beads, daisy spacers, and ear wires. To assemble each earring, string the beaded pendant onto the wire with a daisy spacer at each end. Cut two lengths of chain, each with an odd number of links; we used nine. Use pliers to bend the wire into a wrapped loop at each end, attaching a chain to each end before closing the loops. Wire wrap a 6 mm bead onto a head pin. String a chain, the head pin, the second chain, and an ear wire onto an open jump ring. Close the ring.

Water Lilies: Acrylic on Canvas

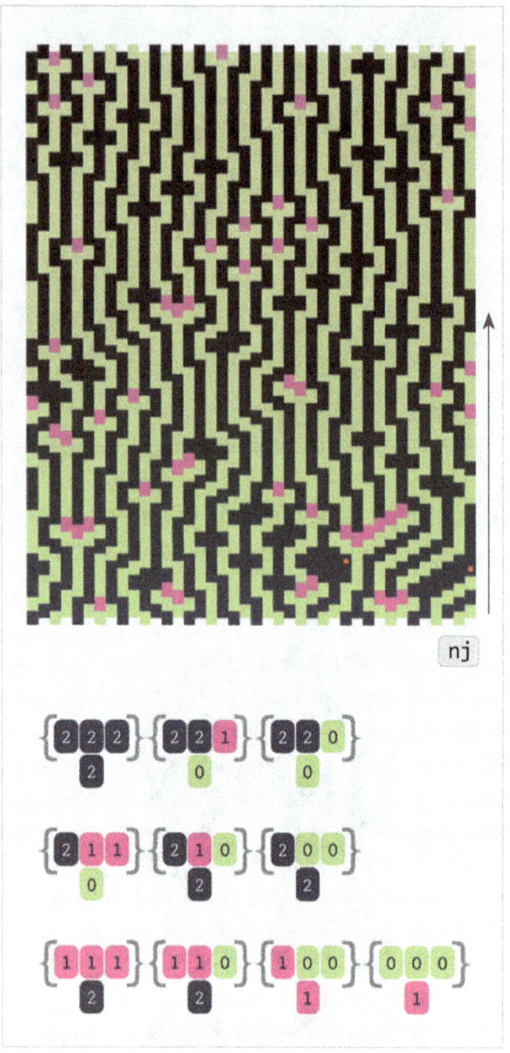

Although the design in the painting looks much like those in the earrings, their rules are different in the details. In fact, there are many rules with three colors on three beads that look very similar to *Water Lilies*, but with subtle design variations. The rule **0202212211** is another example that looks especially nice with a symmetric start.

Grapes

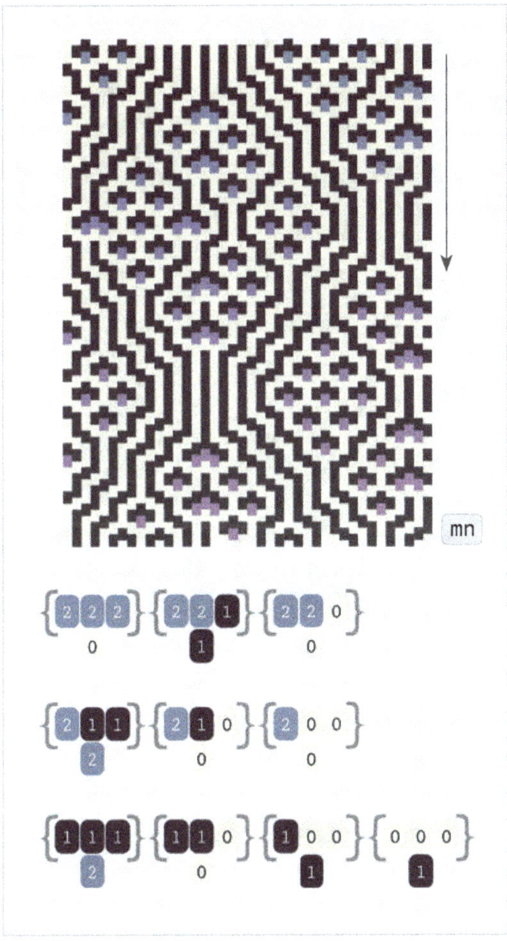

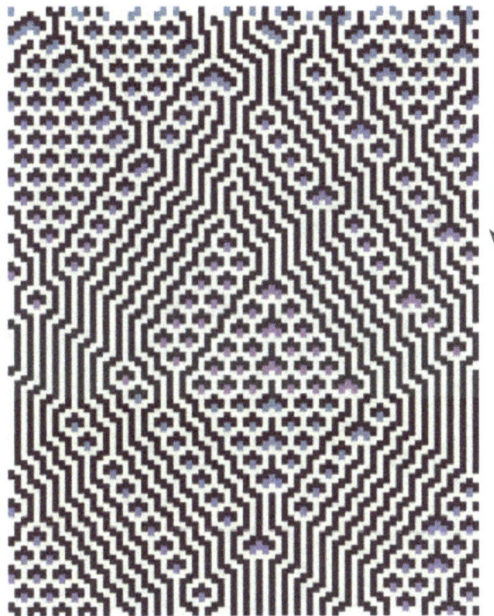

Budding Camellias

0102112110/0202221211/1100021002
1122220020/2002002011/2111120012

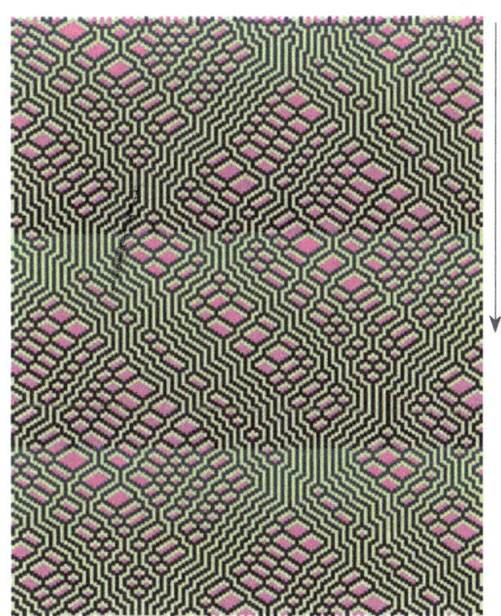

Mountain Tops

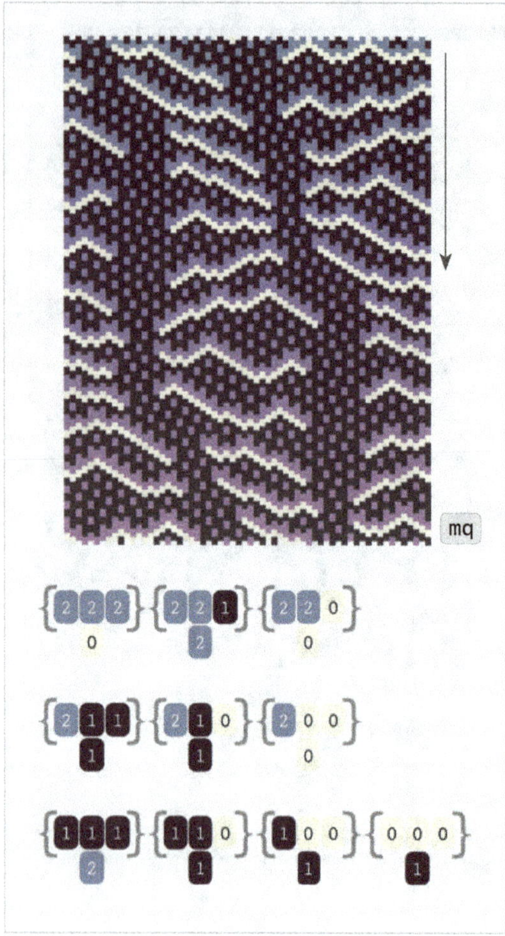

Rich Oscillators

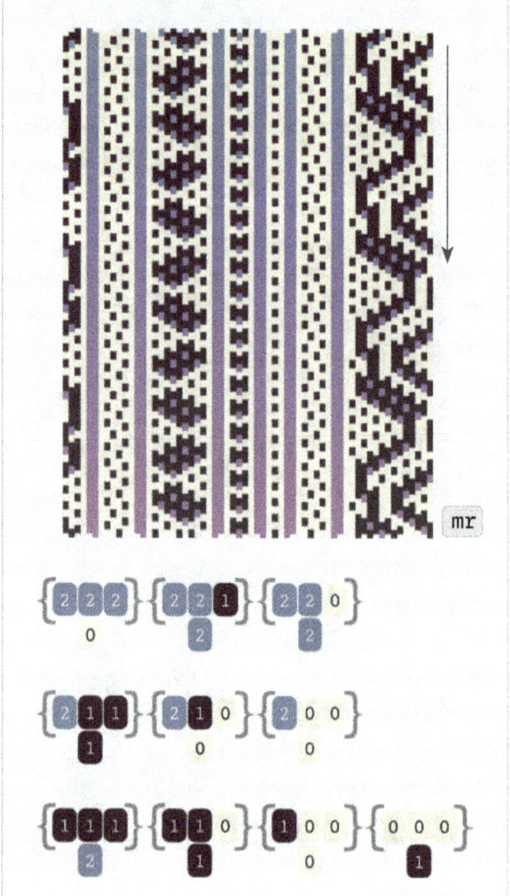

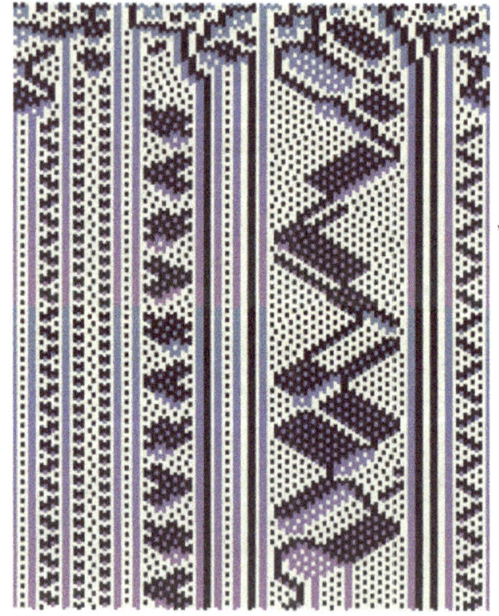

Castle Walls

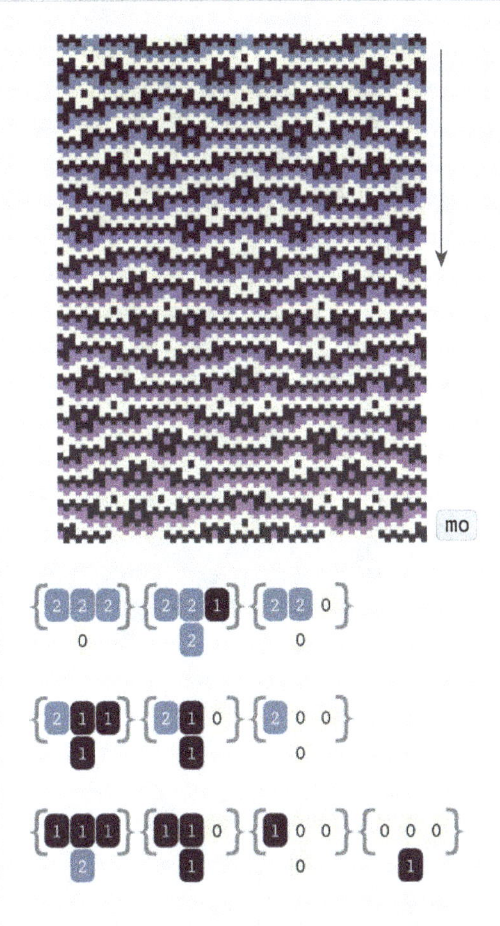

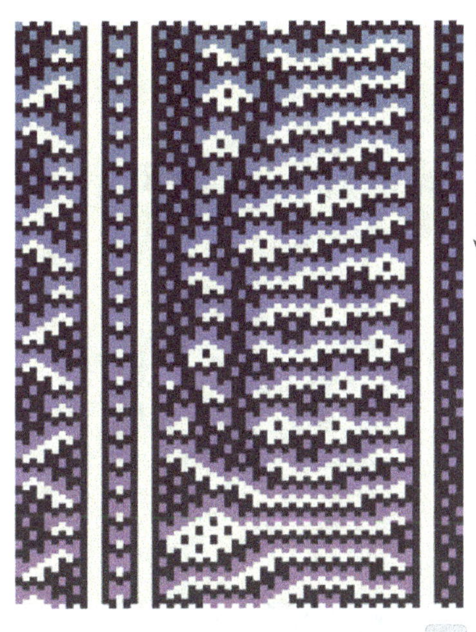

Ziggy's Cat Toys

1222000012/0122220001

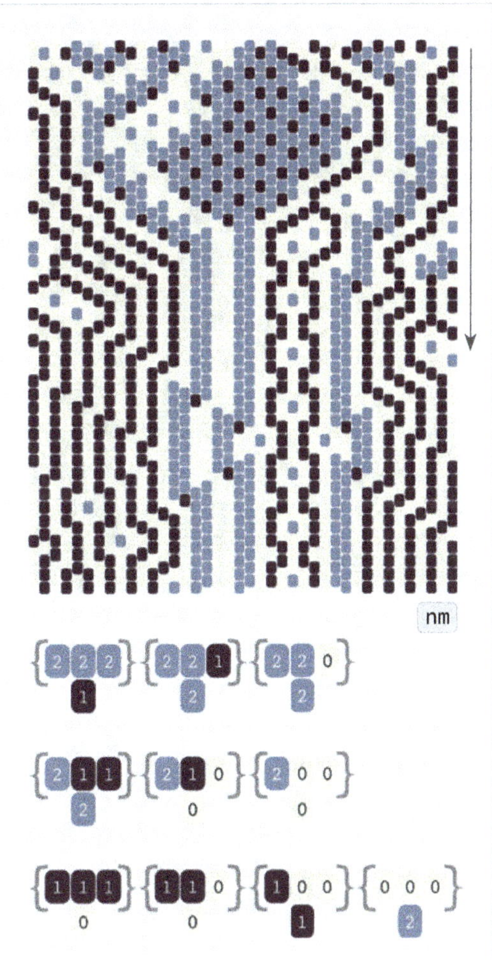

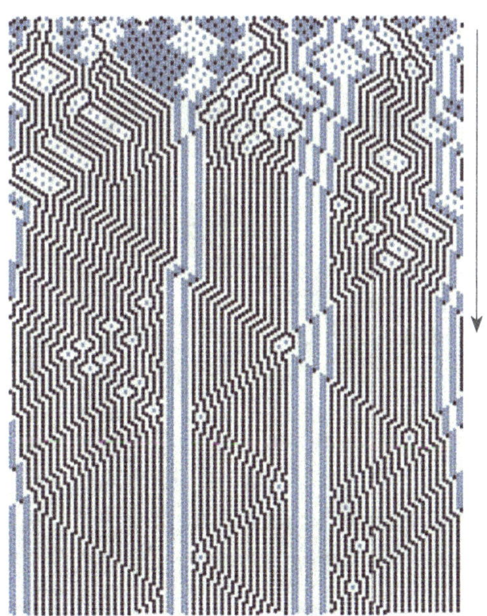

Ziggy's Cat Toys (continued)

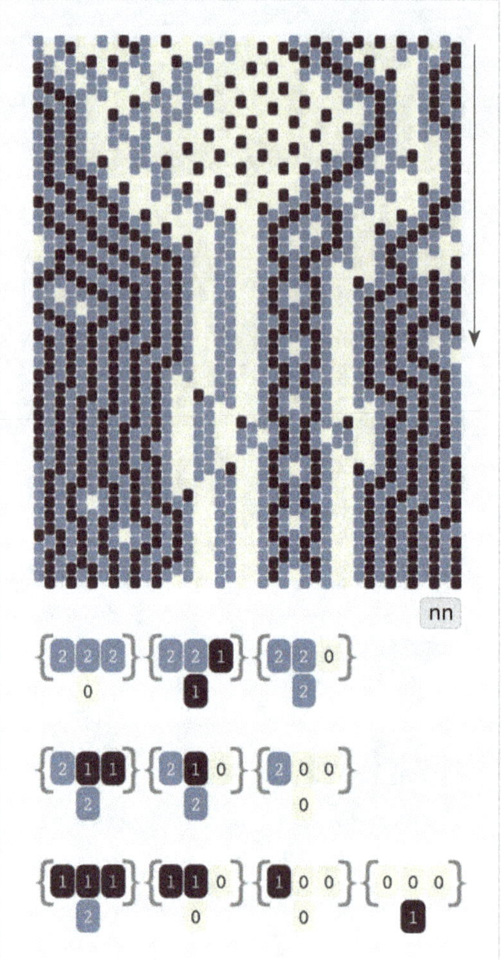

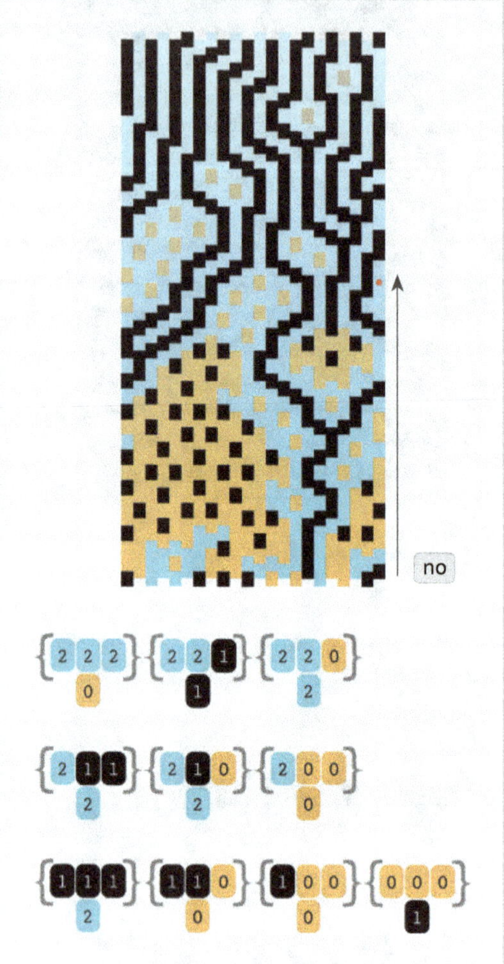

Vines on a Fence
1201102012

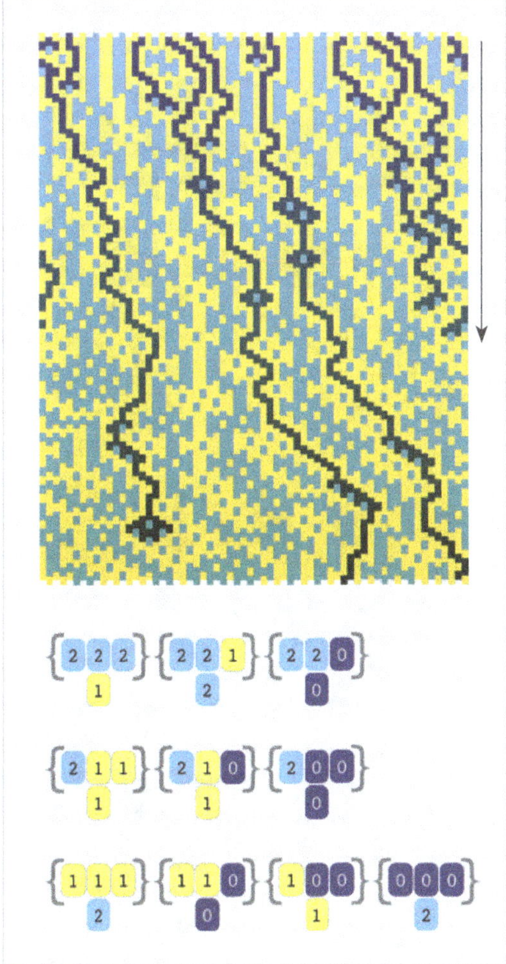

Dotted Checkers
1201002012

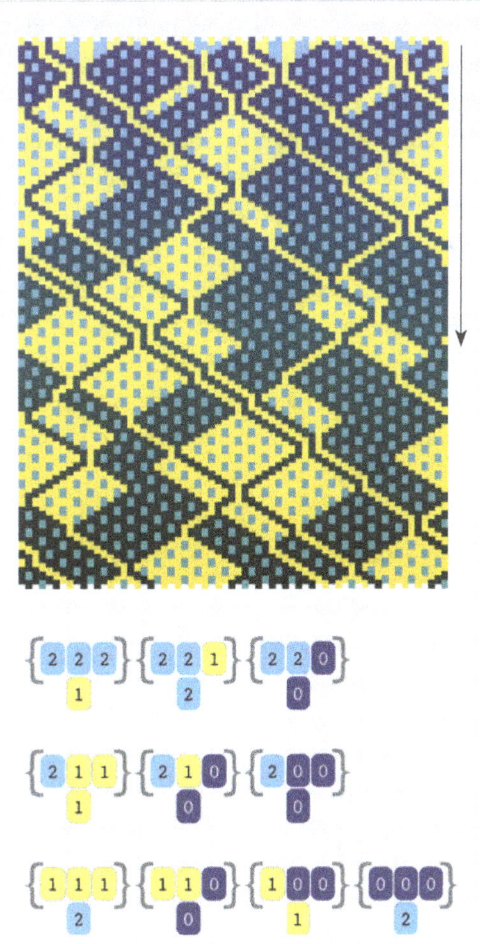

Dotted Torrent Blocks

1201002012

The rule used for this pendant is a combination of the two previous rules, *Vines on a Fence* and *Dotted Checkers*. It is nearly a color split, with color **2** split into **2a** and **2b**. This multiset rule would be a true color split except for the two parts with inputs **{210}**. Depending upon whether **2** is **2a** or **2b**, the output is either **1** or **0**, technically making this a four-color rule. Although the example appears to be three colors, the gold beads are in two finishes, matte and shiny. The colors are shiny gold (**0**), black (**1**), white (**2a**), and matte gold (**2b**).

INPUT	OUTPUT
{222}	1
{221}	2a
{220}	0
{211}	1
{2a10}	1
{2b10}	0
{200}	0
{111}	2a
{110}	0
{100}	1
{000}	2b

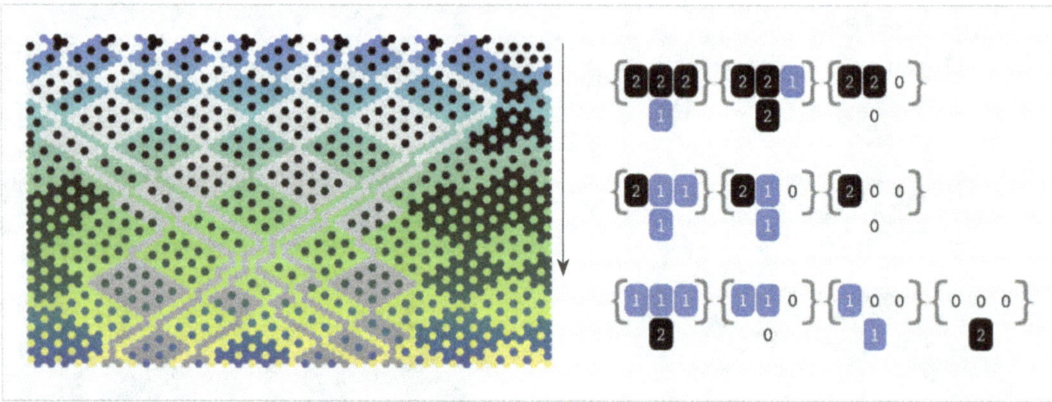

Non-Multiset Rules with Three Colors on Three Beads

Recall that multiset rules are those in which the inputs can be taken in any order, and we use brackets "{ }" to indicate this. If we relax this restriction, indicated by removing the brackets, a rule with three colors on three beads can require up to 27 parts to describe. Of the rules with three colors, these are the most complicated rules we describe.

Triangle Party Cascade

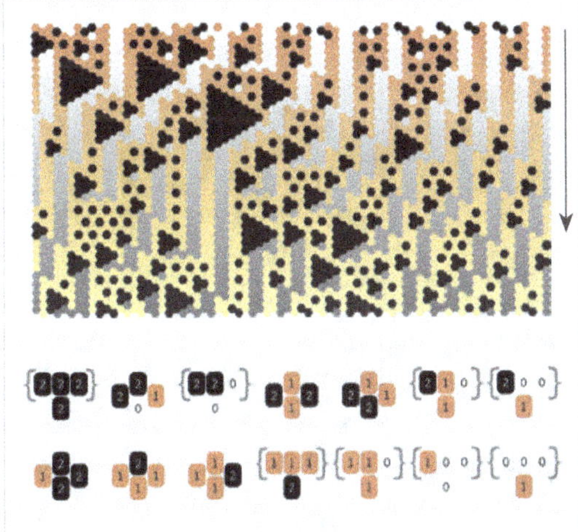

Triangle River

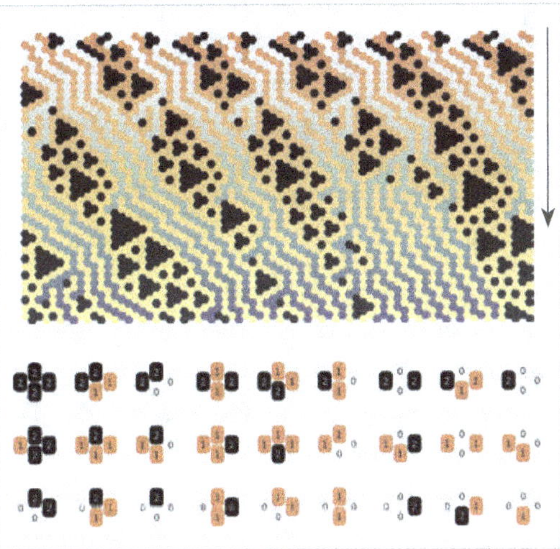

Triangle Drizzle

Bold Triangles

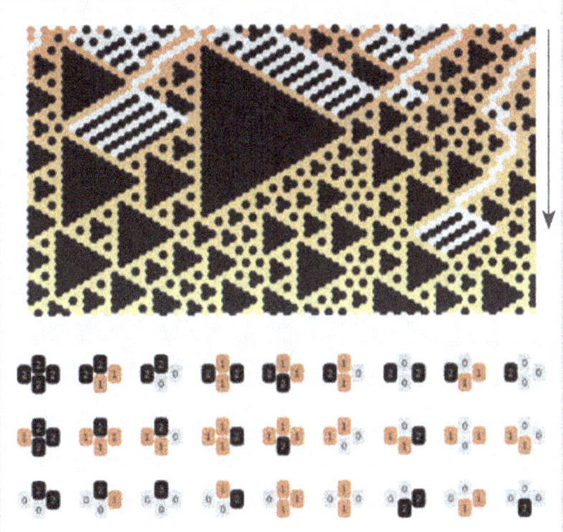

Triangle Streaks

Three Colors on Three Beads: A Symmetric Example

First, we will construct a rule that is not a multiset rule, by starting with a multiset rule.

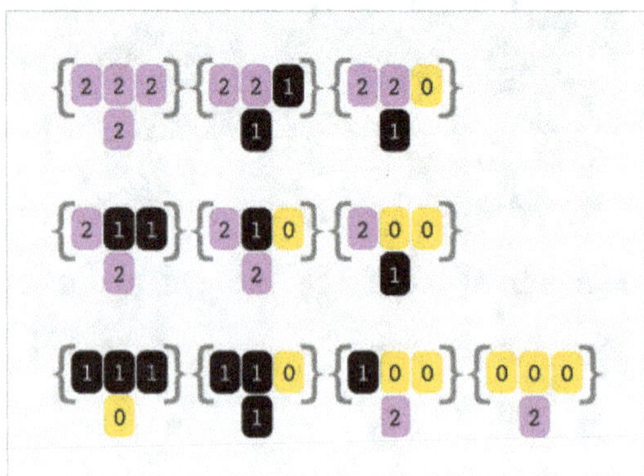

The new rule below is also symmetric, and the designs it generates look a lot like many different multiset rules with three colors on three beads, including the ones described earlier. If we focus above on the output for **{110}**, we see that the output is 1. If we remove the multiset property, as indicated by removing the brackets, we can separately consider the three different neighborhoods: **110**, **101**, and **011**. If we choose the outputs to be **1**, **0**, and **1**, respectively, we obtain the following rule with **12** parts. We call this rule *Mucha* after the great Art Nouveau artist, Alphonse Mucha.

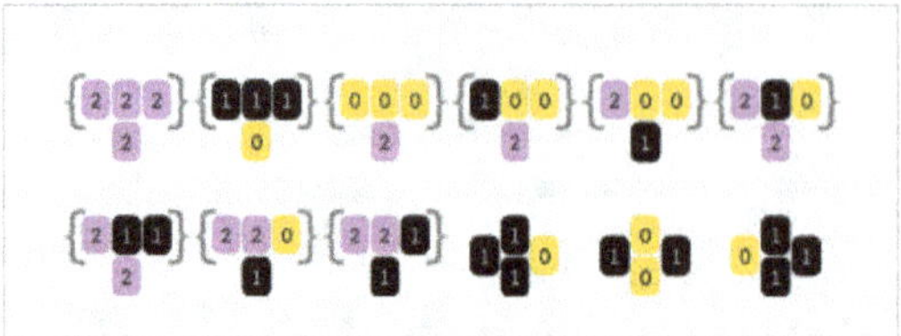

We can expand all of these multisets into their ordered neighborhoods to finish with 27 different three-bead neighborhoods. Each of these can serve as a separate part to a rule. For example, the rule above expands into the following 27 parts when the inputs are taken in order. The 27-digit code for *Mucha* is **211122121 122201202 121212122**.

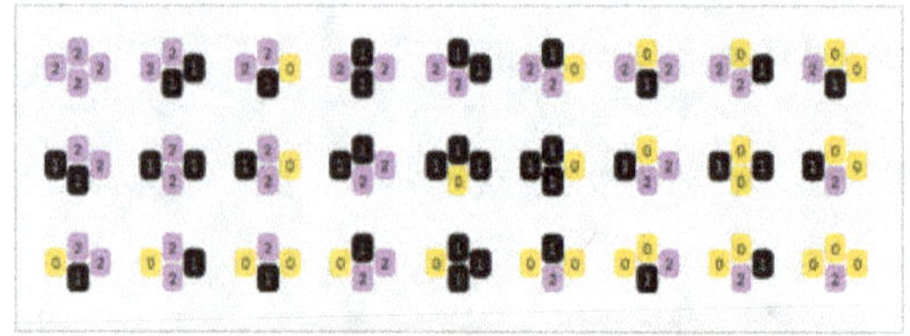

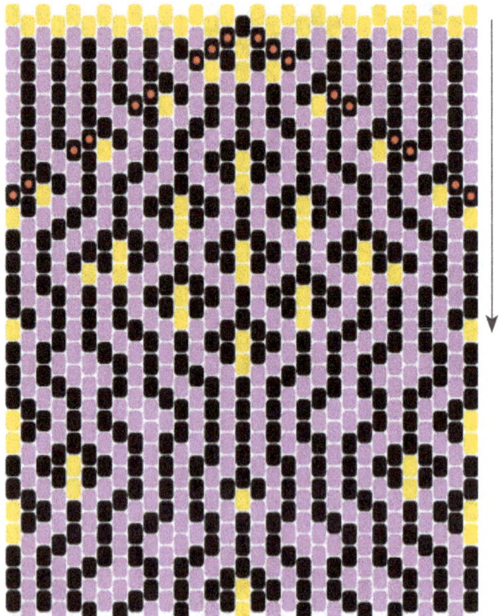

Project: Triangular Beaded Box with Beaded Bead

The rule *Mucha*, with 12 parts, left, was used for the triangular nested box with a beaded bead inside, shown on the next page. For the box, use yellow and orange for **0**, black for **1**, and blue, purple, and green for **2**. For the beaded bead, we swapped the colors for **0** and **2** and kept **1** as black. Color **2** makes continuous parallel stripes against the black. In these pieces, we took advantage of the fact that we can make each stripe a different color. We use the initial color chosen at the increase that starts a stripe to determine the color of the rest of that stripe.

Each piece starts with a triangle of peyote stitch as shown in Chapter 7. We use an increase stitch to make the corner stitches of the triangles, but our rules do not apply to the colors of the increase stitches. Instead, we randomly choose colors, while also keeping the colors symmetric around the triangle. When the triangular base of the box is as large as you like, sew several rounds of tubular peyote stitch without increases; we used four rounds for the beaded bead and six rounds for the box. In the next round, we made a decrease stitch at each corner to add some stability to the beadwork. This shaping with the decrease stitches makes the corners more rigid.

For the beaded bead, make a triangular start with six beads, and stitch the triangle for five rounds with increase stitches. Then, stitch four rounds of tubular peyote stitch, followed by one round with a decrease at each corner. Continue with tubular peyote stitch for 32 rows. Finish the second end to match the first by sewing one round with an increase at each corner, then four rounds of tubular peyote stitch, before stitching the triangle with decreases at each corner.

To make the box and lid fit together, the lid has only one round of decreases at each corner before about 30 rounds of regular tubular peyote stitch. The box has one round with decreases, followed by two rounds of regular tubular peyote stitch, two more decrease rounds, then about 30 rounds of regular tubular peyote stitch.

Field of Grass Bracelet

Field of Grass is reminiscent of *Roots*, but without the large triangles. We present this rule with nine regular parts that use three beads for the inputs, given in order. In addition, the rule has three multiset parts denoted with brackets. These three parts apply to the left and right beads, and the brackets indicate that the order does not matter. Using these three multiset parts, we turned a rule with 27 parts into a rule with just 12 parts.

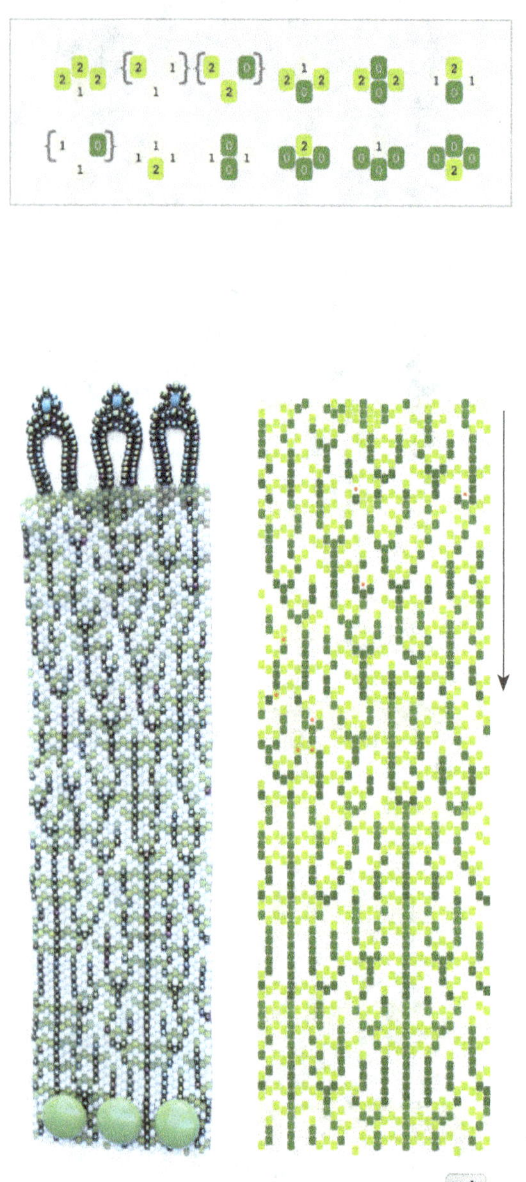

ot

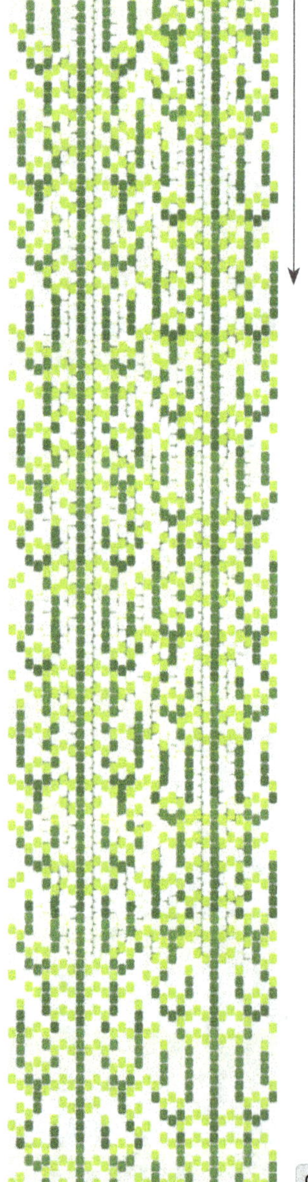

ou

Outlined Baskets

This is another example that uses two different kinds of parts to compress a rule with 27 parts into one with just nine parts. For example, the top left part with input **2?2** corresponds to six different parts in the full 27-part rule. Also, the two parts with inputs **2?1** and **1?2** could be compressed into a single left-right multiset part with the input **{2 1}** and output **2**. This shows how there can be different ways to compress a rule into fewer parts.

Triangle Cascade

With 27 parts, a rule with three colors on three beads can be a challenge to use. However, with some rules, the hardest part is only the first few rows. For example, the rule for *Triangle Cascade* becomes easy once the pattern is established. If you make mistakes in the first couple of rows, you can pick them out later, after the pattern is established.

The presentation of this rule shows some parts combined into multiset parts. Other parts could also be combined using two colors in one place of the input, as shown in the previous example. For example, the four parts on the bottom left with inputs **121**, **120**, **021**, and **020** all have the same output, and could 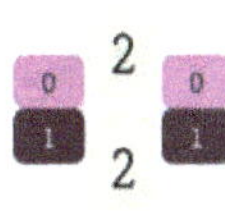 be combined into this one part.

In this example, the three parts with inputs **002**, **001**, and **000** all have the same output. In this case, they can be combined into one part with input **00?**.

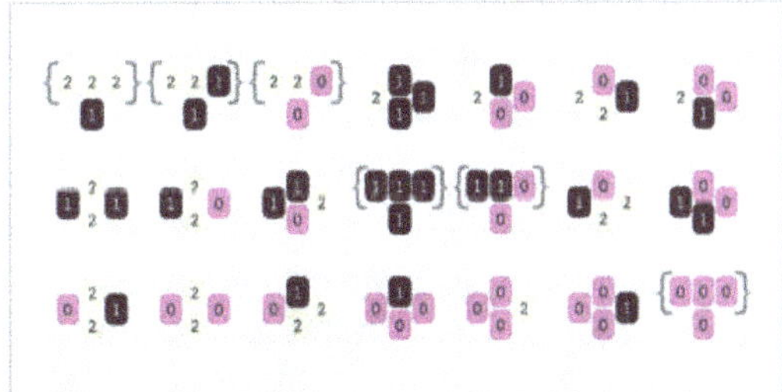

Blossom Cascade

Here are the 27 parts of the rule for *Blossom Cascade*.

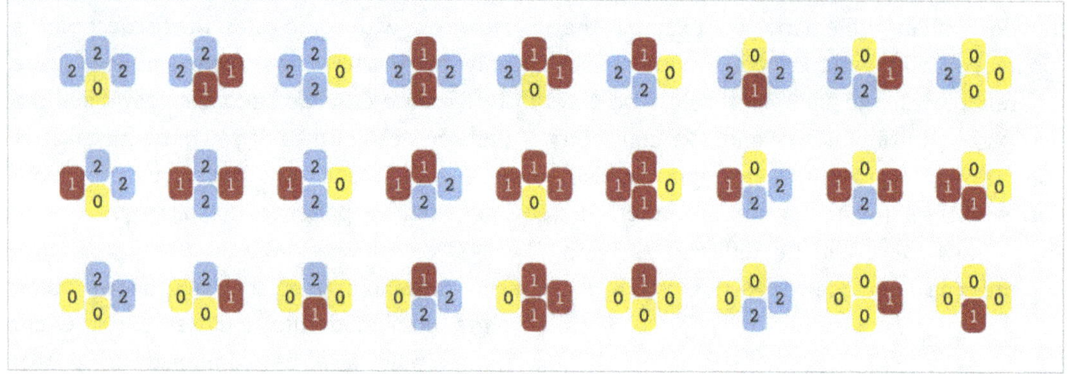

The following two pendants use *Blossom Cascade* with a color split on two of the input colors, to make five colors in all. All of the colors in the two beaded pendants are the same except for Color 2, which is bright blue in one pendant and pale blue in the other one.

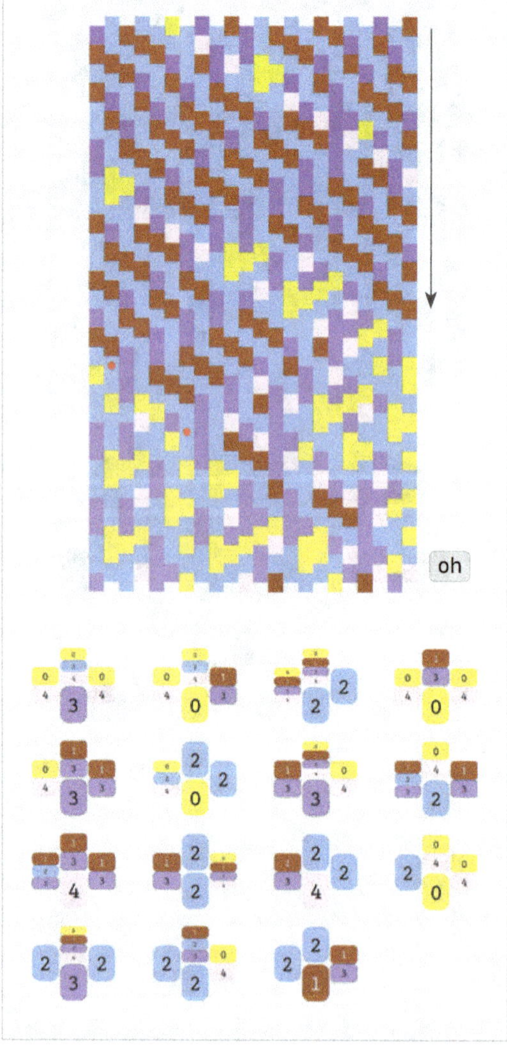

Digital Waterfall

201210021 220100000 021102200

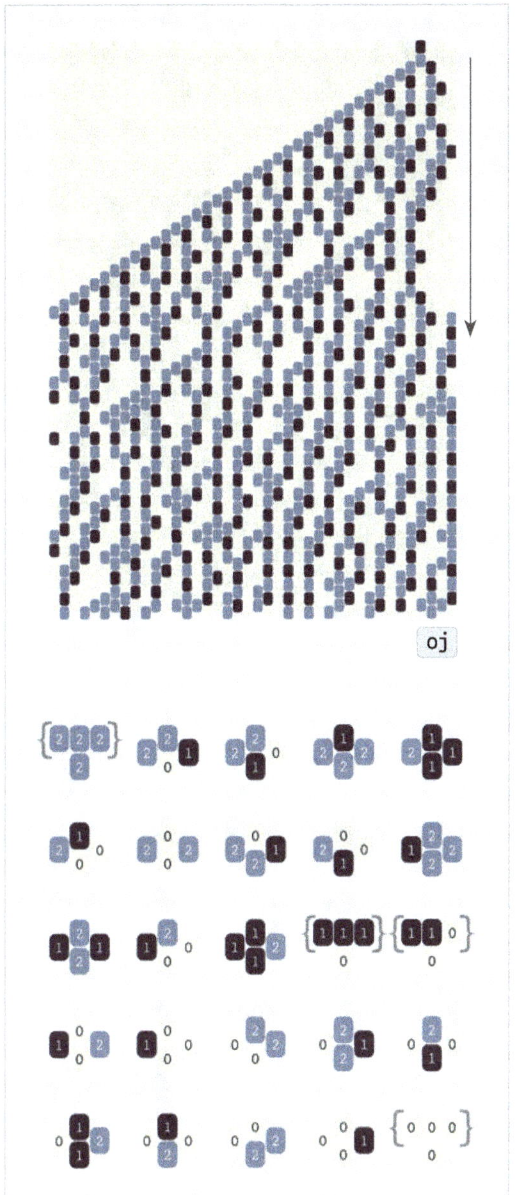

oj

This rule creates a beautiful design with a seed start of color **1** on a color **0** background.

The beaded bead is a tube in which the rows of beads span the length of the tube and the columns go around the tube.

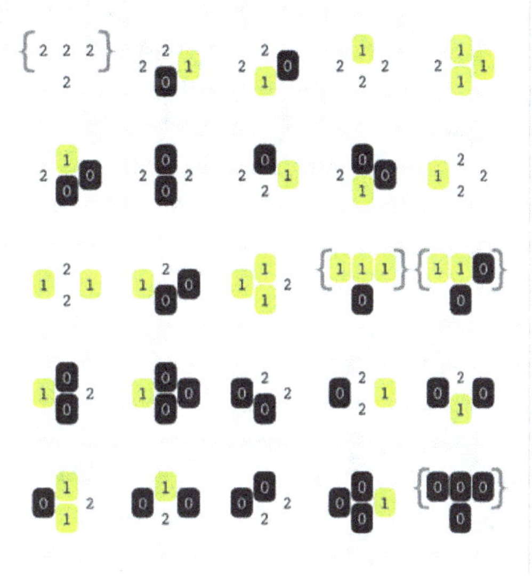

Shingles

120210122 100000002 201021010

Terrace Steps

200102220 120011211 100212101

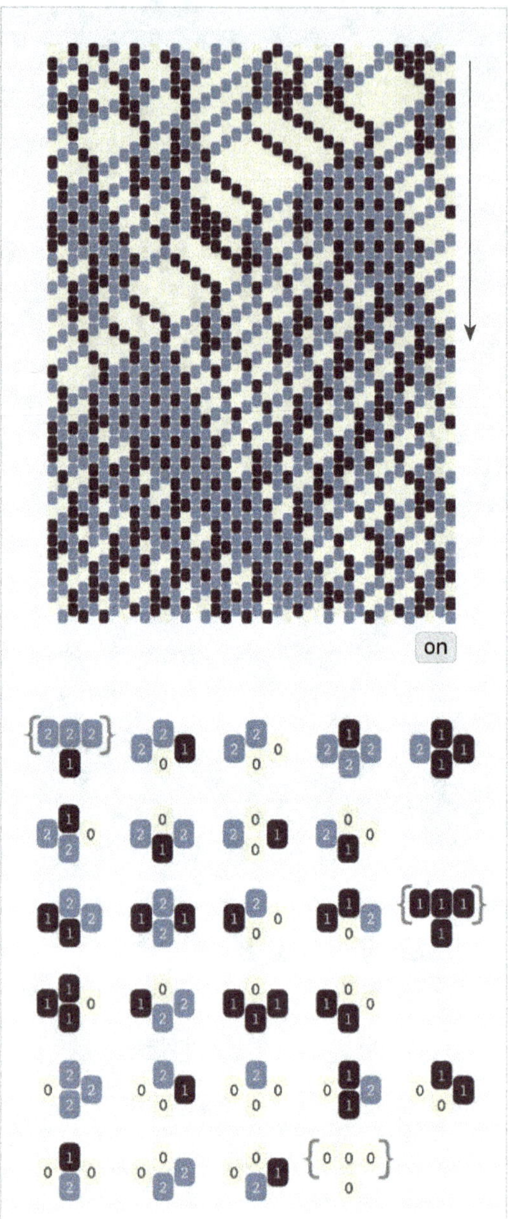

114

Purple Fissures Bracelet

210101001 122222002 011210102

The 27-digit code for *Purple Fissures* gives the 27 outputs of the rule with three colors on three beads. The 27 parts are in the same order as the previous example (*Terrace Steps*), so just substitute the new outputs for those in the *Terrace Steps* chart. For variety, this bracelet uses a color split with five colors in all. The colors include blue/aqua (**2**), purple/pink (**1**), and burgundy (**0**). Learn to make the button and loop clasp in Chapter 7.

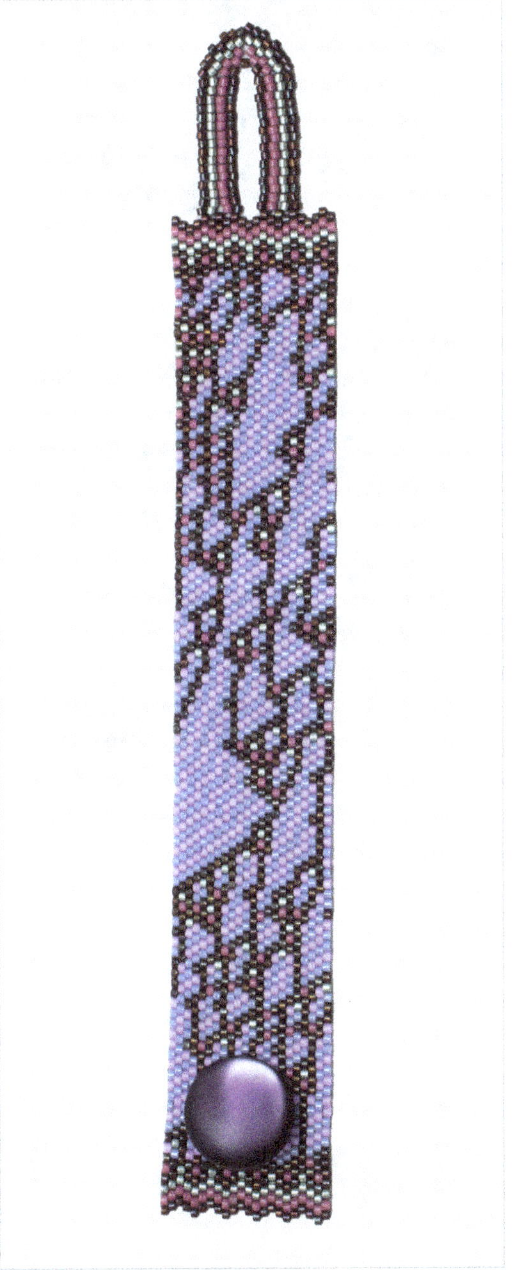

River Rapids

221220200 220220020 002002001

With 27 parts, this rule is asymmetric and a challenge to bead. The three colors for this rule are white (**0**), black (**1**), and blue (**2**), with a split on color **2** that adds interest to the large blue triangles.

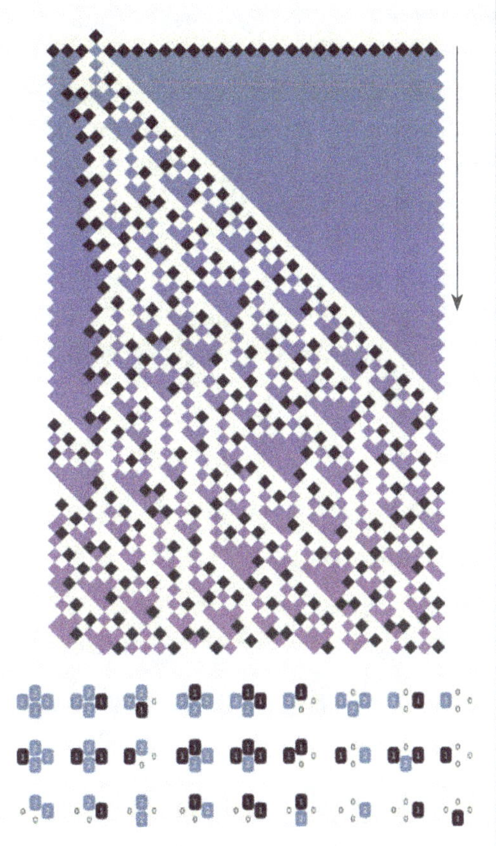

Find-Same Rules

There are numerous ways to define rules without the need for 27 neighborhoods. We can come up with any general way of defining the color for an output, as long as it's not ambiguous. It's best if it's easy to follow.

Here is another way of making an easy rule with three colors on three beads without the need for 27 parts. With only five parts, these rules are easy to learn and use. We call them *Find-Same* rules. We look for pairs (or trios) of beads in the neighborhood (left, above, and right) that are all the same color.

Escher's Staircase

Escher's Staircase is a find-same rule with three colors on three beads. The table gives the rule in five parts.

INPUT	OUTPUT
Left-Right Same	**0** Purple
Left-Above Same	**2** Black
Above-Right Same	**1** White
All Different	**2** Black
All Same	Cycle **0→1→2→0**

The last line means that, if the left, above, and right beads are all the same color, and that color is **0**, then pick up **1**. If that color is **1**, then pick up **2**. If that color is **2**, then pick up **0**.

Beading Tip: Arrange three piles of beads in order: **0**, **1**, and **2**. Label the piles l-r, right, and left/different, respectively.

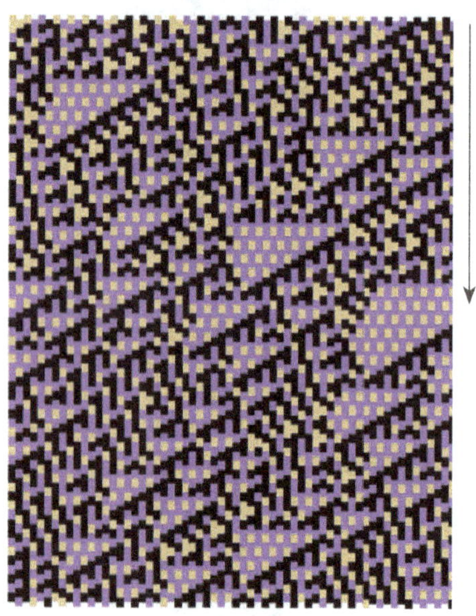

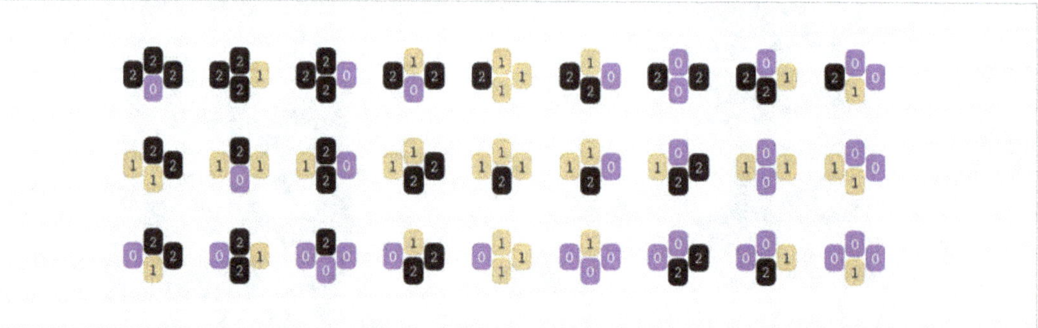

City Lights Bracelet

This beaded bracelet includes a patch generated with another *find-same* rule on three colors. After the diagonal line, we rebooted the design by switching rules to *Hanging Baskets* from Chapter 1.

INPUT	OUTPUT
Left-Right (Bottom) Same	**0** Black
Left-Above Same	**1** Gold
Above-Right Same	**2** Blue
All Different	Above Color
All Same	Cycle **0→1→2→0**

Beading Tip: Arrange three piles of beads in order: **0**, **1**, and **2**. Label them bottom, left, and right.

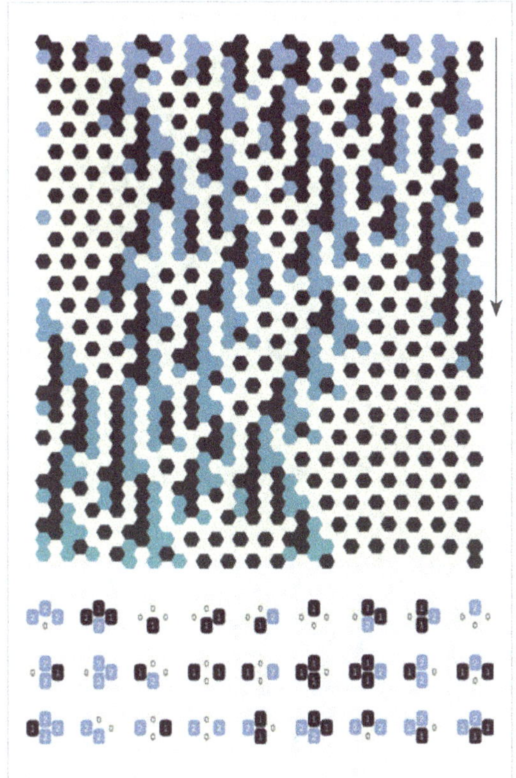

Find-Same Gliders

INPUT	OUTPUT
Left-Above Same	**0** Black
All Different	**1** White
Above-Right Same	**2** Orange
Bottom (Left-Right) Same	**2** Orange
All Same	Cycle **0→1→2→0**

Beading Tip: Arrange three piles of beads in order: **0**, **1**, and **2**. Label them left, different, and right/bottom.

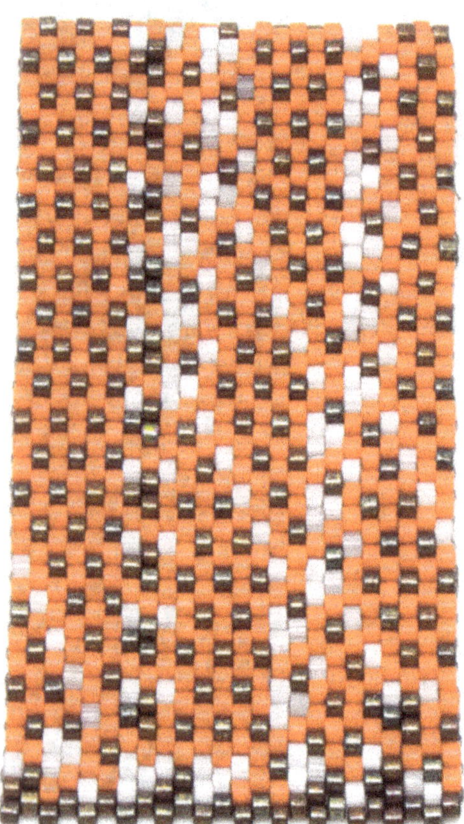

Find-Same Aliens: A Rule with Four Colors

Next are a pendant of seed beads and a wall hanging made with plastic pony beads. They both use the *Find-Same Aliens* rule with four colors on three beads, and both utilize color shading.

INPUT	OUTPUT
Bottom (Left-Right) Same	**0** Black
Left-Above Same	**1** Red
All Different	**2** White
Above-Right Same	**3** Pink
All Same	Cycle **0→1→2→3→0**

Beading Tip: Arrange four piles of beads in order: **0**, **1**, **2**, and **3**. Label them bottom, left, different, and right.

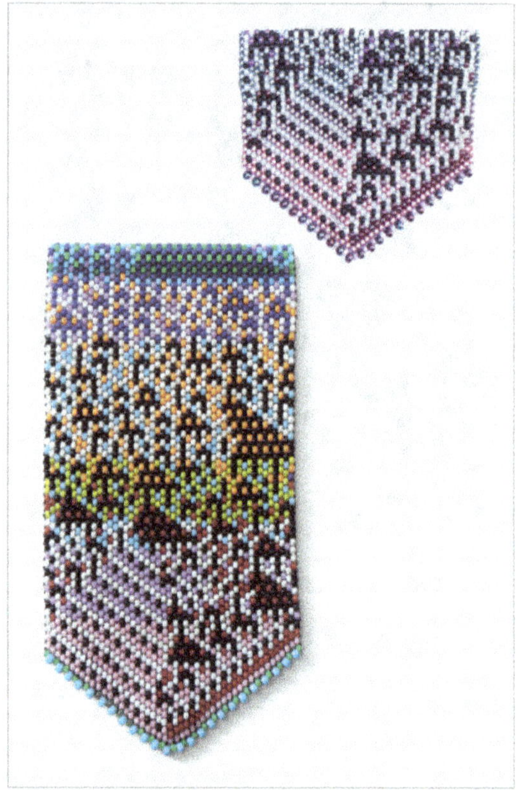

The pendant (top) uses size 15° seed beads and measures 5.4 cm by 5.1 cm. The long wall hanging measures 21 cm by 41 cm.

Chapter Six

FOUR OR MORE COLORS

Unfathomable Possibilities

So far, we have attempted to characterize a few of the 7.6 trillion CA rules for two or three colors. Moving on to four colors, the number of possibilities explodes. With four colors on three beads, there are as many as 4^3 or 64 parts of the rule, giving 4^{64} possible rules. That's 3.4×10^{38} different rules to consider. Of course, we could only begin to characterize that many rules. With five colors, we get 5^{53} different rules, which is 2.3×10^{87}. With six colors, we get 6^{63} different rules, which is so overwhelmingly large that our calculator told us it is not a number. In fact, it is a number that is many orders of magnitude greater than the number of atoms in the observable universe.

In this chapter, we simply aspire to introduce you to a small sample of CA rules on four or more colors. Our favorite is *Tom's Totalistic Rule*, which was one of the first rules that Tom Davis found when employing the software that he wrote using Gwen's ideas. This is a *totalistic* rule, meaning that all of the inputs with the same sum yield the same output. Consequently, this rule is also a multiset rule. As such, it has 20 parts.

Four Colors on Three Beads: Tom's Totalistic Rule

The colors in the beadwork are **0** = black, **1** = dark bronze, **2** = red, and **3** = light bronze.

333	332	331	330	223	222	221	220
3	2	1	1	1	1	0	0

113	112	111	110	003	002	001	000
0	0	0	2	0	2	3	3

321	320	310	210
1	0	0	0

Four Colors on Two Beads: Dihedral Group D2

Another favorite four-color rule is based on the symmetries of a rectangle. The red beads correspond to the identity element. The black beads represent the 180° rotation, and the green and white beads are the vertical and horizontal reflections. The left-right rule used in the beadwork is given here in terms of its Cayley table.

	r	b	g	w
r	r	b	g	w
b	b	r	w	g
g	g	w	r	b
w	w	g	b	r

We started with a random initial state at the top, and then rebooted the design in the middle, with a solid diagonal line in green and white. The bottom of the pendant is finished with a repeating floral trim.

Four Colors on Three Beads: Boogie Woogie Totalistic Rule

The designs created by this rule remind us of Paul Klee's 1943 painting, *Broadway Boogie Woogie*.

The colors used in the beaded bead are **0** = dark purple, **1** = silver, **2** = orange, and **3** = red. Because it is totalistic, it is a multiset rule.

333	332	331	330	223	222	221	220
1	1	0	0	0	0	2	3

113	112	111	110	003	002	001	000
2	3	2	2	2	2	1	1

321	320	310	210
0	2	3	2

Five Colors on Three Beads: Great Wave

This totalistic rule creates designs that look like crashing ocean waves. Because it is totalistic, it is a multiset rule with 35 parts. The colors are **0** = white, **1** = silver, **2** = blue, **3** = aqua, and **4** = navy.

444	443	442	441	440
0	3	2	2	4
334	333	332	331	330
2	2	4	1	1
224	223	222	221	220
4	1	1	4	2
114	113	112	111	110
1	4	2	3	2
004	003	002	001	000
2	3	2	3	2
432	431	430	421	420
2	4	1	1	1
410	321	320	310	210
4	1	4	2	3

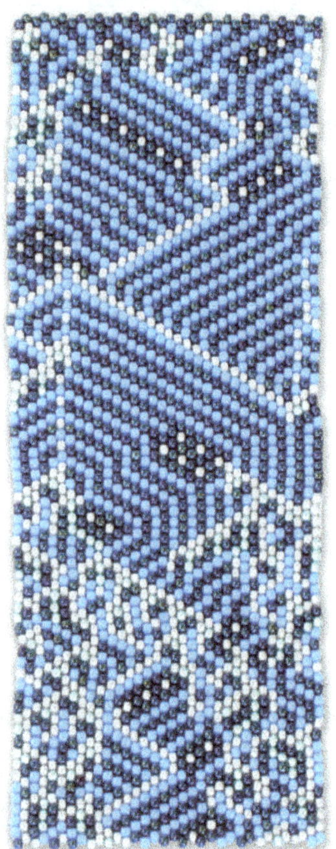

Five Colors on Three Beads: Carnival Gliders

We like this totalistic rule because it creates bold designs with lots of different types of gliders. Also, it looks really different under different initial states. Because it is totalistic, it is a multiset rule. The colors are **0** = gold multi, **1** = black, **2** = gray, **3** = dark pink, and **4** = light pink.

444	443	442	441	440
2	1	4	0	1
334	333	332	331	330
4	0	1	2	3
224	223	222	221	220
1	2	3	4	0
114	113	112	111	110
3	4	0	1	2
004	003	002	001	000
0	1	2	0	0
432	431	430	421	420
0	1	2	2	3
410	321	320	310	210
4	3	4	0	1

Totalistic Patterns

The designs on these two pages give you a taste of the breadth of designs that can be created with totalistic rules on three beads with four, five, or six colors. Some rules create regions or stripes of patterns, as we have seen in previous chapters:

Other designs are total mayhem:

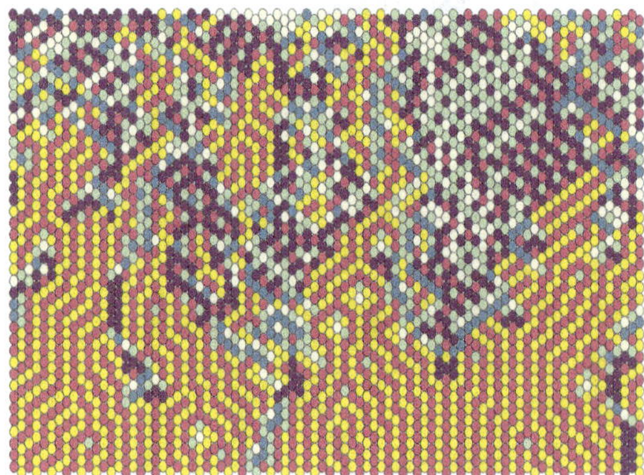
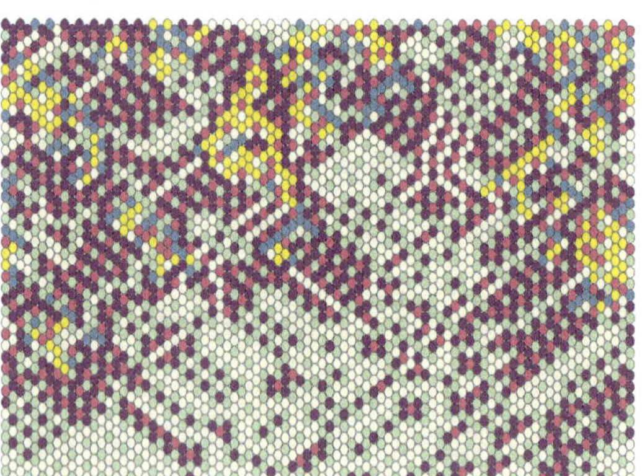

Then there are designs in between:

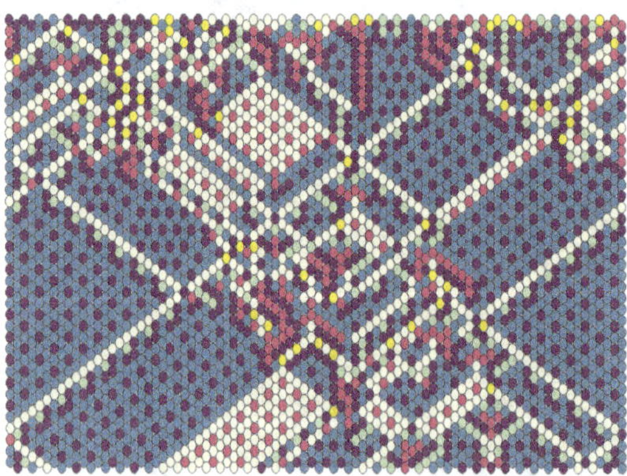
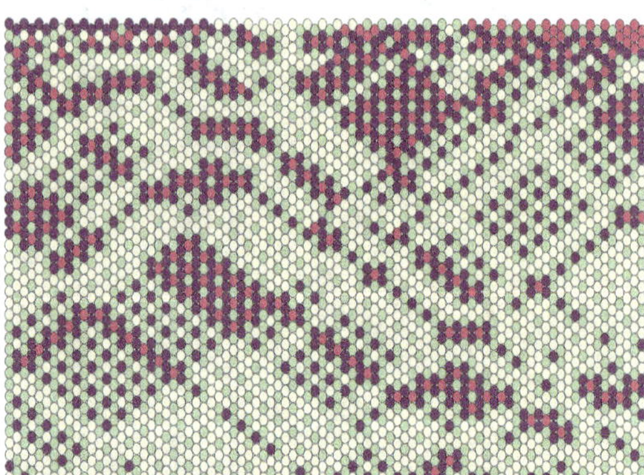

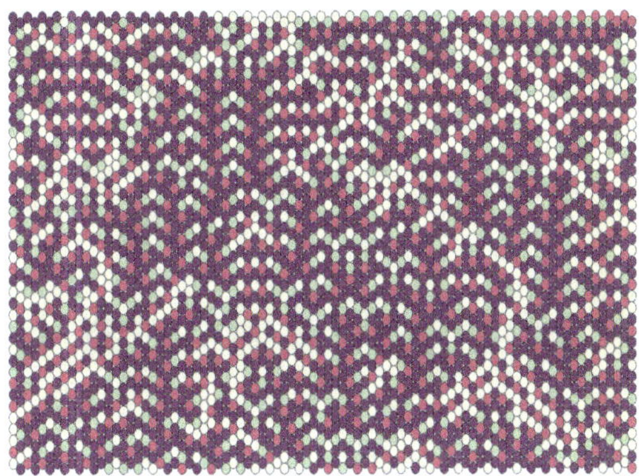

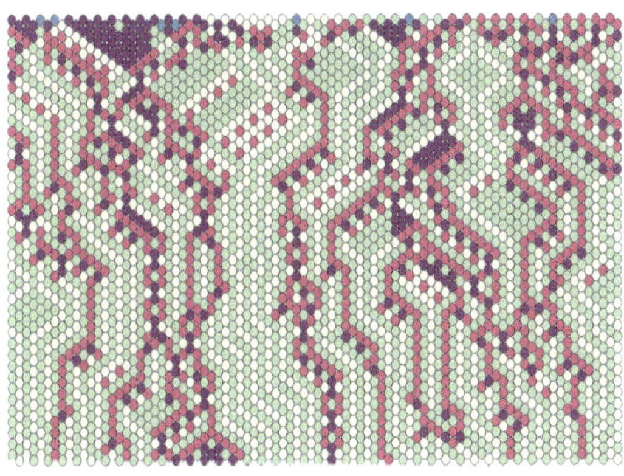

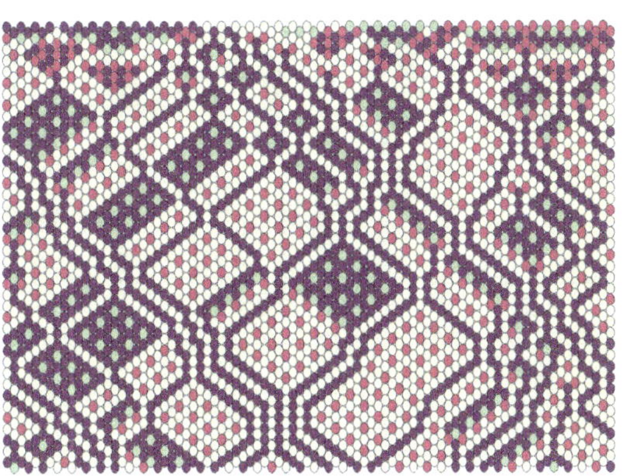

Multiset Rule with Five Colors on Three Beads: Rebecca Plays with Cats

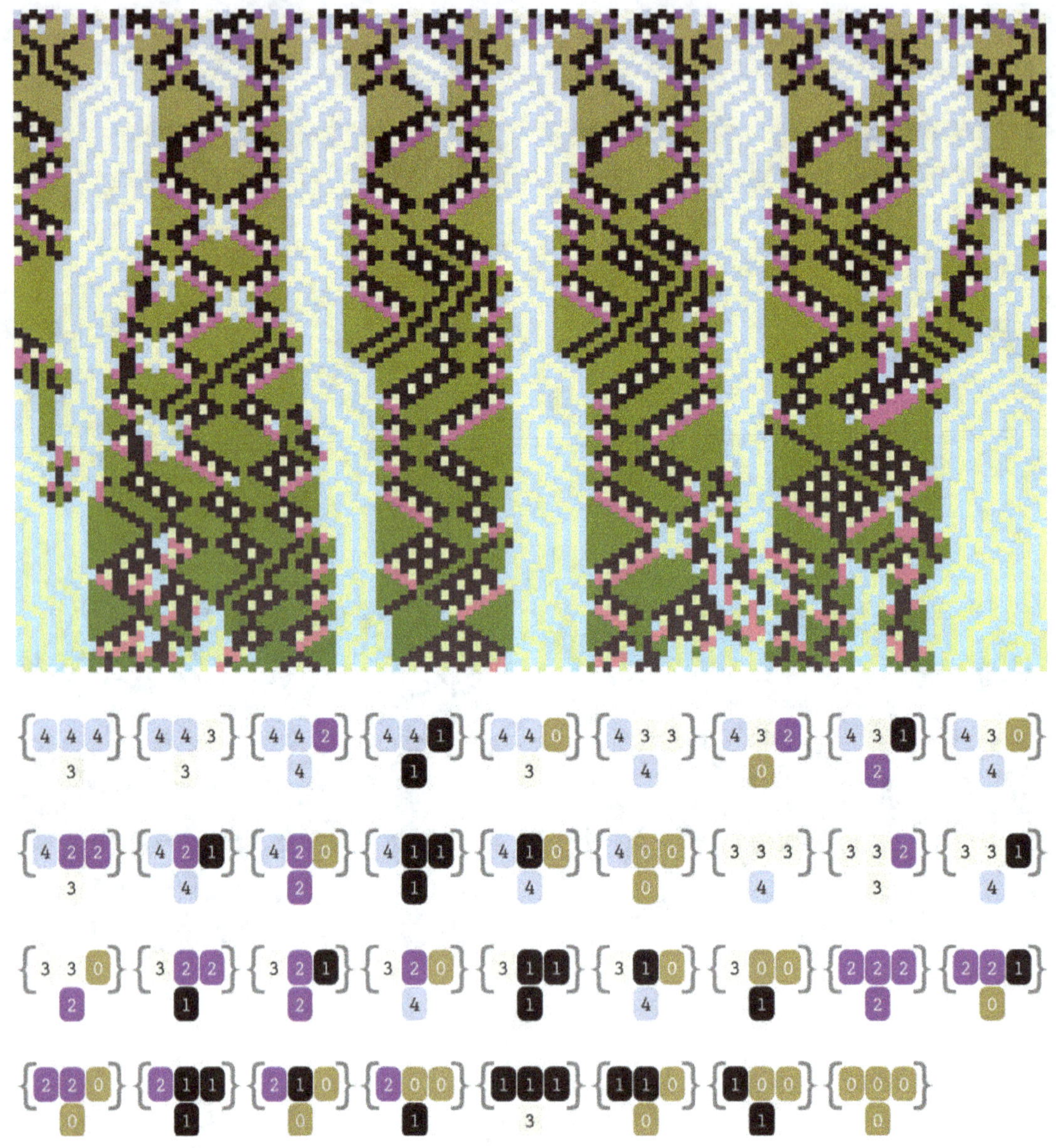

Multiset Rule with Six Colors on Three Beads: Gwen's Volcano

Multiset Rule with 6 Colors on 3 Beads: Zelda's Pet Spider

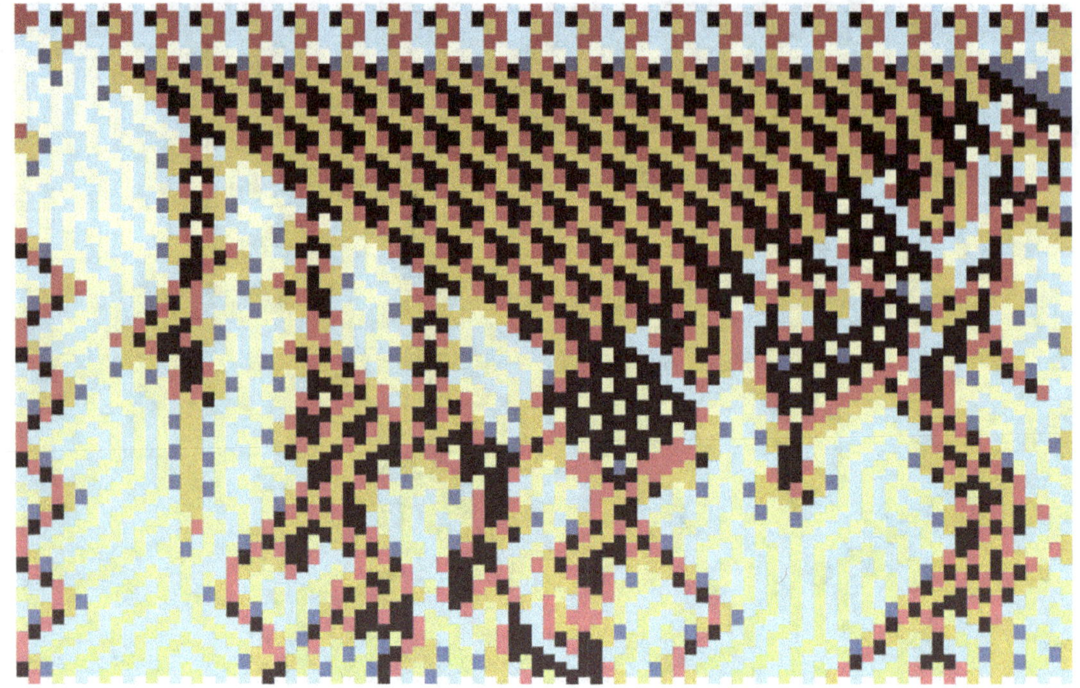

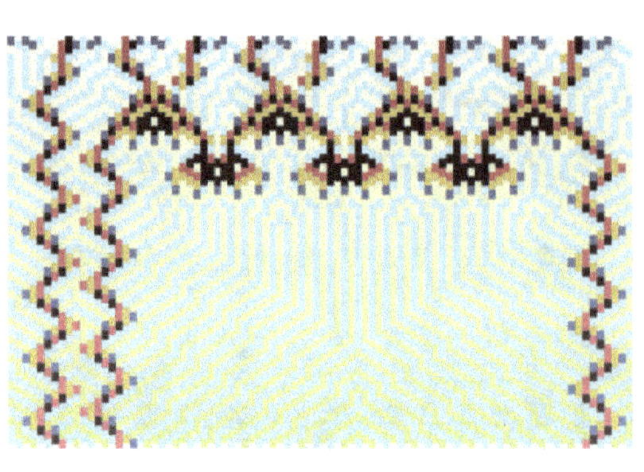

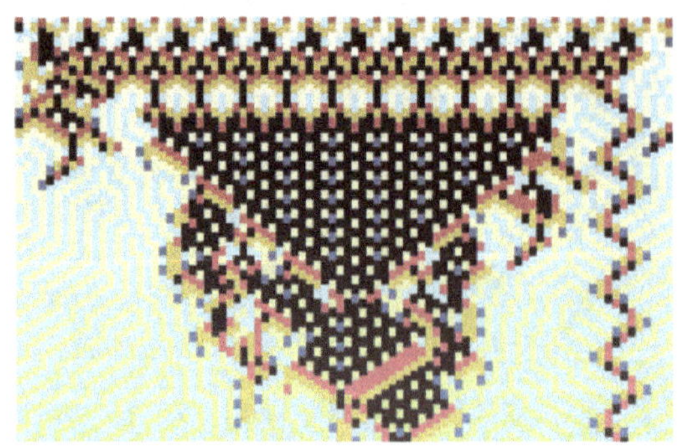

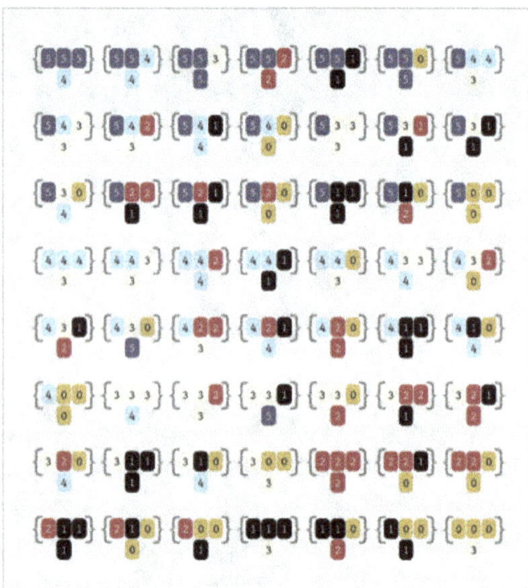

Now go forth and make art.

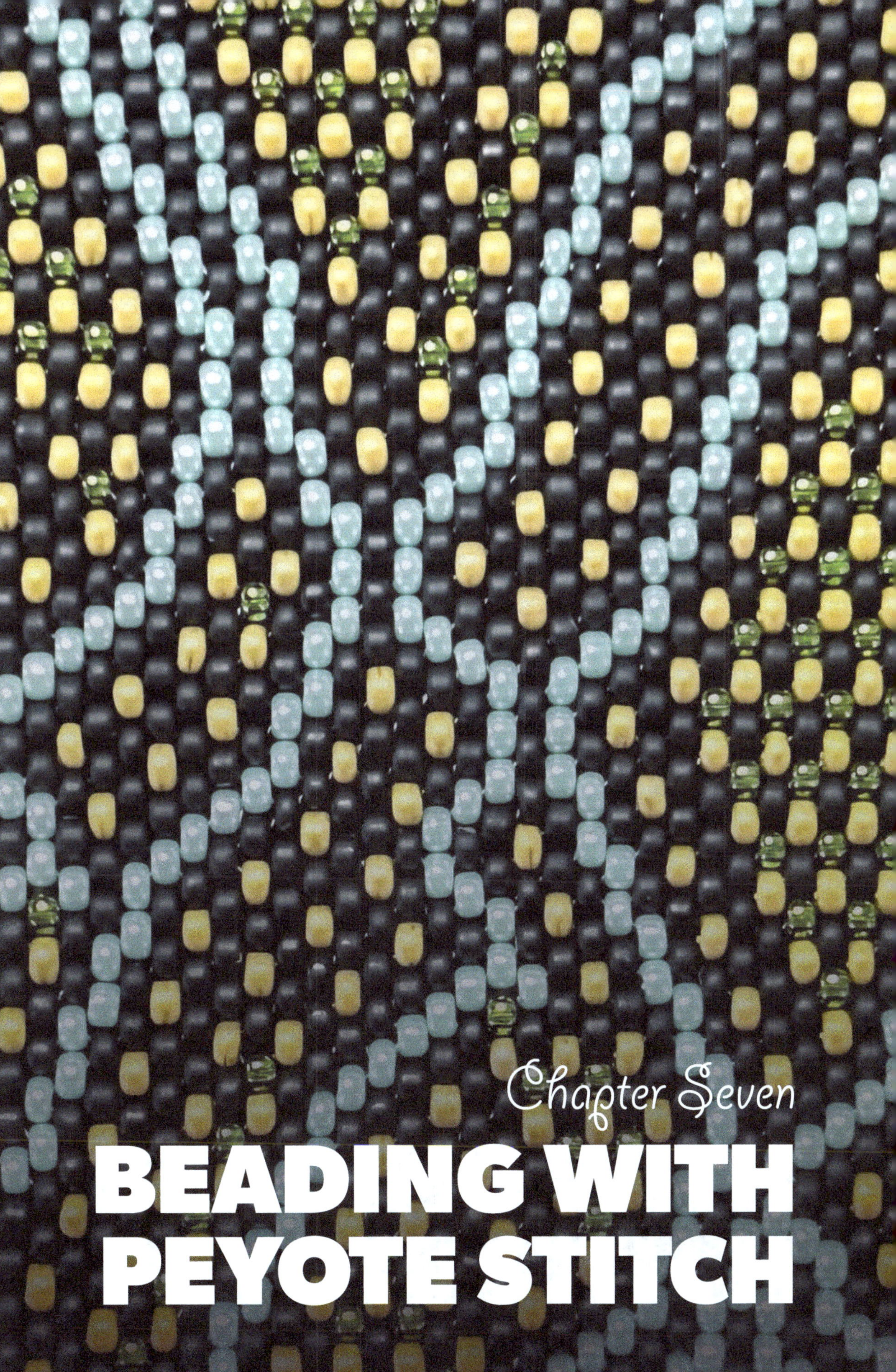

Chapter Seven
BEADING WITH PEYOTE STITCH

Materials, Tools, and Techniques

Bead weaving with peyote stitch is easy to do and requires very few materials. The materials are simple, just beads and thread. The only required tools are a needle, scissors, and a mat on which to place your beads. With these simple tools and materials and a little technique, you will be beading peyote stitch in no time!

As bead weavers, we love beads. We admire the colors and their exotic finishes. Let's start this chapter by talking about the beads!

Materials

Seed Beads

Seed beads are beads that are the size of seeds. Just as seeds come in a variety of sizes, so do seed beads. Peyote stitch requires just one size and shape of bead. To make the designs in this book, you will generally need only one bead size.

SHAPES AND SIZES

Which size should you choose? Mostly, you should choose a size you can see well and easily manipulate with your fingers and needle. Seed bead sizes are numbered, and the larger the number, the smaller the bead. The smallest commonly available size is 15° (read "fifteen naught" or just "fifteen"). The next smallest common size is 11°, then 8°, then 6°. Most of the projects in this book use size 15° or 11° seed beads, except for the wall hanging, which uses larger plastic pony beads. Size 15° seed beads are quite tiny, measuring 1 mm by 1.5 mm. If you are new to bead weaving, I suggest you start with something larger. The advantages of using smaller beads are that (a) you get more detail in your finished project, (b) the finished project is finer, and (c) the cost of materials is less per bead. The advantages of using larger beads are that (a) it is easier to manipulate and see larger beads, (b) the finished project is more substantial, and (c) a finished project of the same size takes less

time to complete with larger beads. So, if you want to make, say, a bracelet that fits around your wrist, it will take less time if you use larger beads, but you will get more detail and pattern if you use smaller beads.

For the projects in this book, choose seed beads that are regular, meaning they are all the same size and shape. In particular, Japanese seed beads tend to be very uniform and will give neater results in peyote stitch than Czech seed beads will. You can still use irregular beads, but the finished beadwork will be more textured and less smooth, and your edges will be a bit wavy.

Seed beads come in two basic seed bead shapes. First are cylinder seed beads, which are shaped like a can, just as their name suggests. Cylinder seed beads tend to be very uniform, light, and more expensive than round beads. The frosted cylinder seed beads, in particular, can be more fragile because they have thinner walls. Brand names for glass cylinder beads include Delica (made by Miyuki) and Aiko and Treasure (made by Toho).

The other common type of seed bead is called round, "rocaille," or just regular. Round seed beads made from glass are typically Czech or Japanese. For the same colors, they are less uniform and less expensive than cylinder seed beads. Japanese round seed beads tend to be more uniform than Czech seed beads. Most of the designs in this book use round Japanese seed beads or Delicas. I typically use size 11° seed beads for bracelets and 15° seed beads for pendants.

Also suitable are larger plastic beads. If you are new to the craft or want to make larger pieces, consider plastic. Plastic beads are also great for beading with children. Plastic beads are larger and lighter than glass beads, and are inexpensive. Large, 5 mm plastic cylinder beads are sometimes called Kandi or melty beads. Large plastic rocaille beads are usually called Pony beads. You can usually find plastic cylinder and pony beads for sale in places that sell craft supplies for children.

DIFFICULT BEADS

Irregular beads can cause even the best designs to look lumpy, so when purchasing seed beads, look for very regular beads. If they are irregular, do not buy them unless you want a textured look to your beadwork or want to spend a lot of time culling (sorting) beads for size and shape. Culling beads can double the time it takes to finish a project, but if you fall in love with a particular color or finish, sometimes it's worth it. Another difficult type is silver-lined beads, which can tarnish over time and change the look of the finished beadwork.

CREATING CONTRAST:
COLOR, VALUE, AND FINISH

Cellular automata designs look good when we use beads with high contrast. Simply stated, a strong contrast makes it easier to see the pattern. Accordingly, look for beads that are very dark, very light, and very bright. Unfortunately, most beads have a tendency to look darker as you weave them together. The light highlight color is a very important component of the design.

A good way to test your color choices is to pour a tiny mix of your beads together in a little pile. If you don't like your combination in a pile, you probably won't like what they look like when beaded.

Using all shiny beads or all matte beads can look nice, but it doesn't create the largest amount of contrast possible. Shiny light beads, such as metallic beads and opaque glass, together with dark matte beads, such as black or jewel tones, provide great contrast. My favorite glass seed beads for the designs in this book are metallic seed beads, to give the look of metal, and shiny opaque glass for their vibrant colors. Matte black is a staple because it's the blackest black. I also use matte metallic (made out of glass) for other dark colors and the matte metallic finishes (on glass) for the lightest colors, especially platinum and gold. These beads are expensive, but very beautiful.

Perhaps more important than color is value, which is the lightness or darkness of a particular color: we say that navy blue has a darker value than baby blue. Especially when working with very small beads, we see contrast in value more than contrast in color. If you try yellow with pale orange and pale green, together with black, most of what you will notice is the black contrast with the blended light colors. So, when you pick out three or more colors, be sure to include some light colors, some medium colors, and some dark colors in your palette (unless you want some of the beads to blend together and read as one value). In a pattern like *Hanging Baskets*, we see the background and everything else: baskets, flowers, and vines. You can make everything else three different colors that read as one value that contrasts strongly with the background.

The value of the beads depends somewhat on the color of the glass that makes the volume of the bead, but also on the finish on the surface of the beads. To look at the finish is to look at how the light reflects off the beads. Does the light reflect back in a focused point, or is it diffused across the surface of the beads? With shiny beads, the light reflects back to a focused point, and this tends to lighten the overall effect of that bead's color. Does the light travel all the way through so that you see what's behind the bead? If so, that bead will appear darker when you weave it into peyote stitch, unless you hold it up to the light. Then it will twinkle.

To make the highest contrast possible, first choose the lightest bead; opaque shiny white is the lightest. Similarly, opaque shiny pearl and pastel colors are very light colors. If you like metallic beads, bright metallic (or matte metallic) silver and gold also look great. The metal-coated glass seed beads can be particularly expensive and beautiful, but other less-expensive metallic options are available, too. Clear (transparent) is not light, as discussed below.

Beads with different finishes tend to contrast more with each other than beads with the same finish, so use a variety of bead finishes. You can get some lovely optical effects by using matte black with a shiny dark gray bead, like a blue or purple iris finish.

The second bead to choose is the darkest bead. The darkest dark is opaque black matte, which I use often. It is inexpensive and gives the deepest contrast. Opaque shiny black is also very dark. Other dark colors include any of the dark matte and matte metallic beads, like navy blue, dark green, or a pearly black with flashes of color. Dark blue, green, and purple beads with a shiny "iris" finish are also nice darks. You can use dark shiny beads with light shiny beads and still get good contrast.

If your design uses more than two colors, full intensity colors are a good choice. Full intensity colors like red, hot pink, bright orange, green, or blue all make great bright beads that contrast well with the dark and light beads.

Some of the less expensive matte finishes applied to translucent glass seed beads appear to suck out all of the light while still creating a saturated color. The richer matte metallic finishes have a more pearl-like quality and subtle variations of color, which add complexity to the finished piece. I also own several mid-tone matte finished beads. I love how they look in the box, but I find them harder to use.

If the bead is not opaque, you can see through the finish by holding it up to a light. Backlit beads will shine in the color of the glass rather than the color of the finish. That is usually not the color you see in most jewelry, except maybe earrings, unless you regularly go around holding your wrists up to the sun to get that perspective.

What about beads that are transparent or entirely clear? Clear and colored transparent beads pick up the colors of whatever is around them. Transparent beads blend into their backgrounds, so they tend to look a lot lighter in their tubes than they do when you weave them into beadwork. To make them more visible, use transparent beads with an AB or "gold luster" finish.

Color-lined beads are transparent glass on the outside and painted with color on the inside. Color-lined beads tend to be less expensive than other finishes, and they come in nice, bright colors. I use them sparingly when I find a particular color I like that I can't find in other finishes.

GALVANIZED AND DYED FINISHES

The old galvanized beads are usually the least expensive of the metallic finishes, and the metallic coating wears off quickly. On a ring, the finish won't last a full day. You will be left with "silver-lined" beads. If the underlying glass is clear, it will look okay, but not like what you started with. I've thrown away most of my galvanized beads, so I won't be tempted to use them and be unhappy with the results.

Fortunately, the bead manufacturers heard about our woes with galvanized finishes. Now they make galvanized beads with durable finishes that are far superior to their older counterparts. Look for beads labeled Duracoat or Permanent Finish. I like these beads for the bright colors, and so far, most of the colors have worn well for me.

Sometimes, we are lured into purchasing dyed beads, especially in bright pinks and purples. For some reason, it's hard to make bright pink and purple glass, so these colors are commonly dyed. Let's just say: buyer beware of bright pink and purple unless they are Duracoat or Permanent Finish.

TESTING BEAD FINISHES

Here's how I check the durability of beads. Using a short piece of wire or thread, I make a ring out of them. Then, I wear the ring. Of all jewelry, rings get the most wear and tear by far; that's why I use rings. If the coating doesn't last a day on a ring, it's not going to last too long on earrings, a necklace, or a bracelet either. If it makes it a week on a ring, it's probably going to hold up well on other jewelry.

Tools

Needles and Thread

Technically, thread is a material, but it makes sense to talk about needles and thread together because the size of your needle should match the size of your thread, and the size of your thread should match the size of your beads. Here is a chart of sizes (smallest to largest) to help you.

BEAD	NEEDLE	THREAD
15°	11 or 12 beading	Nymo: A or B Fireline: 4 lb or 6 lb
11°	10 or 11 beading	Nymo: B or D Fireline: 6 lb
8°	10 beading	Nymo: D Fireline: 6 lb or 8 lb
Pony	18 tapestry	Yarn: Fine size 2

NEEDLES

The size number of a beading needle tells you how thick it is. Bigger numbers are thinner needles. I use Pony brand "Sewing Needles Beading." I prefer the long ones, two inches, because I think they are easy to hold on to. You can also buy short beading needles, sometimes called "sharps," which many other beaders prefer. It's a personal choice. Other popular brands of beading needles include John James and Tulip. Tulip are the most expensive and the strongest.

THREAD

There are many different beading threads on the market. Nymo is an affordable option that gives great results. Nymo is nylon thread that resembles dental floss, but is thinner. It comes on large spools and tiny bobbins, which are not the same thread. Nymo on a large spool has a coating that binds the fibers together, making it much easier to work with than the bobbin version. I don't recommend the bobbin version because it shreds and can make it difficult to thread your needle. Also, the thread on the little bobbins comes from the bobbin in curls. Always pre-stretch Nymo before you start stitching. Just grab both ends and give it a little stretch. If you don't pre-stretch Nymo, it will stretch later, and your beadwork will loosen over time.

When I first started beading, I used Nymo all the time, but at some point, I switched to Fireline. Fireline is several times more expensive than Nymo, but it is easier to thread a needle with Fireline, and it doesn't tangle as easily. Fireline is fishing line and a bit wiry. It comes in a handful of colors, but I only use the color called "smoke," which has a graphite coating to make it slippery. The graphite will rub off on your fingers, but it washes away with a little soap and water. If you are working with light colored transparent beads, you should probably wipe off the graphite before you start beading.

There are still other brands of beading thread on the market, some of which I have tried and some of which we have not. One G is another good brand of beading thread. It's like Nymo but more durable and stretchy. Avoid clear elastic cord used for stretchy bracelets because it is not durable. Feel free to experiment with other beading threads, but be sure the thread you use is designed for bead *weaving* and not bead *stringing*.

THREADING THE NEEDLE

Smash your thread end flat before trying to thread it through the eye of a needle. If you have trouble threading your needle, pinch the end of the thread so that you can just see the end between your thumb and your forefinger. You want just a millimeter of thread to be showing. Pinch the thread tightly and push the eye of the needle over the top of the thread: Needle the thread instead of threading the needle. Also, if the end of the thread is beaten up or not cut straight, trim the end before trying to thread your needle.

Work Surface (Bead Mat)

Do not use a smooth surface to work from. I use a bead mat inside a cardboard box or on top of a large, hardbound book. The bead mat is made of a fluffy fabric like polar fleece, felt, or flannel. The fabric keeps the beads from rolling around while you work. Use a scrap from an old piece of clothing, or go to a fabric store and look in the remnants. You only need a small piece (a square foot is enough). White is best because you can see the true bead colors well on white, but I also have some darker pieces of fabric I use for when I am working with white beads.

Pick up beads with your needle directly from the bead mat. In other words, do not pick up beads with one hand and thread with the other. It is much faster to needle them directly from the mat.

Other Supplies

Use **pliers** for pulling needles through tight spaces. Use **sharp scissors**, **wire snips**, or a **thread burner** for cutting thread.

Many people are wary of bead weaving because they cannot see the tiny beads well. If you are farsighted, try purchasing a pair of drugstore **reading glasses**. They are inexpensive and might be just the thing that will allow you to see what you have been missing. You can go all in and buy illuminated, high-powered magnifying lenses that you wear on your head like goggles. Beware, however, that with magnifiers, your thumbs become the size of golf balls! Alternatively, use larger beads.

Good lighting is useful. We like **full spectrum lighting** so that we can see the true colors of our beads.

More often than not, you will have leftover beads after you have completed your project. Sometimes, we seem to spend as much time picking up unused beads as we do beading. A **little scoop** is an efficient method for clearing a workspace of beads. You can use the top of a tiny gift box, a salt spoon, or, of course, one of the various types of scoops made for the purpose of picking up beads and gems. If your beads come in little boxes, you can also use the lid of the bead box to scoop beads.

We use a **pointed tool** to pull loops of thread into place and untangle knots. If you try to use your beading needles for this purpose, you will likely bend them, so it's good to have an extra pointed tool to help you. Examples include a ball-headed sewing pin, a large safety pin, and a large sturdy needle with a sharp point. The best choice is a thin stiletto or beading awl with a handle, like the ones made by Tulip Needles.

Use an **empty tissue box** as a little garbage collector. It is the perfect size for extra snippets of thread, bead packaging, and throwaway beads.

Techniques

The Structure of Peyote Stitch

The arrangement of beads in peyote stitch is like a brick wall, but built sideways. Imagine rotating a brick wall by a right angle, and building it by placing each new brick in a space between two old ones. Peyote stitch is built in rows, and the rows of beads are staggered, so each row includes beads on only half of the columns. The beads in the interior sit among three adjacent beads in the two rows added before and three more in the two rows added after. The rows in peyote stitch can be counted diagonally.

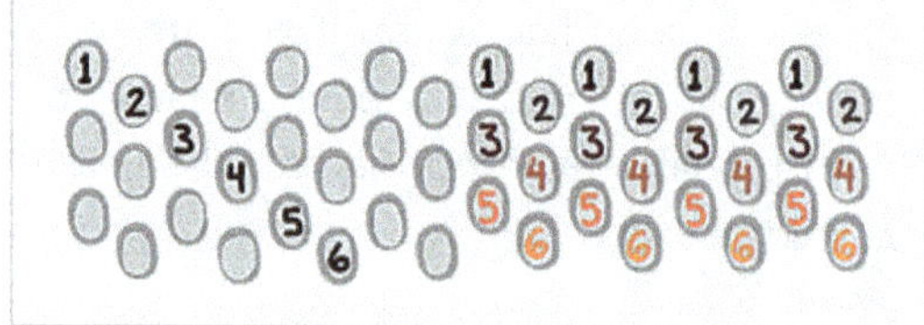

EVEN-COUNT VERSUS ODD-COUNT PEYOTE STITCH

When beading a simple rectangle of beads with peyote stitch, you can use either an even or odd number of columns. The parity of the number of columns (meaning its evenness or oddness) determines whether the count is even or odd. The main advantage of using an even count is that the turn at the end of every row is easy. The main advantage of using an odd count is that your finished beadwork design can have mirror symmetry.

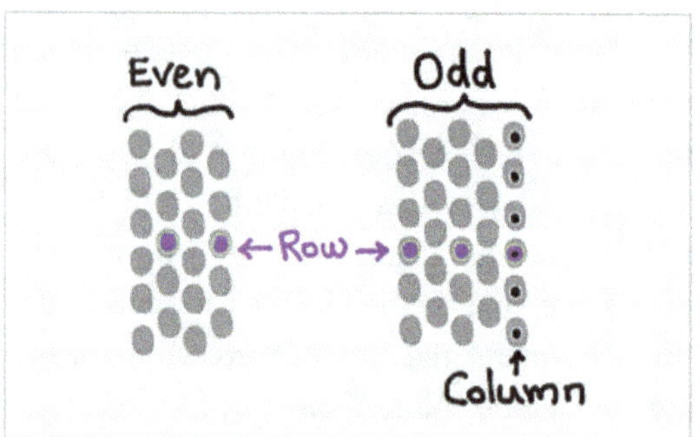

The count also determines whether consecutive rows have the same number of beads (even) or differ by one bead (odd).

Even-Count Peyote Stitch

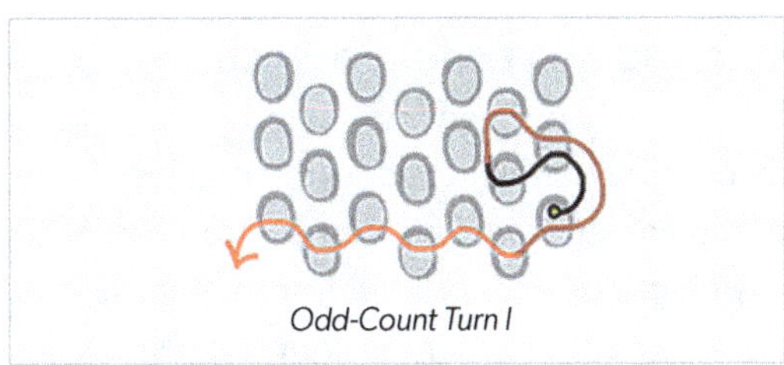

Odd-Count Turn I

EVEN-COUNT

The easiest way to start peyote stitch is at the top of a rectangle with even-count peyote stitch as described in Chapter 1. To review: start even-count peyote stitch by picking up an odd number of beads. Skip the last two beads and pass back through the third-to-last bead. Refer to Chapter 1 for more details.

Pull the thread tight at the beginning of each round, while simultaneously holding down the last bead from the previous row with your fingernail. Sometimes, you can feel the bead pop neatly into position.

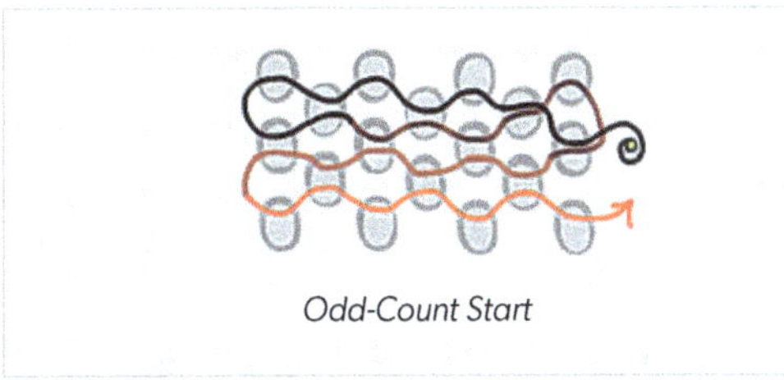

Odd-Count Start

ODD-COUNT

Start odd count peyote stitch by picking up an even number of beads. As with even count, skip the last two beads and pass back through the third-to-last bead. Pull tight, and peyote stitch until you get to the other end. Pick up the last bead, reverse direction, and pass through the very first bead you picked up from the side with the tail. The turn is a little funny as the last bead you picked up sits in the first row, even though you just finished row 3. Rows 4 and 5 are regular peyote stitch until you get to the end of row 5, at which point you can make an odd-count turn.

There are two ways to make this turn. It doesn't matter which type you use, but you should probably pick one and use it for the whole piece. Odd-Count Turn I involves stitching back through previous rows, as shown. A simpler method is to take a stitch under the thread from the previous row on the boundary of the beadwork.

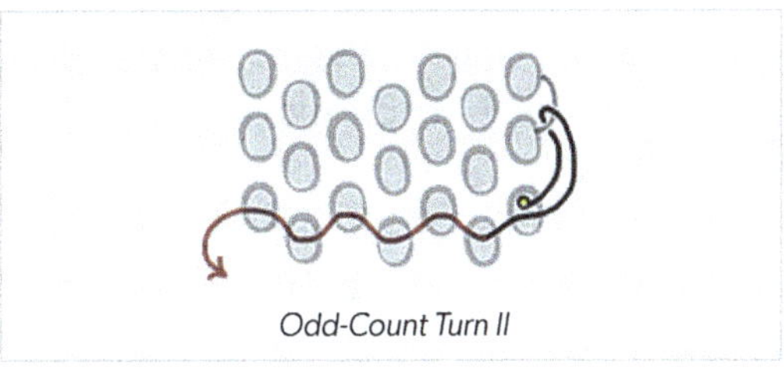

Odd-Count Turn II

At the ends of following rows, you will alternate between even- and odd-count turns.

ODD-COUNT WITH TWO NEEDLES

There is another way to stitch odd-count peyote where every turn is an easy turn. The trick is to use two alternating needles, A and B.

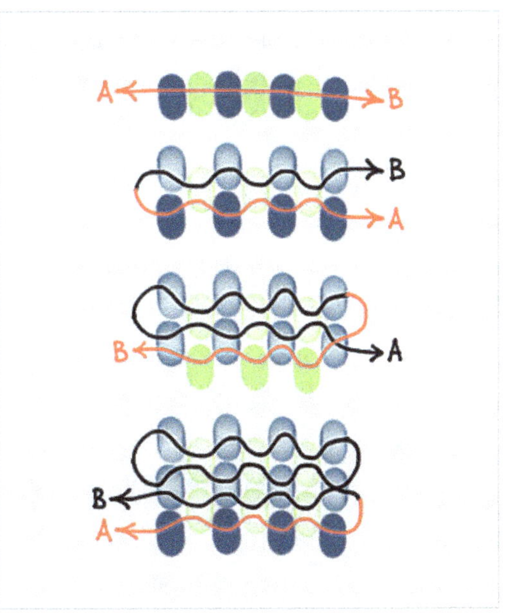

STARTING AND ENDING THREAD

Every patch of beadwork in this book could theoretically be stitched with a single piece of thread. Even so, it's best not to work with anything longer than a wingspan (that is, the distance between your outstretched hands), but shorter is also fine. The longer your thread is, the more likely you are to get tangles. Work with a single strand of thread through the needle, not doubled, and don't start with a knot! You can add a stop bead, which is just a single bead that is passed through twice. The purpose of a stop bead is to keep the first beads in a project from falling off the tail. Stop beads are removed after they serve their purpose.

After threading your needle, string your first two rows of beads, and make a stitch. Then slide the beads down the thread, always leaving a tail end of thread that is 6 to 8 inches long. The tail will give you something to hold on to. You might want to wrap it around your finger on the hand without the needle. Later, when it's convenient, weave the tail into the beadwork.

You don't need to tie knots with peyote stitch. Instead, to tie off, secure the ends by weaving a zigzag through the beads. After three or so reversals, the thread should be securely woven into the beadwork and will not unravel. Cut the end of the thread as close to the beadwork as possible with sharp scissors, pulling the thread tight with one hand while you snip close to the beadwork with the other hand.

To start a new piece of thread, you can weave through the beads on an established thread path, and make a turn or two to anchor the tail. Cut the end of the thread as before.

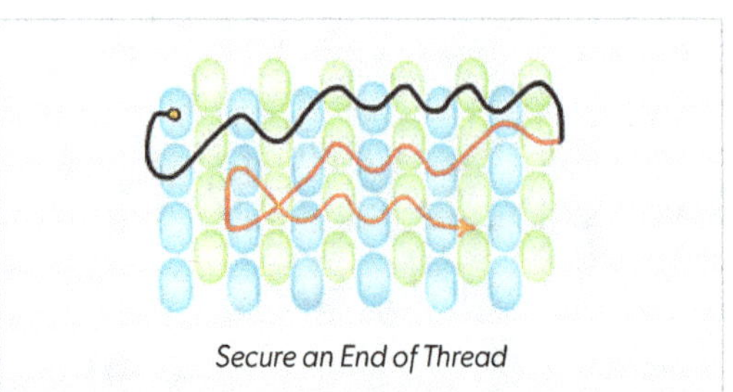

Secure an End of Thread

Pro Tip

Finishing the ends of the thread uses both time and thread. To save on both, here's a trick. You can start beading in the center of a length of thread and work from both ends. To do this, pick up the first set of beads, then measure a wingspan off the spool, but don't cut the thread yet! Instead, slide the beads down a wingspan, leaving a margin of thread between the beads and spool as needed to work comfortably, maybe a foot or two. Weave beads with the free end until it runs out, then tie off. Pull another wingspan of thread from the spool, and finally cut the thread from the spool, giving you a fresh end of thread to weave with.

Beading a Cylinder

A beaded cylinder or tube can be used to cover round objects like candle holders, pens, and lighters. To make a cylinder of peyote stitch, start with a circle of beads. Use an even number if you want to bead in rows, or use an odd number if you want to bead in one continuous spiral. The disadvantage of beading in rows is that you need to step-up at the end of each row, and if you're not paying close attention, you might miss it and end up beading in a spiral anyway. The disadvantage of beading in a spiral is that no matter where you stop, the edge of your beadwork will have a visible jog.

GLASS CANDLE HOLDER

One use for a beaded tube is this glass candle holder. It is made from size 8° seed beads with 44 stitches per round. The glass measures 55 mm in diameter.

These illustrations show how to start an even-count cylinder. Although the diagrams show a disk of beads forming, you will pull each new row tightly to make the cylinder. Start by picking up an even number of beads, in this case, 32. Pass through all of the beads again, starting at the side with the tail, to make a loop, then pass through the first bead one more time. That last pass through is called the **step-up**. The step-up below is shown in purple.

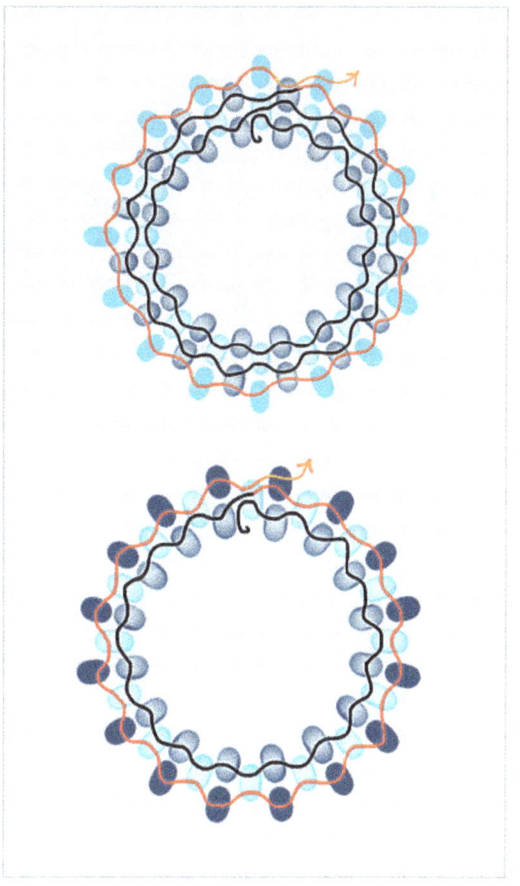

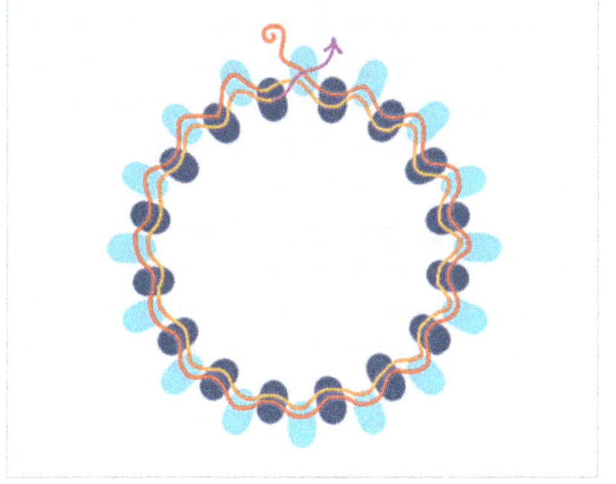

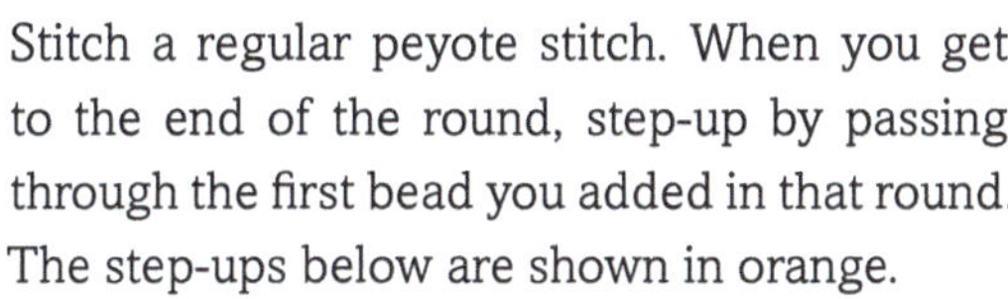

Stitch a regular peyote stitch. When you get to the end of the round, step-up by passing through the first bead you added in that round. The step-ups below are shown in orange.

Spool Beaded Bead

Bead a cylindrical shape to make a beaded bead. The beaded bead below uses size 11° Delica seed beads. Both ends were embellished with round seed beads in sizes 15°, 11°, and 8°.

Shaped Boundaries

Imagine covering the entire, infinite bead plane with cellular automata. Without boundaries, a pattern could go on forever, up and down, or left and right. While it is fun to imagine, here in the finite world of beads, every patch has a shape. Easy shapes to make are triangles and trapezoids. We can shape the border of a patch of peyote stitch by adding or omitting extra beads at the beginning of a row.

To omit a bead is to make a *decrease*.

HOW TO MAKE A DECREASE ON THE BOUNDARY

To make a decrease of one column at the start of a row, make an odd-count turn (type I) as described earlier.

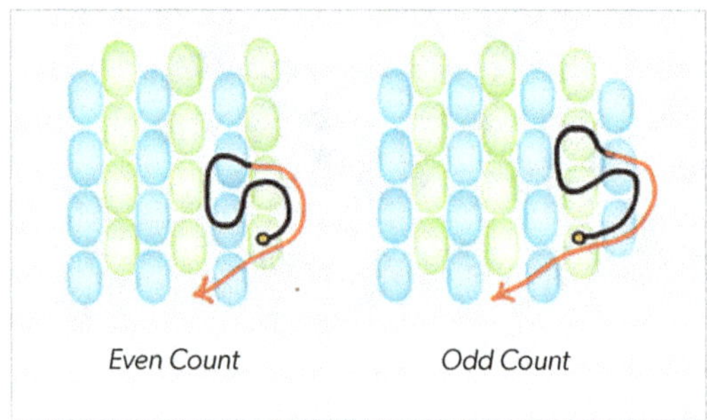

HOW TO MAKE AN INCREASE

To increase by one column at the edge of a row, pick up two beads and pass back through the bead where you started, then through the bead just above it, and then back through the two beads you just picked up. Pull tight.

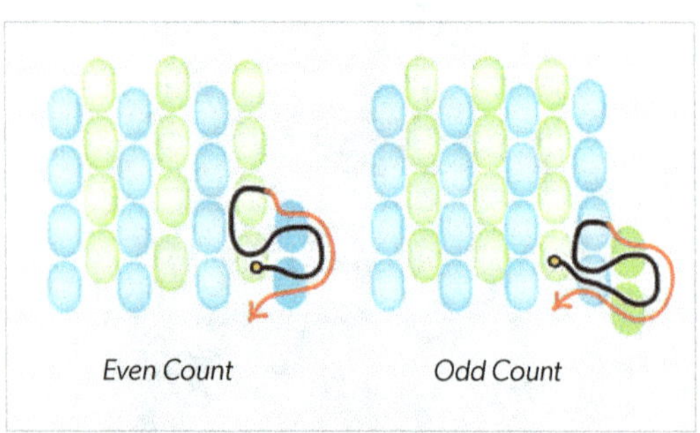

HOW TO MAKE AN OBTUSE ANGLE START

1. Pick up three beads. Pass back through the first bead.
2. Repeat step 1.
3. Peyote stitch to the end of the row (for the first row, this is one stitch).
4. Repeat steps 1 and 3.

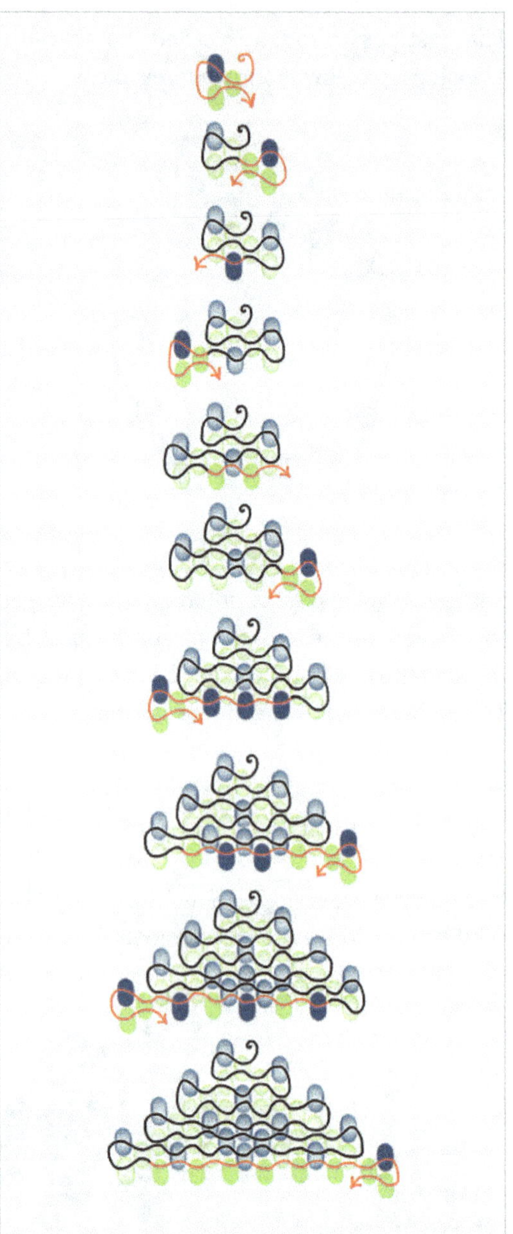

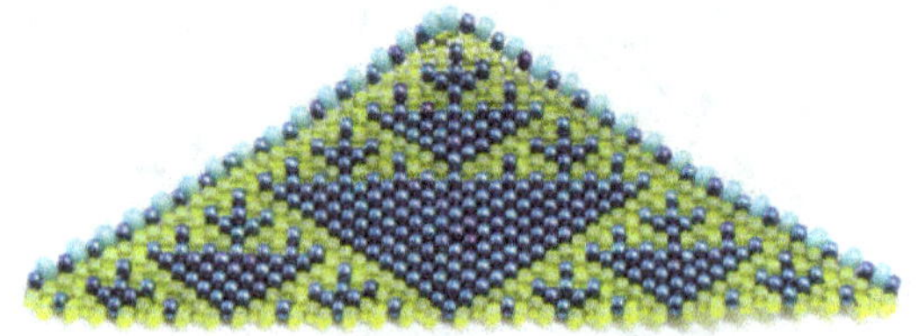

HOW TO MAKE AN ACUTE ANGLE START

1. Pick up three beads. Pass back through the first bead.
2. Pick up a bead, reverse, and pass through a bead.
3. Make an increase by picking up three beads and passing back through the first bead.
4. Peyote stitch to the end of row (for the first row, this is one stitch).
5. Reverse. Peyote stitch to the end of row.

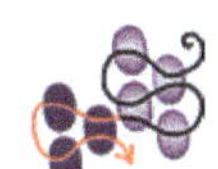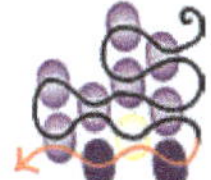

6. Repeat steps 3 and 4.
7. Repeat step 5.

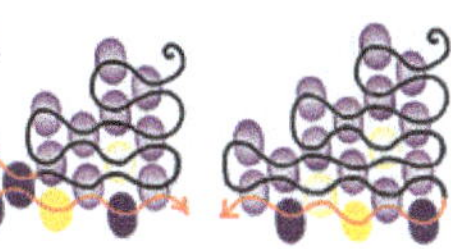

HOW TO MAKE A TRIANGULAR START

Peyote stitch makes nice triangles. Depending upon your tension and the shape of the beads you use, the triangle will either lie mostly flat or cup into a dome.

1. To make a triangle, pick up three beads. Pass through all of the beads again to make a loop, then pass through one more bead.
2. *Pick up two beads to make an increase. Pass through the next bead in loop 1.

Repeat from * twice (three times in total). Pass through the next bead to step-up to the next round.
3. *Pick up two beads to make an increase. Pass through the adjacent bead. Peyote stitch to the end of row (for the first row, this is one stitch). Repeat from * two more times (three times in total). Pass through the next bead to step-up to the next round.
4. Repeat step 3 to make the triangle as large as you want.

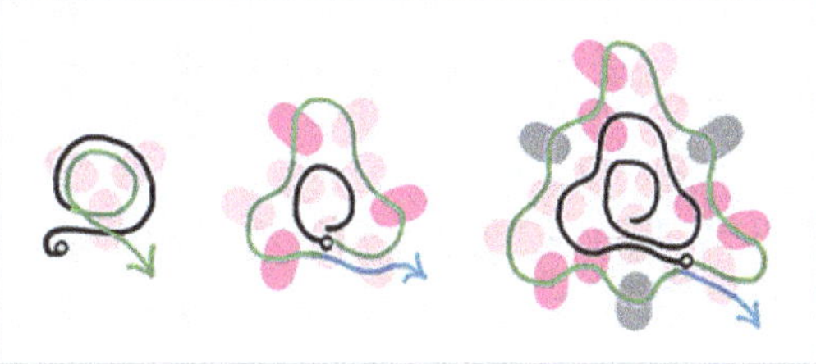

It is possible to make a triangle with a hole in the center, like the one on the beaded bead.

1. Pick up nine beads. Pass through all of the beads again to make a loop, and then through one more bead.
2. *Pick up two beads to make an increase. Pass through the next three beads in a loop 1. Repeat from * two more times (three times in total). Pass through the next bead to step up to the next round.
3. *Pick up two beads to make an increase. Pass through the adjacent bead. Peyote stitch to the end of row (for the first row, this is two stitches). Repeat from * two more times (three times in total). Pass through the next bead to step-up to the next round.
4. Repeat step 3 to make the triangle as large as you want.

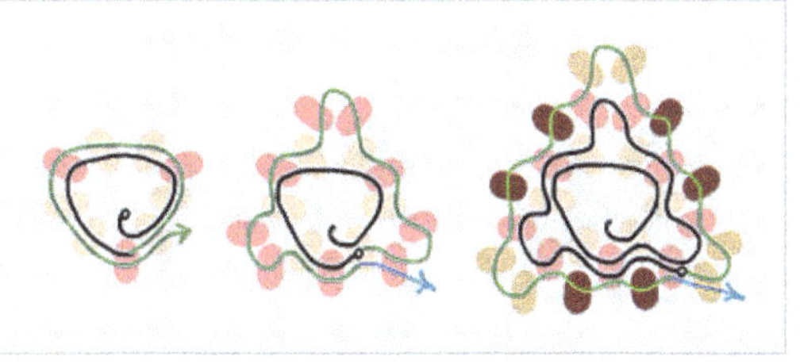

Easy Bails and Beaded Beads

The easiest way to turn a rectangle of bead-work into something you can wear is to fold over the end and zip it up with thread. In this way, you can make pendants, beaded beads, key chains, earrings, and other things. The hole in the tube lets you string it on a cord or chain so you can hang it wherever you want.

THE ZIP!

One of the most satisfactory parts of beading peyote stitch is the Zip! The Zip happens when you weave back and forth, through beads A, B, C, and so on, connecting the two ends of beadwork like a zipper. The result is an invisible join, a connection without a seam. When you zip the first row to the last row, you get a beaded tube.

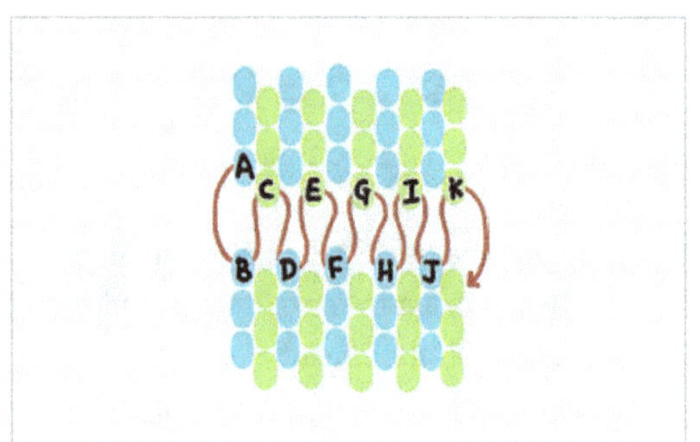

BEADED BEAD

Make simple tubes of beads in any size you want. The counts in the pieces here range from 34 to 58 columns wide, finishing 44 mm to 65 mm wide. The seed beads are all regular size 15° or size 11° Delicas. After stitching the tube, press it flat to find its best view. Run a row of stitches straight down the middle to keep it flat. The finished piece has two long holes running through it, created by the stitches running down the middle.

Here is another way to finish a tube of beads: The beaded bead below has a big, round crystal stitched inside each end to hold it open. We added 6 mm round beads instead of the row of stitching down the center. This beaded bead is more plump than the others.

Easy Pendants

Bead a rectangle of any size you like. Ours are about 20 to 30 columns wide and 60 to 90 rows long, including the fold. The fold contains 20 or more rows, which we count on the edge as 10 or more beads, because the beads on the edge are every other row. To create a fold, beads labeled A, C, E, G, I, K are at the bottom edge of a strip, whereas B, D, F, H, J are in the middle of the strip. Stitch the Zip in alphabetical order, A, B, C, and so on, zigzagging your needle between the two rows.

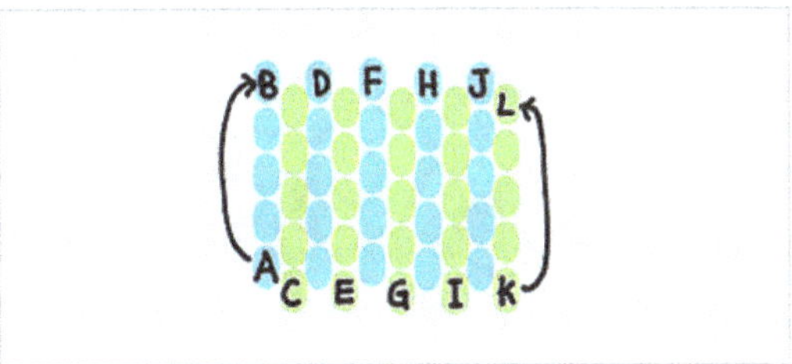

Reinforce the ends of the join, so the thread looks like this in the bead holes.

Earrings

This pair of earrings from Chapter 5 is made from two beaded pendants, wire, chain, jump rings, headpins, ear wires, and round beads.

The pink and lime pendant has a repeating trim in blue and black. The repeat makes the bail into a design element.

Key Chain or Luggage Tag

Make a shape like the one below. You can vary the lengths of A, B, and D to be pretty much whatever you want them to be. Length C should be about 20 to 30 rows (even though the drawing shows 9 rows) so that you have enough space to accommodate a key ring.

When you get to the last row (labeled 15), fold the tab over, and stitch the end to the beginning of the narrow neck (arrow). If you are using a soldered ring or a split ring for the key chain, add it before you zip up the tab. Sew the beads in alphabetical order (A, B, C, and so on). It's just like the bail for the easy pendant, but with a differently shaped pendant.

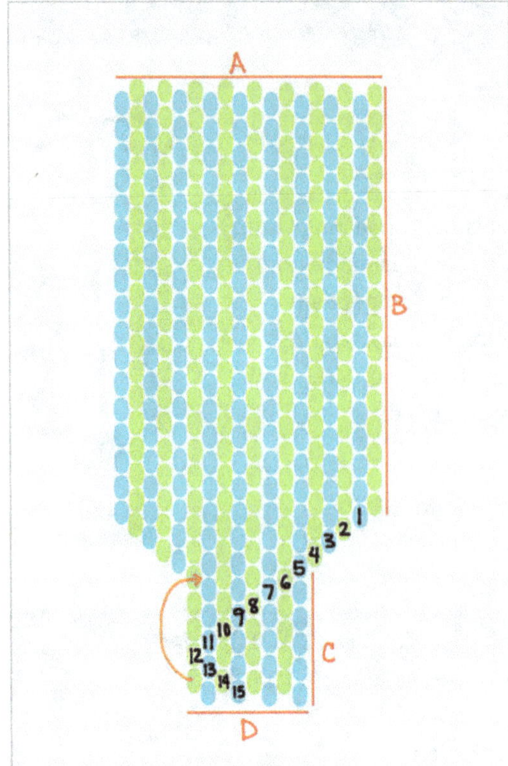

Reinforce the ends of the join, so the thread looks like this in the bead holes.

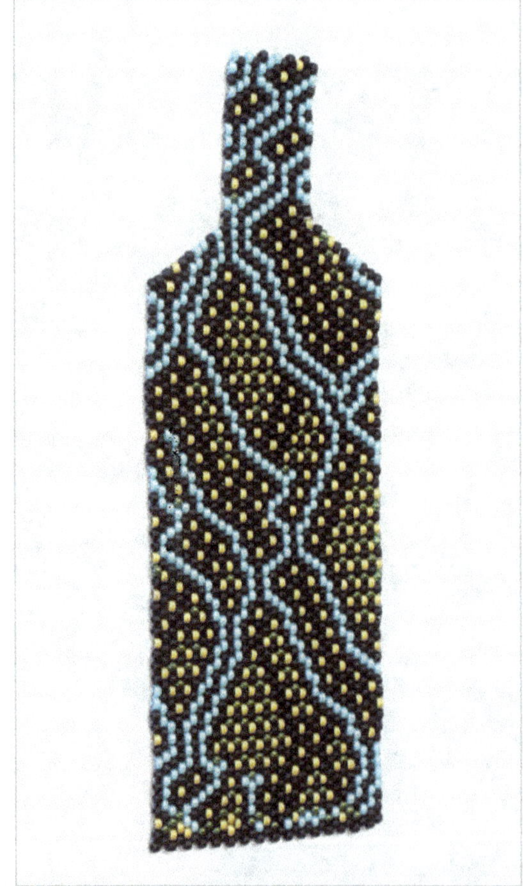

Pill Pouch

A pill pouch makes a great gift for men and women alike. Both the pill pouches shown use size 15° seed beads, but size 11° can also make a nice pill pouch. This one has a small patch of Velcro under the flap to make it very easy to open and close, easier than a button and loop or a snap. We recommend Velcro if it will be used regularly as a pill pouch for vitamins and medicines. You can also make a larger pouch with 5 mm plastic cylinder seed beads.

1. Start at the bottom of the pouch. Pick up an even number of beads. The length of your strand of beads should be a little smaller than the width of the finished pouch. From the end with the needle, skip three beads and pass through the fourth bead to make a picot.

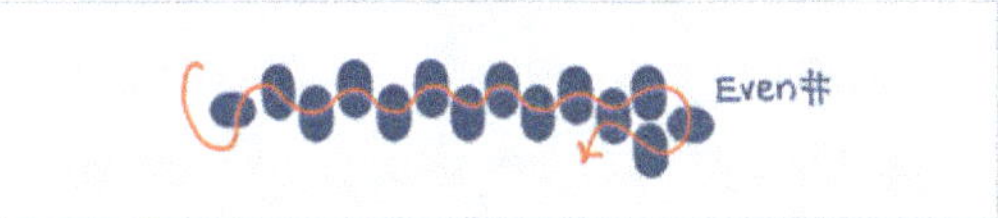

2. Add beads with peyote stitch until you reach the starter rows. For the last stitch, pass back through two beads from the side with the tail.

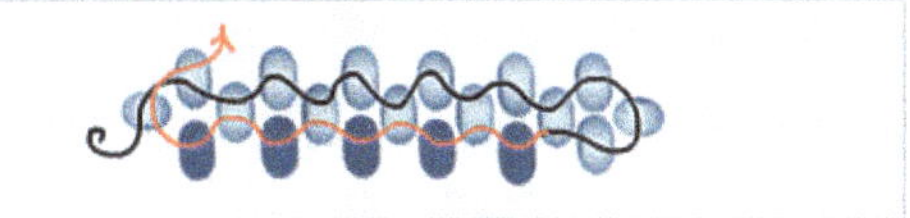

3. *Peyote stitch to the end of the row (shown with five stitches). At the turn, make two side-by-side increases by adding two beads per stitch. Repeat from *. Step up by passing through one more bead.

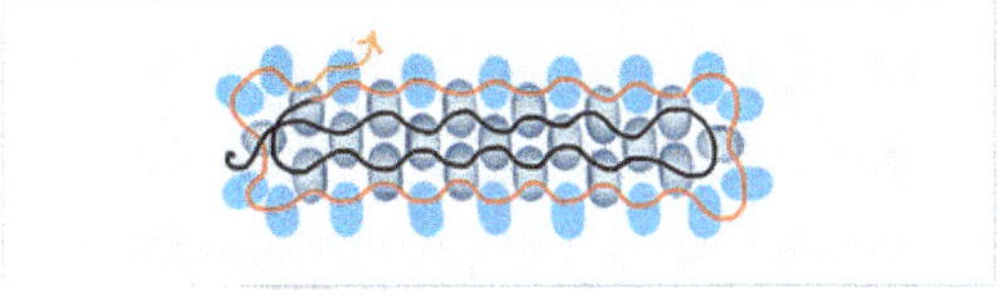

4. *Peyote stitch to the end of the row. At the turn, make an increase, peyote stitch, and increase. Repeat from *. Peyote stitch. Step-up by passing through one more bead.

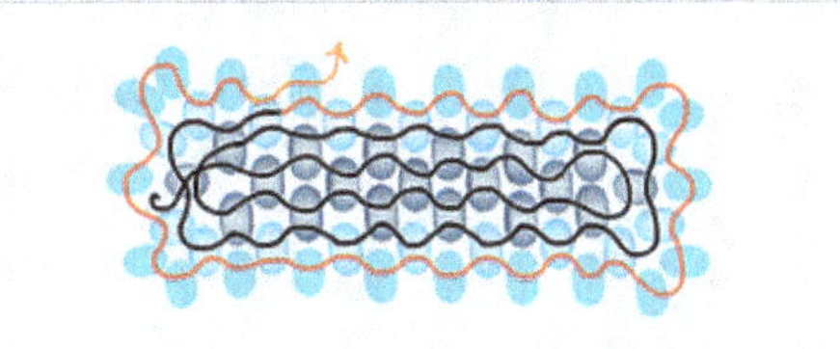

5. Peyote stitch the round. When you get to the increases, add one bead between each pair. This completes the base of the pouch.

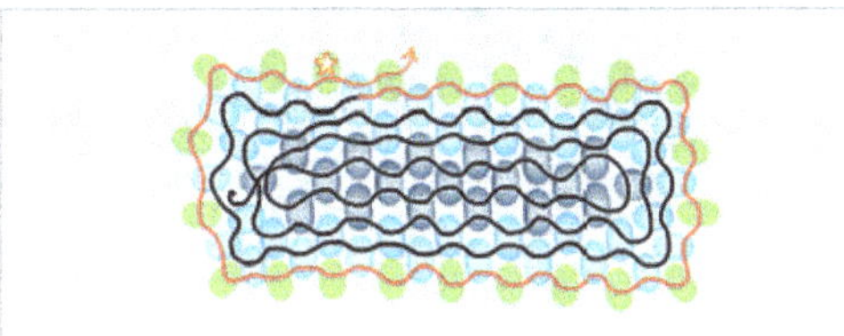

6. From this point, continue with regular peyote stitch to make the pouch as deep as you want. You can stitch in rounds by stepping up at the end of each round. Another option is to add beads in a spiral. To do this, you need to make a half-stitch decrease at the end of a round. The stitch after the yellow star shows a half-stitch decrease, where the last bead in the round lies over two beads instead of one. After the half-stitch decrease, stitches form one long continuous spiral. No steps-ups are needed, and the beading is easy.

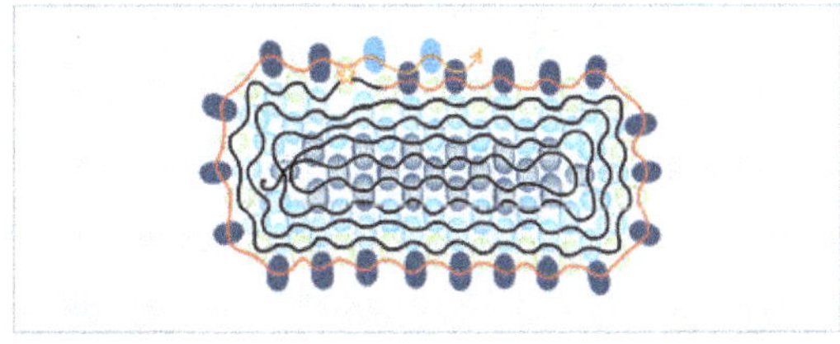

When the pouch is as deep as you want, begin the flap.

The pill pouch below was the first of its kind, and you can see several design changes between this and the pouch just described. First, the prototype does not contain the increases shown on the previous page, and the result is a flatter pouch that does not hold as much for its size. Second, the button and loop clasp, while it looks pretty, takes some nimble fingers to do and undo.

The shaping of the flap is essentially the same as the key chain, and yours doesn't need to be exactly the same as ours.

To make the flap, sew rows of peyote back and forth in a rectangle. The width (columns) of the flap should be less than the width of the pouch folded flat because the filled pouch will have thickness (sides), which reduces the width of the pouch. The length (rows) of the flap should be long enough to cover the filled pouch and then some for the overlap.

After you stitch enough rows to cover the top of the pouch and some more, make decreases on both sides for several more rows. Then stitch regular, rectangular peyote stitch for the little flappy bit that will hide the Velcro (or snap). An optional step is to use a rolled edge at the end of the flap to make it easy to grab the flap, and open the pouch. Simply roll the end of the beadwork and zip the last row to a previous row. Sew Velcro to the pouch front and under the tab, and your pill pouch is done.

Clasps for Bracelets

There are lots of ways to clasp a beaded bracelet, including snaps, hooks and eyes, and, of course, purchased clasps, but our favorite way to clasp a bracelet is with a button and beaded loop. Use one large button or several small ones. Three or more buttons look especially nice on wide bracelets. Here, we show how to weave three different button loops with seed beads, starting with the easiest one first.

BUTTON LOOP 1

The most straightforward way to make a button hole with peyote stitch is to just omit three columns of beads (two or four in an even count bracelet) for the length of the button plus a little bit. To find out how wide to make each side, take the width of the bracelet, subtract three, and divide by two. This bracelet uses size 15° seed beads and a 14 mm button. Read more about buttons at the end of this chapter.

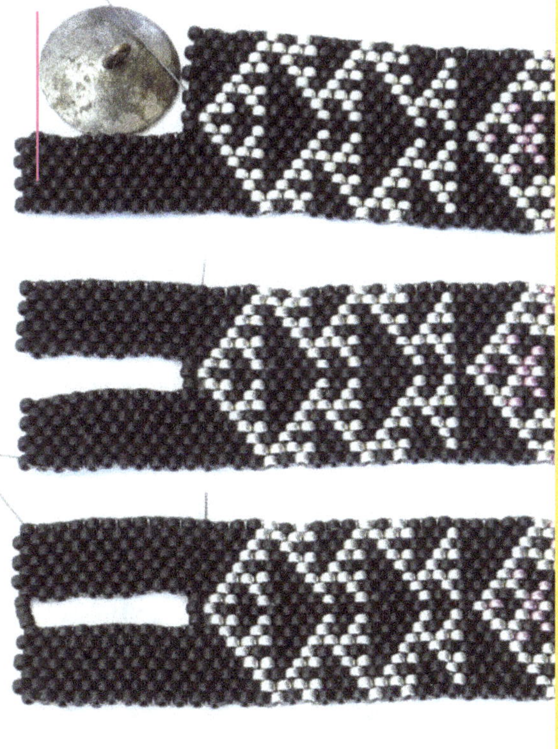

BUTTON LOOP 2

Our favorite button loop works well with buttons from 9 to 15 mm in diameter. The sides of the button loop are made with a stitch called herringbone for its shape, or called Ndebele stitch for the African people, who traditionally used this stitch in their handicrafts.

With herringbone, the holes of the beads in the loop are stitched at right angles to the holes of the beads in the peyote stitch. Use regular seed beads in the same size as your bracelet, plus beads one size larger. For example, if your bracelet is made with size 11° seed beads, then the loops use sizes 11° and 8° (in two colors). With 15° beads in the bracelet, you can use the same or use 15° and 11° (in two colors). Keep in mind that small clasps are harder to open and close than bigger ones.

To determine the spacing, use one button loop for every nine to 12 columns of beads. For example, the bracelet here has 36 columns of beads. While this bracelet has three loops, it would also have looked nice with four. For three loops, the spacing is calculated for six half loops. Since 36/6 is 6, we center the loops on columns 6, 18, and 30, counting from the right. Each loop is stitched over seven columns of beads, centered over a "down" column. Use three or five columns of space between the loops, and zero to three columns at each side.

Once you decide how many buttons you want and where to place them, you can start stitching the button loops.

The orange arrow lies on the line of symmetry of the loop. The orange dot shows where to start. The six red dots show where the loops connect to the peyote stitch.

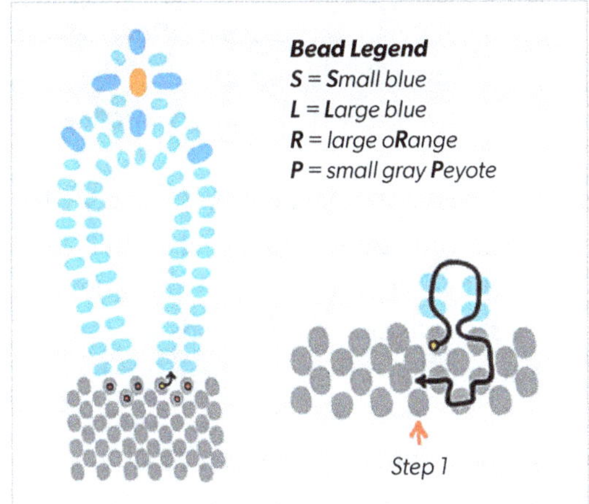

Bead Legend
S = *Small blue*
L = *Large blue*
R = *large oRange*
P = *small gray Peyote*

Step 1

1. Pick up 4 S. Skip the "down" P, and pass through the next "up" P on the edge. Reverse direction, and pass back through 3 P. Arrange the 4 S so that their holes point at right angles to the peyote stitch, and pull the thread tight.

2. Pass right through P and up through 2 S.

3. Pick up 4 S. Pass down 2 S, through P, and up through 4 S. That's a herringbone stitch with an extra pass through the down P.

4. Pick up 4 S. Pass down 2 S, and up through 4 S. That's a regular herringbone stitch.

5. Keep repeating Step 4 until you have a column of seed beads that is 8 or more beads tall. See the green numbers in the drawing and table.

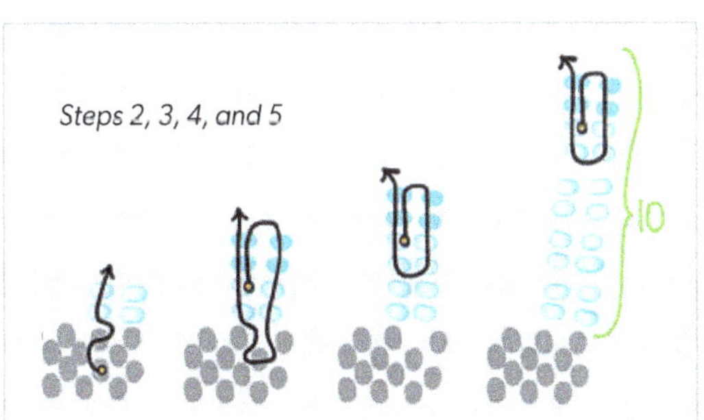

Steps 2, 3, 4, and 5

The table gives examples of different sizes and shapes of buttons and the length of the button-holes we used for them. Dome-shaped buttons require longer buttonholes than flat buttons.

BUTTON DIAMETER	BUTTON SHAPE	GREEN HEIGHT (IN BEADS)
10 mm	Dome	8 size 11°
11.5 mm	Medium	9 size 11°
14 mm	Flat	10 size 11°
12 mm	Flat/dome	10 size 11°
10 mm	Medium	10 size 15°

6. Pick up S, L, and S. Pass down 2 S and up 3 S.

7. Pick up 3 S. Pass down L, S, and up 2 S.

8. Pick up S and L. Pass down 2 S and up 2 S.

9. Pick up 3 S. Pass down L and up 2 S.

Step 6

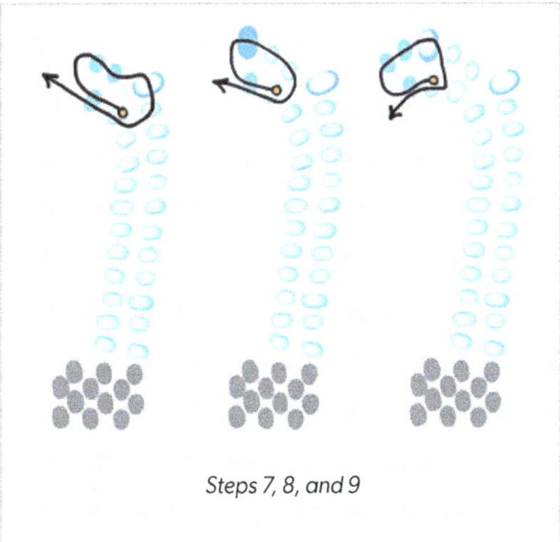

Steps 7, 8, and 9

10. Pick up S, S, and L.
    Pass down 2 S and up 2 S.

11. Pick up 4 S.
    Pass down S L and up 3 S.

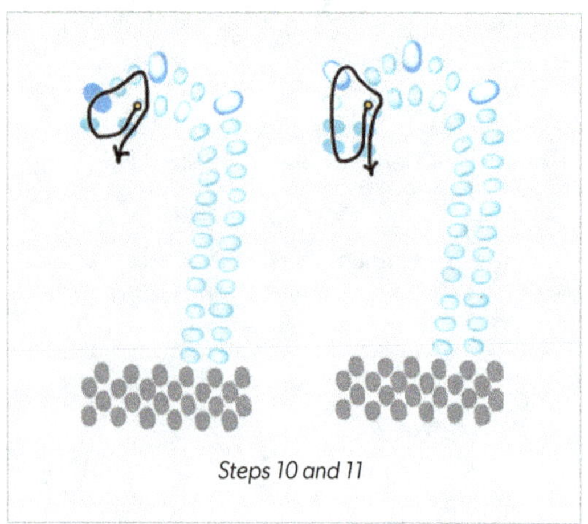

Steps 10 and 11

12. Make herringbone stitches by picking up
    4 S. Pass down 2 S, and up through 4 S.
    Repeat until the second side of the button
    loop looks just like the first.

13. Join the herringbone to the peyote stitch
    by passing through the down P, up 2 S (the
    dotted line), down 2 S, through the same P,
    up S, down S, and then zigzag through 4 P.
    Pass up all the beads on the right side of
    the loop. Pick up 3 S, R, and S. Pass back
    through L and through S and R.

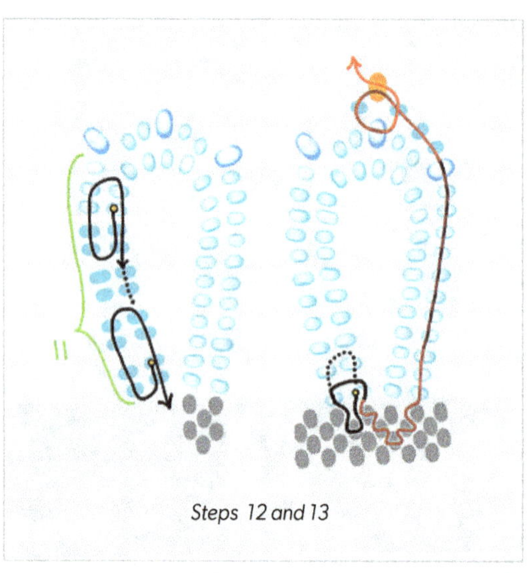

Steps 12 and 13

14. Pick up S, L, and S. Pass through R in the
    same direction as before. Pass through
    S. Pick up 2 S. Pass through L and down
    all of the S, into 3 P, reverse, and zigzag
    through 9 P to the other side. Reverse and
    pass through 2 P, and up all of the S, L,
    and 3 more S, stopping just before the R.

15. Pick up L. Pass through S, L, and S. Pick
    up L. Pass through 3 S and L. The loop
    now has all of its beads. We recommend
    you weave through the beads to reinforce
    the stitching to strengthen the beaded
    loop for repeated use. Read more about
    buttons at the end of this chapter.

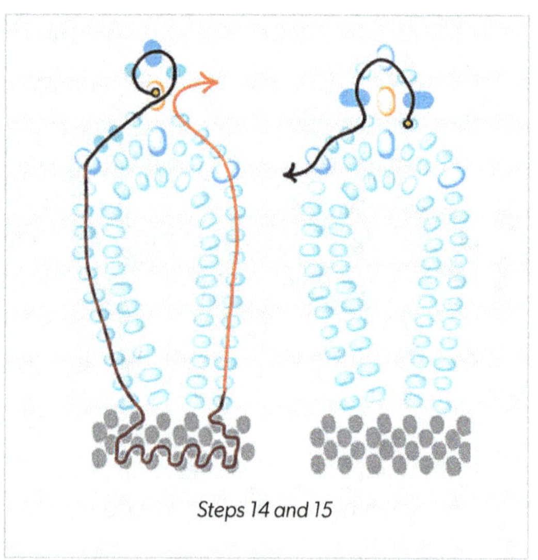

Steps 14 and 15

BUTTON LOOP 3

This button loop is suitable for use with a single larger button, 19 mm (3/4 inch) in diameter. For a larger or smaller button, you can easily adjust the length of the loop to fit. The stitches used include herringbone and peyote.

Both bracelets shown with this button loop are made entirely with Delica beads in size 11°. The width of each bracelet is 22 columns.

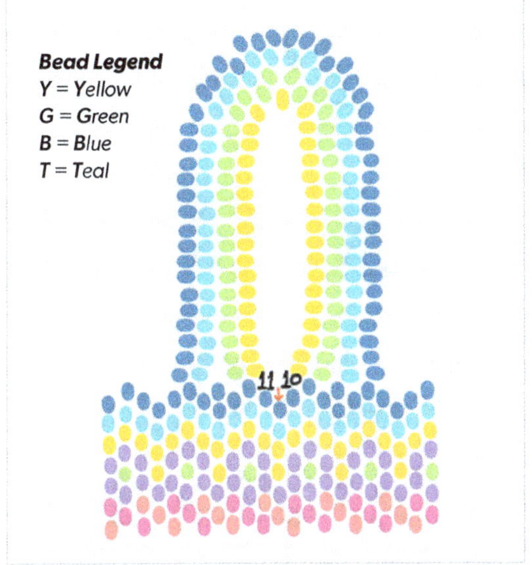

1. Newly added beads are shown with pink dots. You can skip the first and the last new beads if you aren't using the repeating trim. *Pick up T, pass through 3 T. #Pick up T. Pass through T. Repeat from # once more. Repeat from * twice, stopping short when you get to the end of the row. Reverse, and pass through six beads as shown.

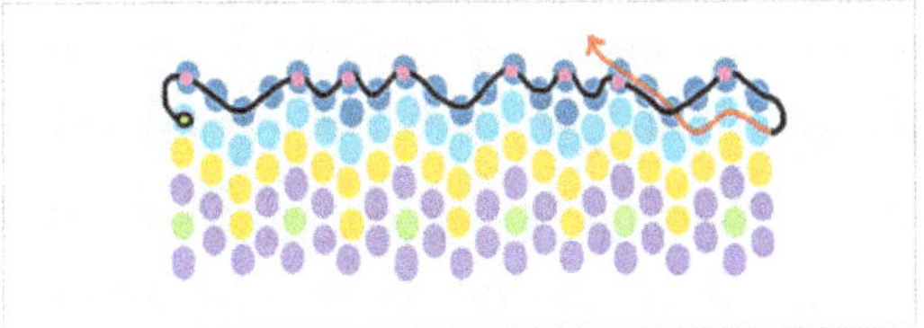

2. Pick up 2 B and 2 T. Pass through 3 T. Pick up 2 G. Pass through 2 B and 3 T. Pick up 2 Y. Pass through 2 G and 5 T. Pick up 2 G and 2 Y. Pass through 3 T. Pick up 2 B. Pass through 2 G and 3 T. Pick up 2 T. Pass through 2 B and 2 T.

3. Reverse and pass through 4 beads in the peyote stitch. Reverse and pass through 3 beads in the peyote stitch. Pass up through 2 T. Pick up 2 T and 2 B. Pass down through 2 B, T, and up 2 G. Pick up 2 G and 2 Y. Pass down through 2 Y and 5 beads in the peyote stitch. Pass up through 4 T.

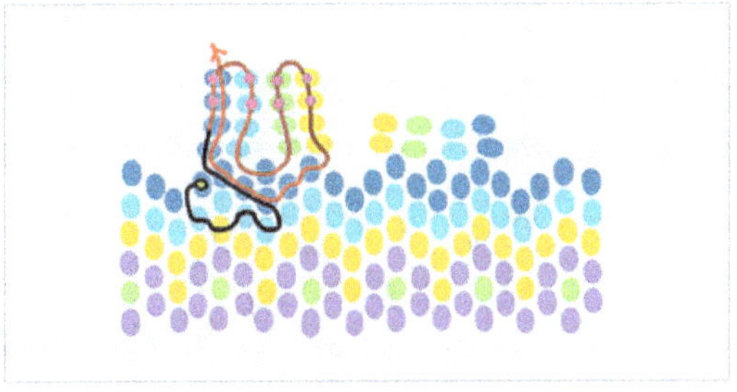

4. Pick up 2 T and 2 B. Pass down through 2 B and up through 2 G. Pick up 2 G and 2 Y. Pass down through 2 Y, up through 4 G, down through 4 B, and up through 4 T.

5. Repeat step 4 until the herringbone strip is a little longer than the length of your button; here, it is 16 beads. Repeat steps 3 and 4 to make the second side of the loop to match the first.

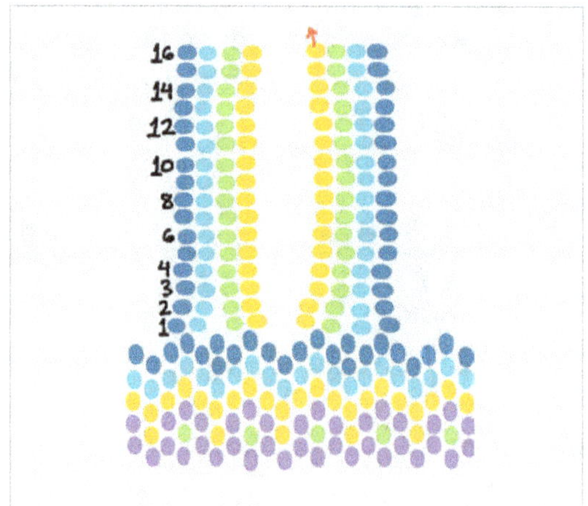

This shows the top two rows and where the thread should exit.

6. Pick up 3 Y. Pass down 2 Y and up 2 G.

7. *Pick up G. Pass through Y. Repeat from * 2 more times. Pick up G. Pass down 2 G and up 2 B.

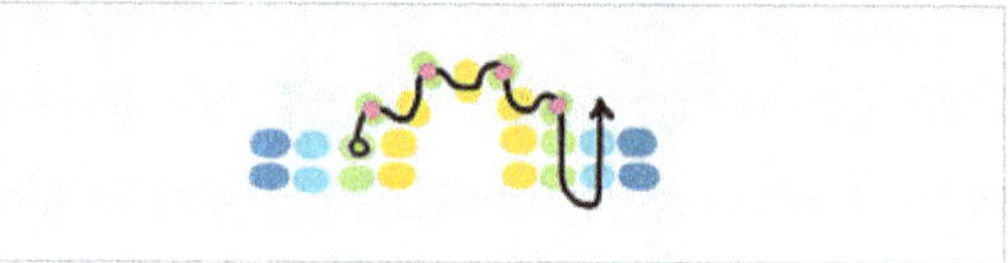

8. Pick up B. Pass through G.
   Pick up G. Pass through G.
   Pick up 2 G. Pass through G.
   Pick up G. Pass through G.
   Pick up B. Pass down 2 B and up 2 T.

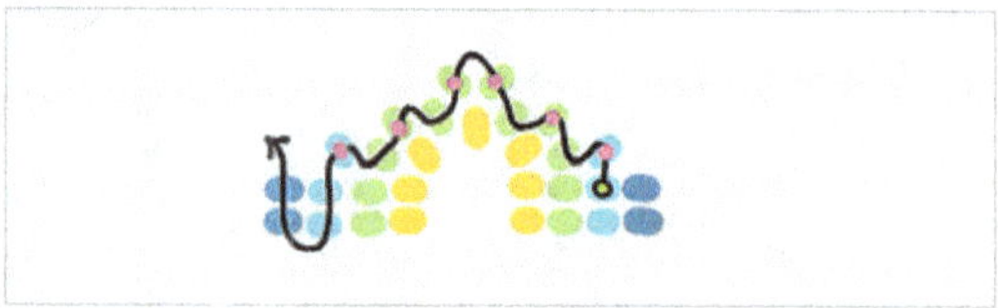

9. Pick up T. Pass through B.
   Pick up B. Pass through G.
   Pick up B. Pass through G.
   Pick up 2 B. Pass through G.
   Pick up B. Pass through G.
   Pick up B. Pass through B.
   Pick up T. Pass down through 2 T.
   Pass up through B and 2 T.

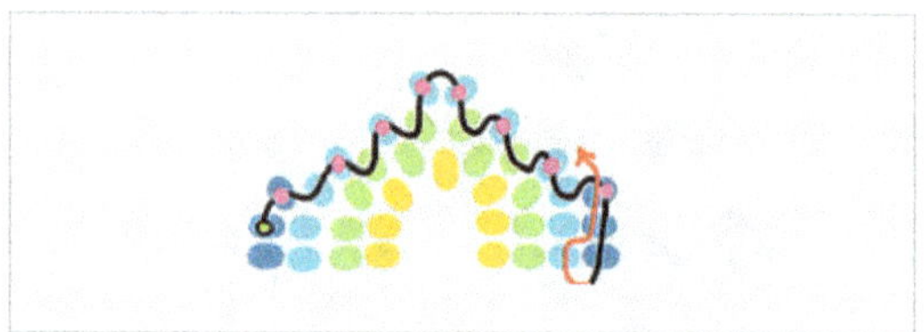

10. Pick up T. Pass through B.
    Pick up B. Pass through B.
    Pick up B. Pass through B.
    Pick up 2T. Pass through B.
    Pick up B. Pass through B.
    Pick up B. Pass through B.
    Pick up T. Pass down through 3 T.
    Pass up through B and 3 T.

11. Pick up T. Pass through B.
    Pick up T. Pass through B.
    Pick up T. Pass through 2 T.
    Pick up T. Pass through B.
    Pick up T. Pass through B.
    Pick up T. Pass down through 4 T.
    Pass up through B and 4 T.

12. Pick up T. Pass through T.
    Pick up T. Pass through 4 T.
    Pick up T. Pass through T.
    Pick up T. Pass down through all T.
    The loop now has all of its beads. We recommend you weave through the beads to reinforce the stitching and strengthen the beaded loop for repeated use.

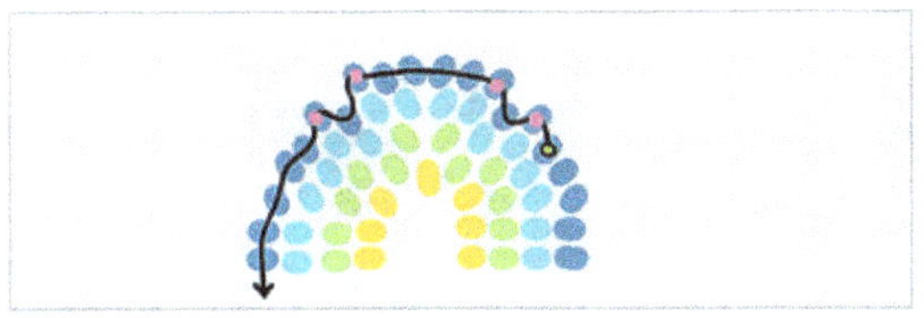

BUTTONS

When you shop for buttons or toggles to go with any of the button loops in this chapter, look for buttons with shanks. You really need a shank to go with these beaded button loops because the beaded loops have thickness. The shank gives extra space for the beaded loop to rest neatly between the peyote beading and button. The good news is that if your button doesn't have a shank, you can make one with seed beads by simply adding a seed bead under each hole in the button to act as a shank.

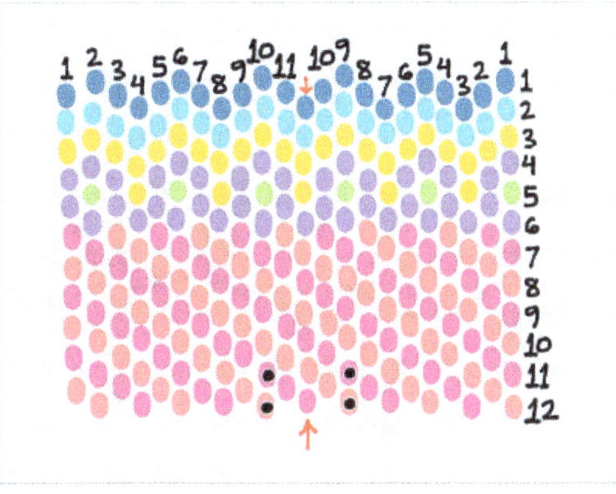

Center your button on the opposite end of the bracelet, deciding how far to place it from the edge based on how you want it to fit your wrist. We like to leave an even "frame" around all sides of the button. The black dots in the illustration show button placement in the rainbow bracelet and the one on this page.

Attach the button with the thread path shown. If you pull the thread crazy tight when you attach the button, you will probably deform the beaded fabric. So don't do that!

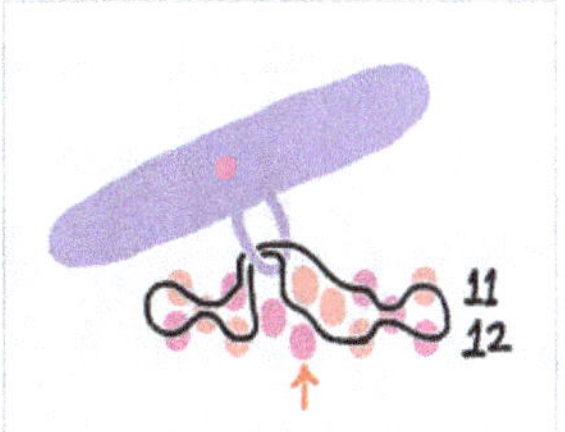

COLORING PAGES

BEADING WITH ALGORITHMS

BEADING WITH ALGORITHMS

BEADING WITH ALGORITHMS

BEADING WITH ALGORITHMS

BEADING WITH ALGORITHMS

BEADING WITH ALGORITHMS

About the Authors

Gwen Fisher

Gwen Fisher earned her M.A. in Mathematics from the University of California at Santa Barbara and a Ph.D. in Mathematics Education from the University of Wisconsin at Madison. She was an Associate Professor of Mathematics at California Polytechnic State University at San Luis Obispo, specializing in the mathematical education of teachers. There, she wrote and taught a full course on mathematics and visual art. Around that time, in 2005, she began weaving beads. Soon thereafter, she started writing about her discoveries. She has served as an editor and reviewer for academic journals and as a speaker and exhibitor at conferences. She has published academic papers on mathematical bead weaving, felting, quilting, and mathematical art. She has sold thousands of tutorials for bead weaving on her website *beadinfinitum.com* and on Etsy at *etsy.com/shop/gwenbeads*. Find her as "gwenbeads" on social media.

Roger Antonsen

Roger Antonsen served as an Associate Professor in the Department of Informatics in the research group Analytical Solutions and Reasoning at the University of Oslo, Norway, in the research group Logic and Intelligent Data (LogID), and as a Visiting Scholar at UC Berkeley, California. He earned his Ph.D. in Computer Science, within the field of mathematical logic, automated reasoning, and proof theory. Roger's interest in cellular automata overlapped with his interest in logical calculi, proof theory, mathematical logic, complexity theory, combinatorics, and the philosophy of mathematics. Roger engaged in many forms of science communication and outreach, from writing a column for Norway's largest printed newspaper to giving talks all over the world and creating mathematical videos. See more of Roger's work on his website *rantonse.org*.